THE
LITTLE
BOOK
OF
DATA

THE
LITTLE
BOOK
OF
DATA

Understanding the

Powerful Analytics That Fuel AI,

Make or Break Careers, and

Could Just End Up Saving the World

JUSTIN EVANS

HARPERCOLLINS
LEADERSHIP

AN IMPRINT OF HARPERCOLLINS

Design by Neuwirth & Associates, Inc.

ISBN 978-1-4002-4836-0 (eBook)
ISBN 978-1-4002-4835-3 (HC)

Library of Congress Control Number: 2025931628

Printed in the United States of America

25 26 27 28 29 LBC 5 4 3 2 1

CONTENTS

Introduction   *vii*

PART ONE: HOW WE GOT HERE · 1

1: Data Is Everywhere: 3
    "Here's My Number"

2: Life After the Data Revolution: 15
    The Library

3: Data Science: 27
    Data During Wartime

4: Artificial Intelligence: 41
    A Sport for Cyborgs

PART TWO: GOOD AND BAD DATA PEOPLE · 57

5: Data Bullies: 59
    A Story Where Bankers Are the Heroes (No, Really)

6: Data People and Why I Love Them: 71
    The Day Priya Saw the Line

PART THREE: SUPERPOWERS · 85

7: Omniscience: Solving One Big Problem: 87
    Skate the Lake

8: Omniscience: Solving Many Small Problems: 99
    "But It's a Map!"

9: Data Directs Resources to Where They Are Needed: 109
    A True Spartan

10: Data Is Light in a Dark Room: 123
    Tiny Submarines

11: Data Crystallizes Complex Information: 137
    The Railroad Nerd

PART FOUR: HOW WE USE DATA • 151

12: Counting: 153
    The Idea of Three

13: Tracking: 165
    The Power of One Number

14: Anomalies: 179
    Hunter of Earthquakes

15: Identity: 189
    "The Greatest Business Day of My Life"

16: Matching: 201
    The Coupon and the Cancer Genome

17: Scoring: 215
    The Loneliness Score

18: Certification: 227
    The Pope of Meat Grading

19: Performance: 237
    King Ben

PART FIVE: CONCLUSION • 249

Index   265
About the Author   271

INTRODUCTION

Is it weird that I cried so much writing a book about data?

Data is supposed to be dry. It's proverbially nerdy, boring, technical. Yet here I am, hanging up after interviewing one of the subjects of this book, not just shedding a tear but full-on pressing my hands to my face, weeping.

What's going on?

Data is not something we touch. It's abstract. It's invisible. Yet it has a powerful impact on our personal and professional lives.

I first truly understood this when I heard my boss addressing his leadership team with a cracked voice.

I had been brought in to help the TV advertising division of the cable company Comcast. This division was being slaughtered in the advertising marketplace by Google and Facebook, who had created all sorts of tools that used data. Comcast had its own data, but they hadn't put it to much use. So they hired me to cook up ideas of how to use their own data to help advertisers, sell more ads, and beat back the tech onslaught.

Little did I know, my hiring was only the first step in a massive changeover in the company.

Soon, the division president—a handsome, polished leader, never seen out of a well-fitting gray suit, whose office displayed pictures of him and his pretty wife grinning with Bill Clinton—was addressing his leadership team by speakerphone from the tower office in Philadelphia. Clearly he had just been fired.

Some of what he said was boilerplate. "Time to move on . . . Proud of our many accomplishments together . . ." And then he went off script, stumbling over his words. "The business has changed," he lamented with sudden passion. "Now it's about . . . data. Algorithms." His words steamed with frustration. *I don't understand what these words mean or why they matter*, he seemed to be saying. *But I know the world changed on me, and I'm getting canned for it.*

Others soon followed. And unlike the division president—whom I found kind of inscrutable—these were folks I adored. Leaders of huge lines of business—in the billions of dollars—with thousands of employees—empathetic, kind, hardworking leaders you'd follow into battle any day, who were my friends, who would text me updates on their kids, or audiobook recommendations. They started taking early retirement. In their fifties. And each time, on their way out—always in those well-fitting suits—they'd give me, their data guy, a kind of melancholy wave. Sort of like, *Good luck, kid. We've done our bit.*

In their *fifties*. Isn't that supposed to be the new thirties?

And then I started noticing this phenomenon more and more: Clever, admirable people not knowing the first thing about data beyond what they read in a news headline. My beloved friends and neighbors in New York City, smarty-pants with college degrees and impressive careers as doctors, screenwriters, editors, therapists—they didn't know data either. When I'd raise it as a topic, they'd go sour, like I was asking them to clean out my garage or eat sea urchin.

What was the problem? Didn't my friends and colleagues and neighbors know that data had become the way we solve problems in the twenty-first century?

That AI too was trained on a data set larger than the Bible, Shakespeare, Agatha Christie, *The Lord of the Rings*, and Philip Roth—times twenty-three thousand.

When you get cancer treatment, your doctor can reference 2.5 petabytes of genomic, epigenomic, and proteomic data to help cure you.

When you see a little french-fry-sized ad on your phone, it has been cranked through machine learning algorithms and has chosen your profile from a hundred million others.

When we fret about climate change, we do so because we've seen weather data from 750,000 weather stations in 180 countries.

Finding a coffee shop on a map.

Your daily step count.

Whether the subway will be on time.

All those things—now enabled by data.

And the fact that some of the best and most competent people I knew were turning their backs on that? Abdicating that knowledge to somebody else, some rando with a computer science degree they'd never met? They were letting *that* person take control?

Why were they giving up that power?

I think I knew why. We can call it the four layers of data denial.

The first layer is: *I don't need to understand data. It's like high cholesterol. If I have a problem with it, I'll study up on it. Until then, I have other things to worry about.*

But data is how we solve problems. And you, likely, have some mission in your career, or your organization, that makes you a problem-solver. So you can't afford to ignore your most promising tool.

The second layer is: *Data is complicated. I'll never understand it until I go back for a master's degree or learn how to code with Python. Which I will never do. So I'll just take a pass.*

But the fact is, data is not about number crunching. It's about ideas. It's about what you use it for, not all the little details of how you use it.

The third layer of data denial is, by most people, unspoken: *It's intimidating. It makes me feel stupid when I hear people using fancy terminology, and I can't follow.*

Fair. Everybody feels this way when they start. Twenty years ago when I started in the data business, I walked around with a permanent blush because I was certain everything I asked or ventured was idiotic.

It wasn't. And now I get exasperated when I witness people getting intimidated about data. Because there's usually some nerd bully, some twerp, on the other side of that discussion. An expert lording their acronyms and technical terms over a person with less knowledge. To hell with that. Anyone can understand this stuff. You can't give power to the twerps.

And the final level of data denial is pretty dark: *It's that people think data is evil.*

There are several reasons for this.

The reason people think data is evil is that data is invisible. It is a force *behind* the applications we hold in our hands. In our stock trading, we focus on the graphs, the alerts, the interface. Not the massive databases that link ticker symbols to their hundred million daily trades. We don't *see* the data, and certainly not its origin.

And with this invisibility comes suspicion. We don't understand what our relationship to data is. We understand, vaguely, that we inadvertently create it every day. Those credit card purchases are recorded somewhere. Same with our phone calls and texts. Or the pulsing blue dot we manifest on the mapping app. But we know that we, ourselves, are not processing that data. So somehow we are shedding data, and someone else is using it. That's problematic.

In this gap, there is room for suspicion. I regret to say, as a member of the digital advertising community, that creepy advertising experiences like "retargeting"—when you look at a pair of sneakers on a website for ten minutes once and then see those sneaks in nineteen different ads for a week—affect people's assumptions about the use of data.

And, thanks to the massive, society-damaging misdemeanors of spineless, unethical, greedy creeps like Mark Zuckerberg, we leap to the assumption that our data is being treated as respectfully as the way Facebook treats data. Which is to say, as a source of profit and without regard for algorithms that split American communities or foist eating disorders on teens; and without regard for, or a sense of dignity about, its point of origin: Us.

Aspects of this narrative are real and infuriating, and have been written about powerfully by authors like Shoshana Zuboff, Cathy O'Neil, and others.

Yet this can't be the whole story.

If data is nothing more than a scheme by surveillance capitalists to wring billions out of the masses, why do we, as a society, bother with it at all?

The answer is that data—like the mythical fire bestowed by Prometheus or the historical leaps in agriculture and industry—is a kind of superpower. One that charges us with amazing productivity and insight. And charges us, in a second sense, with responsibility.

And if it is a superpower, and if it is available to everyone (and it is), then all the more reason for everyone to understand it.

I feel a sense of mission to help people understand this power, which led to the writing of this book. I felt I had a unique ability to do so because I came to data not from a technical perspective but from a business perspective and, also, because I am a storyteller. I don't have a degree in computer science or applied mathematics. I was an undergraduate English major who sat in the front row of Shakespeare lectures. This nontechnical background became a strength in my career. I became the person called upon to explain the data to the clients (who, themselves, were expert in their businesses—but not in data). Which meant I had to make it clear.

Oddly, it helped that I started in the data business as green as anyone, struggling with impostor syndrome and sweating through that first high-profile product launch based on my idea. Yet in a career spanning the Nielsen Company (creator of the TV ratings), a venture-backed start-up, Comcast/NBCU, and Samsung Electronics, I have conceived of countless ways to use data to help clients; led teams of data scientists; and made hundreds of millions of dollars for my employers. And I did it without writing a single line of code. (Which no one would want from me anyway, believe me.) I was able to do this because once you wrap your head around the core ideas of data, you can be as effective—maybe more so—than the most technical wizard.

You merely need to understand what we can achieve with data.

This leads to the last challenge of writing the book, and takes us back to my crying jag at the start. How could I communicate the core ideas of data to a nonprofessional, nonexpert reader? There are a zillion online courses you can take. Another zillion books about data science and AI and using data in business. Most will quickly involve formulas and advanced terminology and code. But those won't help us.

If data's superpower is to help us solve our biggest problems as a civilization, well then, I thought, let's meet some problem-solvers. Let's understand how they used data to achieve something extraordinary.

The chapters you are about to read introduce a few dozen characters, many of them colorful, who are, in a word, seekers. People passionate about data, serious about their craft, and who decided to use data to solve a problem no one else had solved before.

How can we track pollution and polluters?

How can we protect New York City from an epidemic?

How can we cure loneliness?

It was in meeting these seekers that I grew emotional. Their seriousness. Their humility. Their dedication. Their generosity in sharing their stories with me . . .

. . . and now, with you.

It is through their eyes that we will explore the superpowers that data confers on us and the ways we can use it to make our world a better place.

PART ONE

How We Got Here

"This must be a simply enormous wardrobe!" thought Lucy, going still further in and pushing the soft folds of the coats aside to make room for her. Then she noticed that there was something crunching under her feet. "I wonder is that more mothballs?" she thought, stooping down to feel it with her hand. But instead of feeling the hard, smooth wood of the floor of the wardrobe, she felt something soft and powdery and extremely cold. "This is very queer," she said, and went on a step or two further.

—C. S. LEWIS, *The Lion, the Witch, and the Wardrobe*

CHAPTER 1

Data Is Everywhere

"Here's My Number"

I t is Tuesday at 5:45 a.m. I am stumbling around my apartment in the dark. I just turned fifty. Recently I passed the grim milestone of having my third close friend diagnosed with cancer. It's time, at last, to get a colonoscopy. When I get the results, the doctors will tell me if I have colon cancer. Or not.

It's just a standard screen, I tell myself.

And because I have made my career in data and because there is something metaphorical in a colonoscopy—the invasiveness of it; the fact that it's so personal—I have decided to use the morning of my colonoscopy as an opportunity to turn the tables on my data. Today, *I* will track *it*.

TO GET A colonoscopy, you have to show up with an empty colon. That means thirty-six hours without food.

And I love to eat.

My Greek mother-in-law favored me because I always went back for fourths. At one summer barbecue, she goaded me to finish an entire platter of chicken. "I can't, Kleri, I've had three pieces already."

"Oh, come on."

In this way—one thigh, leg, and breast at a time—I ate till there was only one piece left.

"Finish it!" my mother-in-law scolded me.

"Kleri, I can't!"

"There's only one piece! You're a young man!" So I choked down the last piece of chicken. Without missing a beat, my mother-in-law turned to my wife and in Greek griped, *"Oooh, then aphise dipote yaton skilo."* Translated: "He didn't leave anything for the dog."

In my state of colonoscopy preparation, I am inhabiting an uncool nook of the multiverse. The one where I don't get fed.

And it's not just not eating. It's purging. A few days prior, a kit arrived in the mail with three pouches of an evil, salty-tasting medical Kool-Aid. I mixed them with water and drank them. Since then, I have been expelling the contents of my intestine at regular intervals. Like, very regular.

My apartment got into the act. As anyone who has lived in New York City buildings knows—especially those grand old ladies built in the 1940s—something is always breaking.

Last night, fatefully, it was the pump in my toilet.

It didn't just malfunction. The toilet pump took to *shrieking*. So here I am, starving, trying to sleep in the summer heat with all the audible flotsam of city life passing under my open window—the yelling drunks, the pitiable madmen raving, the urban motorcycle gang pulling wheelies on the boulevard—and I am getting up every five minutes to purge my colon with my toilet screaming like a teen in a Blumhouse slasher.

So my day starts at 5:45 a.m.; I'm dehydrated, sleep deprived, and starving.

My data, however, is perky.

At 5:45, my phone alarm rings. I take it off airplane mode. The phone connects to the internet.

Humans may not want to talk to anyone before coffee. But apps are like good sons. At 5:46 and 13 seconds, my Google email app calls its mother.

The app pings Google servers five times in that first *second* it is awake. It has a lot to say. For starters, it tells Google servers what my IP address is (100.38.252.205). And it reminds them what my Google ID is. Google calls these "Gaia" IDs. Gaia is a lovely name from Greek mythology. She is the mother Earth, who succeeded Chaos and gave birth to the gods and the Titans. According to Hesiod, Gaia "first bore starry Heaven. She bore also the fruitless deep with his raging swell." In Silicon Valley, Gaia is an acronym for Google Accounts and ID Administration. My Gaia ID is 965299537481.

While I pee—wondering how I can still have water in my body—my Gmail app pings Google another forty-two times. Each time it does so, it creates an entry in a database 250 miles away at the Google Cloud Data Center in Northern Virginia, a windowless commercial building that might be a furniture warehouse or a shipping hub. And each ping makes a small mark in my name—okay, 965299537481's name—in the history of data.

HOW, AT THE start of one generation, did data live only in mainframe computers, thrumming like some caged monster in the depths of a giant corporation like IBM, and at the end of that generation live in our pockets, casual as a set of keys?

And how did that happen so gradually that none of us really noticed?

Electricity started with a bang. One September day in 1882, Thomas Edison lugged six twenty-seven-ton dynamos into a warehouse on Pearl Street in New York City and threw the switch to start the electric age. A brilliant PR man, Edison's first client was the *New York Times*.

"The 27 electric lamps in the editorial rooms and the 25 lamps in the counting rooms made those departments as bright as day," gushed a *Times* reporter.

But after that sudden twilight dawn of the electric age, electricity had to weave its way into our daily lives. A zigzag trip.

The direct current (DC) Edison originally used had too much juice. Arc lights—the great banks of light we use for night ball games—lit the first electrified homes. Victorian early adopters would squint under the glare and flinch when the overhead light emitted a periodic snap like it was going to burn their hair off. Tesla's AC current had the power to "step down" the juice. Easier to use. By the 1920s, if you lived in a city, chances were you had electricity. When the US passed the Rural Electrification Act in 1936, farmers got it too. Soon, the Blue Grass Rural Electric Cooperative of Nicholsville, Kentucky, was holding a funeral for the kerosene lamp. (Seriously—a funeral. They had a casket and everything.) And that was the end of the gas age and the start of the electric age.

In those fifty-four years, electricity changed the way humans live. We had primitive robot helpers in the form of electric clocks, clothes washers, dishwashers, irons, floor polishers, freezers, lawn mowers, radios, refrigerators, sewing machines, tea kettles, and vacuum cleaners. On the farm, there were electric animal clippers, corn shellers, cream separators, dairy sterilizers, sheep shearers, and vegetable washers. At first electricity was just a way to replace the sooty kerosene lamp. But it became a platform to solve any problem.

Data is like electricity in three ways.

First, it is invisible. We don't see it working. We don't see it being made.

Second, it gives us superpowers. Robotic extensions of ourselves and our knowledge. I will talk about those superpowers in later chapters.

Third, it is revolutionary. It has changed our civilization.

But the Data Revolution is unlike electricity in one important way.

With electricity you have to sign up for the ConEd account. You have to pay the bill. You have to flip the switch. Electricity, in other words, is voluntary.

Data just happens.

Data does not wait for you to flip a switch or pay a bill.

A diligent, blank-faced stenographer, it simply records.

Data is Andy Warhol.

Data is a voyeur.

Data is subject to a paradox like the subatomic particles under the mysterious rules of the Heisenberg Uncertainty Principle. Data can exist only if the thing it observes exists first.

Today, I am that thing. Me, my phone, and my intestines.

I AM GOING to take a car to East Side Endoscopy. I call an Uber at 6:16 a.m.

To find me, the app uses location data.

Location data uses one of three methods. All three of the possible methods employ triangulation.

Triangulation is a weirdly simple technique. Let's start with the cell tower version because it's the most intuitive.

Because I use my mobile phone to make phone calls (duh), my phone constantly pings Verizon cell towers to find out which one is closest. So I'll have the best possible signal. When the data comes back, my phone knows the time it took for the signal to return from the tower—the "round trip time." If there are three towers nearby, my phone will know the distance to each one. A triangle. My phone knows I am ten thousand meters from Tower A, and five hundred meters from Tower B, and two thousand meters from Tower C. Map that on a piece of paper like a middle-schooler with a protractor, and my phone knows it is in my kitchen on Eastern Parkway in Brooklyn. While I daydream of the breakfast I am not allowed to eat.

A slightly creepier version of triangulation is based on Wi-Fi. Instead of triangulating to cell towers, my phone pings nearby Wi-Fi routers. The signal strength of each router triangulates where my phone is. For some reason, I dislike this one. Wi-Fi was my friend. Now it's talking behind my back?

The last version is the space age version—GPS.

As I stand in my kitchen, six satellites operated by the United States Space Force whirl overhead at heights ranging from 288 kilometers to 1,400 kilometers above the earth, and at speeds ranging from 11,000 mph to 17,000 mph. The satellites are talking to my phone. Their names are Globalstar, Asgardia, RiSat, Technosat, Proxima I, and Proxima II. They are telling my phone how far away they are and what time it is according to the atomic clocks they carry. My phone converts those distances into Cartesian three-dimensional space—using the center of the earth as the origin point—and calculates not only where I am (40.672520 latitude, -73.964180 longitude), but also my altitude above sea level.

So my Uber knows where to pick me up.

My driver is Luba. She is from Georgia—former Soviet, not Allman Brothers, Georgia. She wants to practice her English. She tells me she was a pediatrician in Georgia. "No money," she tells me, anticipating my unasked question about why she moved. The Uber app feeds her directions in Cyrillic. She tells me about her husband's job managing a laundromat. But I am staring out the window. New York scenes. In Chinatown, dry leaves and little white napkins skitter up the gutters in the hot breeze. In NoHo, two policemen hold their hands over their eyes to peer in the darkened windows of a vegan restaurant. Was there a break-in? Suddenly, as if summoned like film extras, young women in yoga pants appear. A class at some hidden gym. Their water bottles are as large as their forearms.

I arrive at East Side Endoscopy. When I typed my destination (380 Second Avenue) into Uber, Uber *knew* that the address 380 Second Avenue belonged to East Side Endoscopy. How did Uber know that?

Uber buys data from FourSquare. FourSquare has an app where you check into places. When you check in, you are helping to build FourSquare's database of "points of interest," or POI, data. (In the FourSquare entry for East Side Endoscopy, the bearded poster included a selfie of himself in his paper gown. Why?)

On my way down the clinic's elevator, I accidentally start iTunes. It plays a Mozart piano concerto I had listened to last night. (I am not usually so highbrow. But when I am working and the family is around, Mozart filters out the voices and doesn't fill my head with catchy lyrics.)

I am so zonked at 6:51 a.m. that I think the music plinking from my phone is actually Muzak playing in the elevator. There is someone else in the elevator. She has press-on nails so long and pink she looks like a predator version of Dolly Parton. I catch my mistake and turn off the music. I make an apology and a self-deprecating joke to Dolly. In my addled, famished, dry-mouthed condition, I sound like a stoner trying to talk through a rag. Predator Dolly couldn't care less.

The encounter took 11,393 milliseconds, not including the apology. I know this because Apple was alerted to the fact that user 2026862198—which is associated with my device ID, email address, phone number, and postal address—was listening to Mozart's Piano Concerto No. 21 in C Major.

Second movement.

Andante.

From IP address 2600:1017:b42a:69dc:6466:9dad:581:d1e.

In the office, I sign consent forms with a stylus attached to a signature pad manufactured by a company called Topaz Systems, Inc. Topaz has a software development kit (or SDK) that allows the doctor to capture my signature electronically. I consent to the "use and disclosure of health information"; I acknowledge privacy practices, my financial responsibility, and informed consent. Topaz Systems stores my signatures as an electronic file in a drive in the doctor's office computer marked "consent forms colored." (Each form is yellow, pink, and white.)

A nurse guides me to a gurney enclosed by a curtain, like in an emergency room. I strip and put on a robe with my bare behind facing the flap. Easy access for the docs. *Aw, man,* I think. *Getting close to showtime.*

I do not take a selfie.

I am wheeled into a procedure room. My gastroenterologist, Dr. Mojaver, has a great head of hair. He is making jokes to put me at ease. The technician, aware of how starving his patients are, is asking me where I want to eat when I'm done. This is probably his standard patter. I tell him I am from the South. What I crave is soul food. Fried chicken, collards, biscuits. At that moment he is injecting me with propofol. I can see it, white and creamy, in its plastic container.

"Hey," I say, thinking of soul food. "This anesthesia looks like Crisco." I think this is hilarious. I am instantly unconscious, so I don't know if anyone laughed.

THERE ARE 95,528 standardized descriptions of medical conditions. Each has a unique number. The documented conditions range from "Cholera" (number zero) to "post COVID-19 condition, unspecified" (number 95,528). In the middle you might find "Infection of amputation stump" (number 3,785) and "Major laceration of right kidney" (number 39,383). A team in Geneva, Switzerland, updates these descriptions frequently. The World Health Organization runs the program and coordinates with sister organizations in every region. For North America, the coordinating authority is the Centers for Disease Control and Prevention. As a data person, I find the whole apparatus both elegant and impressive.

In a blink, my screening is complete. I am still high on propofol.

A hasty nurse has shoved a printout of my Patient Health Record into my hand. The printout shows color pictures of the insides of my intestines. My first thought is: *How do they get such good lighting in there?* My second thought is relief. My intestines are pink and clear.

Which is great from a health perspective. But my relief is also that of a host. I was oddly afraid my guts would be messy. Seeing my pink, clean intestines on camera is like having unexpected company and finding your children have made their beds.

The photos were produced as part of my treatment. Treatments also have WHO codes. This is code Z12.11, screening for malignant neoplasm of the colon.

Dr. Mojaver did not find any cancer or polyps. But he did find K57.30, diverticulosis of the large intestine, which are these weird little pockets in your intestine, like cloakrooms, that serve no purpose and offer no health risk. Fine.

They also found K64.8, which is "other hemorrhoids," the WHO term for "internal hemorrhoids," which is gross, but I suppose better than having them on the outside. The hasty nurse tells me I need to eat more fiber.

"Feeling okayyyyy?" she says, in a tone border collies employ with sheep. She really wants me out of this bed.

I am dazed. I want soul food. I open Google Maps. I search for "soul food." There are no soul food places in the East 20s in New York City, which I think is a damned shame. I am at latitude 40.73719 and longitude -73.9812. The Google Maps app pings the Google servers 136 times.

"Feeling better?" The nurse has ripped back the curtain. If she were in possession of a posthole digger, she would scoop me up and cast me aside like a muddy divot, hairy with grass. "Ready to get up nowwww?"

I put my clothes on. Because of the general anesthesia, you have to be picked up. My wife arrives in a tender mood. We take another Uber home, this time with Hector, a muscular kid driving a souped-up Camry with red leather seats playing a Lite Hits station. The propofol is still in my system. I gaze out at the day with a glowing, universal goodwill. "Call Me Maybe" . . . what a wonderful song!

I arrive home at 9:05. I have been on a southern food cooking jag and have leftover South Carolina white grits in Tupperware. I reheat them in butter along with tomatoes I roasted last week. I scramble eggs. I sprinkle them with kosher salt and grinds of pepper. To hell with fiber. I wash it all down with a fresh pot of hot coffee. It is the best meal anyone has eaten, ever.

And I have earned it. I have created data for Apple, Google, Uber, Topaz Systems, and a company called eClinical Works has recorded my personal health record. The data was generated using Space Force, Verizon, Android, iOS, the International Classification of Diseases Clinical Modification system from the World Health Organization and the CDC, and the FourSquare Points of Interest database. The data is connected to my IP addresses, my lat/long, my altitude, my iPhone device ID, my email address, my Verizon mobile number, and my postal address.

And it is not even ten o'clock.

HOW DID MY world become so steeped in data? Both inside my colon, where I am known as K57.30 . . . and out, where I am known as 965299537481?

To answer that question, we will need to witness a great fire, count people using clocks, and help scientists smash together subatomic particles.

KEY POINTS IN CHAPTER 1

- Data has crept up on our civilization like electricity did in the twentieth century: Gradually becoming part of the fabric of life and business.

- Smartphones bring data into our daily lives through GPS, location data, and app usage, and data penetrates as deep as our health records.

- An infrastructure of IDs, codes, data centers, and calls between "smart" devices and servers has built up to support it all, even if it is largely out of sight.

THOUGHT STARTERS FOR YOU

- As citizens, we must: Be aware that we shed data like dandruff in virtually every aspect of our lives.

- As a professional, I can put this same data to work. What aspect of life or commerce are you interested in describing? Inquiring about? Assume the data is there.

WHERE DO WE GO NEXT?

We need to better understand how we got here—to this place where we are making and storing data at such volumes.

CHAPTER 2

Life After the Data Revolution

The Library

I f you were standing at the Port of Alexandria in Egypt on a fateful November night in 48 BCE, you'd be terrified. Smoke would choke you. The great glow of a hundred wooden ships burning would threaten to fry your corneas. You'd see embers and sparks flying into the night sky.

Some idiot in Julius Caesar's army had set the fire. What was Julius Caesar doing in Alexandria? It was all a little complicated. How Caesar fled there during the Roman civil war. How he got on the bad side of his host, the Emperor Ptolemy. How he got mixed up with Ptolemy's sister Cleopatra. And why the Romans thought burning the whole Egyptian fleet was a good way to protect themselves, when they themselves were encamped on land.

The main thing to pay attention to is the embers. One rises, lazily rides the breeze a short distance, lands on a large nearby building, which happens to be the Library of Alexandria, and sets it aflame. Thirty thousand scrolls and half of Greek civilization goes up in smoke.

A tragedy of ancient civilization.

A tragedy of data.

And more precisely, for our purposes, a tragedy of data *storage*.

Pick a Greek tragedy that survived the fire. *Antigone*, by Sophocles. If you add up all the type and text that goes into *Antigone*—setting aside the genius and all that—it's about a half megabyte. Today, you can download it as a pdf to your phone in about twenty seconds.

In 48 BCE, the storage of *Antigone* required the wealth of an empire.

The Library of Alexandria was not a library like we think of libraries today. A place you go to snack and text while pretending to do homework. The Library of Alexandria was basically Stanford University. A lavish campus, with landscaping, sculpture. Scholars with bad hygiene puttering around the grounds, thinking great thoughts, living off a stipend. The collection itself was a multigenerational achievement, requiring the obsession and the treasure of the entire Ptolemaic Dynasty, from Ptolemy Eurgertes, who started it, to Ptolemy Philodactus, who had his ships burned by Caesar. At its peak, it contained seven hundred thousand scrolls.

And it is not a flight of twenty-first-century fancy to equate the library with a giant database. Its greatest librarian, Zenodotus, invented a system for labeling the scrolls. Each scroll would have a plate next to its storage slot with its title, the name and birthplace of its author, and the first line of the book. So our slot would read:

Antigone
Sophocles
Kolonos
My sister, my Ismene, do you know

With this plate system, which was called *pinakes*, Zenodotus had invented *metadata*. Data about data. We'll come back to that in later chapters.

For now it is enough to understand that the storage of half a megabyte of data in 48 BCE is impossible to put a value on. It would be like putting a value on storing the *Mona Lisa*. You'd have to value the entire Louvre Museum, all 650,000 square feet of central Paris real estate, not to mention its value as a historic landmark or its annual operating budget for staff and climate controls and cafeterias and parking and tourist security. Everything required to keep the *Mona Lisa* up there half-smiling on her hook, day after day, for generations.

Data storage to Ptolemy in 48 BCE was, literally, priceless.

And so it would remain for two millennia. Until a nineteen-year-old Columbia engineering grad named Herman Hollerith went to Washington, DC, and got frustrated.

"FEW, WHO HAVE not come directly in contact with a census office, can form any adequate idea of the labor involved in the compilation of a census of fifty million persons." So wrote Herman Hollerith. The son of German immigrants, schoolteachers, he looked like a schoolteacher himself. Skinny neck. Weak chin. Pale. He wore a bushy walrus mustache in the style of the time. You can just see him growing it out to try and look older.

Now twenty-nine, Herman had spent a decade laboring at the census. And he was exasperated. Because the United States had outgrown its own census. The 1880 census—which Herman had been working on for years because the process was so manual—counted "fifty million persons." Herman expected the 1890 census, which he was preparing for, to cover sixty-two million people. Twenty-four percent growth in ten years. And look at all the data they were gathering! Race, sex, age, marital status, employment, disablement, literacy, children. And now, Congress was asking *not* that the census team bucket Americans into age groups, like eighteen to twenty-four. Instead they now wanted every age *by year*! That could mean a hundred items for the age category alone. And in the racist ways of the time—this was the Jim Crow era—they wanted race to be "enumerated and tabulated with reference to the distinctions of blacks, mulattoes, quadroons, and octoroons."

That's four race categories, just for Black people! Herman wasn't so much outraged by the requests or their motivations. He was sputtering at all the *combinations* he knew Congress was going to ask for. He just knew they would be asking for a count of the White, female, literate, and employed, who also had kids. And then they would want to know how many of them were under age twenty-four. And over age forty-nine. And so on. And the requests would never stop. "It would then take a strip of paper over 500 miles long to contain such records," he wrote.

So Herman basically said, "To hell with it. I'm inventing a computer to calculate and store all this data."

To be more specific, he invented the punch card.

What if, he mused, you created a piece of paper for every citizen you wanted to count. You made it out of sturdy manila stock. Then the census taker—the *enumerator* in Hollerith's language—the person who went around door-to-door asking citizens about themselves, would merely have to punch a hole for each answer provided by each citizen.

And then, when the enumerator brought his bag of cards back to the census office, what you'd do is, you'd shove that card made of manila paper under a press. Kind of like one of those big paper cutters you see in a copy shop, where you pull the handle down. Only here, you pull the press handle down to stamp each census card and that press has a little plate of metal pins. The pins connect to a circuit. So when the pins pressed against the card, *and they punched the card in a certain spot*, they would complete a circuit. The circuit would be complete only for that one spot. All those other possible spots had not been punched. So: No completed circuit. No record. But for that one data point you punched—completed circuit. The data point—maybe for "literate" or "disabled"—would be recorded.

Recorded how? By a bunch of clock-like mechanisms Herman Hollerith had invented. The clocks would be over here, to the side, stacked in a specially made wooden cabinet. Only instead of hands for the minutes and hours, like a regular clock, it would have hands going to the ones and hundreds. These clocks would record the results of every stamped punch card. A tally.

And then, when you wanted to track *combinations* of data points— the ones Herman seemed very nervous about, all those requests for literate + White + women + over forty-nine—you had this other apparatus called the Sorting Box.

You set the machine to go ping when it finds the specific combinations you want. Like White + women + literate. And you set those aside, close them up in a box, and shove the box to the side to count later.

An elegant system.

The United States Census Bureau followed Herman's recommendation for the new system and used it for the 1890 census. Then Canada, France, Russia, Austria, Norway, Puerto Rico, Cuba, and the Philippines all used it for their national censuses. Herman founded The Tabulating Machine Company, an enterprise we know for its later name, International Business Machines, or IBM. They used punch cards for another hundred years.

Herman Hollerith reduced the cost of calculating and storing data from priceless to manageable.

And the cost of storing data kept falling. Storing our half-megabyte copy of *Antigone* in a 1950s IBM computer would have cost millions. Storing it today costs a fraction of a penny.

Herman Hollerith had successfully changed *part* of our relationship to data: How we store it.

The other half of our relationship to data changed in 1989, in the Swiss countryside . . .

How we make it.

PARTICLE COLLIDERS ARE a peak achievement of human science. They are massive facilities. Their mission is to whip subatomic particles around in a figure eight shape, faster and faster, until they smash together with such force that they re-create the conditions of the Big Bang. Then we can measure and understand what happened at the dawn of the universe. The biggest collider on the planet, the Large Hadron Collider, located in the CERN lab in Switzerland, is a collaboration of twenty-three countries, staffed by thousands of scientists.

It should be very hard to upstage a particle collider.

Tim Berners-Lee, a mild-mannered Englishman, worked at CERN in 1989—the year Madonna's "Like a Prayer" was a top hit, as was, in Switzerland, a bizarre mash-up called "Bring Me Edelweiss." But Tim didn't focus on the dawn of the universe. His job was "data acquisition and control." Tracking what all the brilliant scientists came up with. (The brilliant scientists being the other people employed at CERN—not him.) What bothered him was how hard it was to access information. Everybody had different computer systems. Different mainframes, running on different systems. "Often it was just easier to go and ask people when they were having coffee," he said.

When he expressed his frustration, colleagues would shrug. Wasn't email a sufficient platform for sharing information?

It wasn't. "I wanted to access different kinds of information," Tim said. "Such as a researcher's technical papers, the manuals for different software modules, minutes of hastily scribbled notes, and so on."

Tim Berners-Lee pictured a kind of neutral space—*between* all these scientists, between these many different *types* of information—where information sharing could happen. Between all the makers of information (like the scientists) and the receivers of information (like him). And that space would be able to handle the number and variety of information makers and receivers, and the variety of information types, necessary to advance a gigantic, complex scientific program like CERN's.

So Tim wrote three pieces of code.

One was a standard way of formatting documents.

With a standard format, any information—whether scribbled notes in a technical paper—could be shared. Since the text was shareable, in the lingo of the day, that made it "hypertext." So he would call that standard for formatting information a "hypertext markup language." He abbreviated that as HTML. But once you formatted the information properly, how would you transfer it from the particle physicist one flight up to Tim's desktop? Tim created some code for that, too, for transferring information from one computer to another. It was still the hypertext that was being shared. So he called that a "hypertext transfer protocol." Doesn't roll off the tongue, either, so they abbreviated that as well: HTTP.

And then, he needed a way of filing the data. Chasing down the Swiss particle physicists when they were on coffee break was annoying and stressful. Tim needed that particle physicist—or at least their technical papers—always to be in the same break room, drinking coffee, at the same time, forever. So he created a system for locating each file, each information source. Freezing the particle physicist's coffee break in space and time! A universal record locator. Or URL.

A format for the information.

A way to ask for it and receive it.

A permanent address so you could always find it.

And . . . the European scientists hated it.

So Tim Berners-Lee moved to the United States and started the World Wide Web Consortium at MIT. And along the way he had, of course, achieved something far beyond a means for mad scientists to share technical papers. He had solved the other end of Herman Hollerith's census problem.

All those enumerators, going from house to house with cards, asking questions, punching holes in manila paper. So slow. So costly.

Tim Berners-Lee had made it so that anyone—make that, *everyone*—in the world with a computer device who could make any kind of file, could become an enumerator. A creator of data.

. . .

TWENTY-TWO YEARS LATER, nearly 80 percent of the US owned a personal computer. Twenty-four years later, internet penetration broke 80 percent. Thirty years later, smartphone penetration reached 80 percent. Three hundred thirty million people with a computer for making and sharing data. Globally, six billion people.

Now each person with a smartphone is an enumerator. Listening to music. Posting photos. Posting comments. Writing. Reading. Searching. Shopping. Calling. Texting. Meeting. Even just moving around. We are data creators. Our actions, our movements, our mere fingers typing, create data, which, thanks to Herman Hollerith, we can store. Cheaply.

And it is not just people that are data creators. A *person* does not need to punch the card anymore. Because our devices are "smart," they, too, are enumerators. More than seven thousand satellites circle the earth, taking pictures of every tree, road, hill, and canyon on the planet, every minute, generating 950 terabits a day. Road sensors passively capture traffic data in "continuous count" programs. Stock markets track the flow of trades each day, creating a hundred terabytes of data. Ocean sensors bob in the deep tracking every patch of ocean the size of Texas. Oil and gas exploration uses sixty types of seismic sensors to plumb the earth.

We're taking the pulse of our planet.

Add it all up, and, as a civilization, we produce data at the rate of seventy-nine zettabytes per year. What the heck is a zettabyte? In volume, that's thirty-five billion times the works of Shakespeare . . . every minute. The planet doth protest too much.

We produce it. And then we *keep* it.

Why?

One reason is because we can. Thanks to the tabulating machine, storing the data is affordable.

But the deeper reason lies back in the Library of Alexandria.

Around 240 BCE, the Ptolemaic emperor who started the library, Ptolemy Eurgertes, sent an envoy to Athens. The request was to borrow the original scroll of *Antigone*. Also the original scrolls of Sophocles's other works: *Oedipus Rex*, *Oedipus at Colonus*, *Ajax*, *Women of Trachis*, *Philoctetes*, and *Electra*. Also the works of Aeschylus. And the works of Euripides. Pretty much the canon of Greek tragedies. The Athenians said yes. The only reason they did so is that Ptolemy Eurgertes plunked down an enormous deposit, the equivalent of millions and millions of dollars.

When the scrolls came back to Alexandria, Ptolemy Eurgertes had copies made.

Then sent those *copies* back to Athens.

He kept the originals. What a bully.

Because he wanted the originals in his library.

And the Ptolemies kept adding to the library. Book buyers spread out across the globe, buying scrolls, whole collections. If you were a visitor to Alexandria you'd find that your ship would be searched. Goons, employed by the Ptolemies, would empty out your trunk and confiscate your books. (In their fashion, they would keep the originals and give you back copies.) When the city of Athens was starving, an Egyptian envoy pulled up to the harbor at Piraeus with a ship full of food aid and said, "We'll happily unload the food to feed your starving people—if you give us books in return." Literary extortion.

Why?

Greed, clearly. The Ptolemies lusted for books. They were thieves, even. Literary gangsters. But *why* did the Ptolemies need all the books? Why did they need to amass a dragon's hoard, with Zenodotus prowling the stacks, labeling it all, counting it?

To me, the answer is simple. *Because they might need it.* There might arise some unexpected problem to solve. Some question to answer. Like the tragic hero in another Sophocles work, *Oedipus Rex*, Ptolemy Eurgertes, leader of his people, successor to both Alexander the Great and the Pharaohs, might come upon a sphinx—c'mon, he was Egyptian; of course it would be a sphinx—posing him a riddle, standing between him and something he desperately needed. Some terrible problem that threatened his people. Life, and history, has a way of doling out such problems all the time. And Ptolemy Eurgertes wanted to be able to go to the library, sniff all of Zenodotus's plates, and be able to find an answer.

The vast storage of data, and the incomprehensible speed of data creation, are new. The desire for data—for information just in case—dates back at least to Ptolemy Eurgertes.

Two thousand years later, in 2012, a big data expert named Edd Dumbill spoke what no doubt Ptolemy Eurgertes felt in his data-greedy heart:

"When you can," he said, "keep everything."

KEY POINTS IN CHAPTER 2

- Systematic data labeling and storage goes back to ancient times with the *pinakes* in the Library of Alexandria.

- The early computer systems of the US Census Bureau consolidated data and made it query-able.

- Internet protocols laid the groundwork for unlimited data creation and sharing, with tools for electronic formatting (HTML), transfer (HTTP), and storage locations (URL).

- Then, when our "smart" devices connected to the internet, the data creation, sharing, and storage revolution began in earnest, as every connected human became a data generator, and data quantities exploded.

THOUGHT STARTERS FOR YOU

- Where, in your world, can you start building a data asset?

- One way to look at it is: Where is it *easy* for you to build a data asset? Where are you, in the course of your business, logging transactions of some kind, tracking activity, measuring an output?

- Another way to look at it is: Where do you have a *valuable* data asset? Where do you have contact with a consumer or an industry or a space that *only you* (or your organization) touch? If you're privileged to have such a position, that's where you have a unique database to build.

- Learn from Zenodotus: A building with a bunch of scrolls is just a building with a bunch of scrolls. It's only when you meticulously tag everything with *pinakes* that it becomes a library. You must clean, organize, and tag your data. Without that, it's just a pile of parchment.

WHERE DO WE GO NEXT?

So far we have gotten to know data through the ages and through a single day. But we've been talking about data like it's some static thing: An asset, a pile of treasure for a Ptolemy. But that's not what data is about. At a certain point, we put it to work. Data is too precious, and too expensive, merely to hoard. In times of crisis, we learn how valuable it can be.

CHAPTER 3

Data Science

Data During Wartime

Data science seems to leap forward during moments of life and death.

London in 1665 was a city of fear. The plague had broken out in Amsterdam. Londoners knew their city could be next, and it was vulnerable. Overpopulated. Poor folks lived jammed thirty or forty to a house. And filthy: The ditch-like drains down the center of the main streets served as the sewage system and garbage disposal combined. People dumped buckets of waste out of windows. People attached little metal platforms to their shoes so they wouldn't track other people's feces into their homes. And because of the epidemics of 1603, 1625, and 1636, they knew what plague would do to you. Headaches, fever, vomiting. Lymph nodes in your armpits and groin swelling to the size of eggs and bursting with pus. When you got sick, the pain could drive you to screaming. It would kill everybody in your home. In this environment, folks frantically read the daily Bills of Mortality (a kind of late edition newspaper focused on deaths in each parish) like 2020 urbanites poring over the *New York Times* trailing-seven-day COVID heatmap.

Only one man kept his head.

John Graunt was a haberdasher, or clothes maker, who, perhaps after so many hours spent with measuring tape, had grown obsessed with numbers.

And amid the chaos, he said to himself, *The city authorities are spending a lot of time staring into these Bills of Mortality. But they don't seem to be putting them to much use.*

To Graunt, this left critical questions unanswered. How many Londoners was the plague killing? How long should anyone expect this to go on? Was it time for the people (who could afford to) to retreat to the countryside, where there was less crowding and survival rates were higher? What should businessmen in London do, to plan?

Graunt knew the methodology for the Bills of Mortality was a little rough and ready.

"When any one dies, the tolling, or ringing of a Bell," he wrote, would serve as an alert. That bell would call to action a group of people Graunt called the Searchers: "ancient Matrons, sworn to their Office." These matrons would "repair to the place where the dead Corps lies." And then by looking at the dead body, and by "view of the same, and by other enquiries," the Searchers would "examine by what Disease or Casualty the Corps died." These "ancient matrons," were, in other words, a kind of old-school medical examiner. You can only imagine the immune system required to play that role. And what a strange, indomitable force those ladies must have made, trundling to the church whenever the bell rang. (It always rang for them.) In the language of Herman Hollerith, they were *enumerators*. But if their immune systems were tough, they were not immune to payoffs. Landlords didn't want their buildings slashed with the red X that marked a plague house. So a tip to the ancient matron could have your house corpse tagged with the relatively chill label "consumption," that is, tuberculosis. Better than plague.

Still, there was a system. The Searchers would report the body count and cause of death to the parish clerk. The parish clerk in turn would make a report, every Tuesday, to the clerk of the hall. They published consolidated reports on Thursdays. Every year there would be an annual tally.

Graunt, a proud Londoner, felt he could do better. He gathered all the annual bills. He consolidated disease definitions. He cleaned up the geographies—which parish was in, which was out. Then Graunt made the death counts consistent and comparable year over year, so you could see trends.

Maybe it reveals a ghoulish character, but I find something Monty-Pythonish about Graunt's entries. Sure, you have death counts of, in 1665, "Murdered and shot, 9" and "Poisoned, 1," which are straightforward (and decidedly quaint from the point of view of a modern American, where 800 people die from shooting every week; but I digress). But then you have deaths by "King's Evill, 86" or because they are "Distracted, 5" or have "Collicke and Winde, 134," or they are simply "Frighted to death, 23." This is before you get down to the business of the plague, which that year carried off people at a whole different level: 68,586. I'm not laughing anymore. And neither, presumably, were the London authorities.

Graunt's efforts were so early in the history of data interpretation that he is credited for being the first demographer; first epidemiologist; first to make a time series analysis; first to create a statistical sample; first to focus on infant mortality rates.

Graunt, humble haberdasher though he was, published his work, as *Natural and Political Observations Made Upon the Bills of Mortality.* Samuel Pepys bought the first edition. It became a hit of sorts. The Royal Society recruited Graunt. After his work, civic leaders across Europe began counting their living and dying populations to make better decisions. To *make more use* of the information.

Even so, Graunt grappled with the idea that data was somehow a means to tackle real-world problems. He compares his work to that of a "silly Scholeboy." He frets that he is not academic enough. He tries to justify himself.

"I proceeded," he explains, "that I might present the world with some real fruit from those airy blossoms."

The airy blossoms in this case were not the thousands of bodies, dead of plague. One historian wrote, "The whole city reeked like a giant privy." Nothing blossom-y there.

No, the airy blossoms were the tables he had gathered. The data describing the dead.

No weight, no substance, really. This wasn't medicine for the sick or pesticide for the fleas that carried the plague or some scrubbing or sanitizing tool for hygiene. These were just tables of printed numbers. Ephemera. Ether.

Fruit, on the other hand, is nourishing. Practical.

Note that Graunt doesn't choose some other kind of metaphor. Anything related to truth or purity. Like, "Present the world with diamonds from this dirty coal." Or, "Present the world with fresh water from these muddy depths." He wished to present the world with fruit from airy blossoms.

Fruit.

Something you can bite into.

I AM A late bloomer. I took my first job managing people at the age of thirty-seven. By this age most people who go into management have at least, like, managed a shift at an ice cream parlor. I hadn't. I'm not sure why. I just avoided it. Or it avoided me. So managing people was new to me; the new job was an executive role, and it was part of a division of the Nielsen Company that did statistical modeling, which was also new to me. The division was called Claritas. The company had achieved nerd fame for a consumer segmentation scheme called PRIZM that placed every home in the United States into a segment based on the demographics of its neighborhood. The segments had cute names like

"Shotguns and Pickups" or "Blue Blood Estates." Each segment had a little picture of the people in the segment. And then, all the pictures would be stuck together in a poster. Clients loved the poster. It was color coded. Fun. And it told a story.

But I was struggling—trying to learn how to manage people, be an executive, and wrap my brain around something called multivariate division partitioning all at the same time.

So thank goodness for Dave Miller. Dave, a thirty-year veteran of the business and a statistician, was as patient, gentle, and wise as I was overcaffeinated, anxious, and snarky. I needed a little refuge in the storm. And the time I had with Dave helped me. I had this notion, pretty much right off the bat, that we could use the PRIZM segmentation scheme, which had been used exclusively by direct marketers—targeting mailers for Best Buy or Allstate insurance—to target digital advertising.

I was at a conference. I was about to pitch the idea for the first time. The meeting was in an hour. I had grabbed Dave because I was still wrapping my head around my own idea. (This happens to me. I'm not sure if others are the same way. I get an intuition, then try and prove it right or wrong.)

JUSTIN:
I'm just worried about whether it will work in digital.

DAVE:
It works in direct mail. We just won an award for the best model.

JUSTIN:
How did the contest measure it? How did they know our model worked best?

DAVE:

They measured the open rate for the direct mail. Each piece of mail has a unique code. So when the customer calls the 800 number and gives the code, the marketer knows which campaign that response came from.

JUSTIN:

Okay, so our model had the best open rate?
The most people who called the marketer?

DAVE:

Right. The highest percentage of people.

JUSTIN:

Okay, so how will we know if it works in digital?

DAVE:

There's only one question to answer.
[with a big smile]
Is it better than your next best alternative?

What was Dave's smile for? He knew I wanted a fancy answer. Or an answer that would sound fancy to the client I was about to meet. Preferably an answer containing words like *multivariate division partitioning*. But Dave was confident enough in his craft to know when to give a simple explanation.

Is it better than your next best alternative?

In other words: Your answer, using data, doesn't need to be perfect. It just needs to be a better answer than the one you had yesterday. If it is, then the answer you have now has value. Maybe even a lot of value.

I never forgot the exchange. (Clearly.)

What I didn't realize, at the time, was that the concept was already decades old.

· · ·

JOHN TUKEY WAS a wartime statistician. During WWII he worked on technical challenges for the B-29. He worked on battlefield range finders and on breaking the codes of the Nazi Enigma machine. In the Cold War, he worked for Bell Labs and helped create the U-2 spy plane so the US could detect a surprise Soviet nuclear attack.

Maybe it was this wartime thinking that drove him to blow up statistics.

In 1962, Tukey published a paper that no one in the field of stats ever got over. He called it "The Future of Data Analysis." "The Future of Data Analysis" is so famous it has an acronym: FoDA. A prominent journal published it, alongside a lot of precise and mathematical research. And who the heck was John Tukey to blow up his own chosen field? Sure, he was a wartime statistician. But he was a statistician. He grew up in New England. His dad was a high school Latin teacher. His mom was a substitute teacher at the same school. He went to Brown University. He adored Brown and wore the Brown tie all the time. He got a teaching and research job at Princeton and spent his entire career there. John Tukey was married. He loved his wife. He met her folk dancing. Decades later when she died, he lamented the way only a statistician can lament. "One is so much less than two," he said. In photographs, John Tukey wears a blazer and a shirt with buttoned-down collars and a tie; his gray hair is cut short, and he's a little thickset and looks like an earnest, committed, successful, East Coast, twentieth-century White male, with a flicker of wit in the smile and the remote gaze of someone who very well might be calculating a big number while he's talking to you. But a revolutionary?

"For a long time," John Tukey begins in FoDA, "I have thought I was a statistician."

Wait, past tense? You *thought* you were a statistician?

Right from the get-go, you know something is coming.

"But as I have watched mathematical statistics evolve," he goes on, "I have had cause to wonder and to doubt."

We pay statisticians to doubt, yes. Poke holes. Apply rigor. But John Tukey was also a statistician who *wondered*. And what he dreamed up in his paper was a whole new vision for statistics, where it would break off from its role as the most boring subdepartment in the Department of Mathematics and become its own science. Data science. Tukey doesn't coin the term—that would happen later—but he lays out passionately what he means.

- "Data analysis must seek for usefulness rather than security."

- "Data analysis must be willing to err moderately in order that inadequate evidence shall suggest the right answer."

- "Data analysis must use mathematical argument as bases for judgment rather than as bases for proof."

It was revolutionary. He was saying the discipline should not be about professionals combing through small samples and using careful, cautious, correct math to make a defensible projection. To hell with cautious and correct! Make errors! (Moderate ones, anyway.) Use inadequate evidence! Use your math as a tool—as a means, not an end. The idea is to make something useful. Collaborate with people who might not know math the way you do but are experts in the domain you're working in.

Can't you just hear John Graunt cheering? Don't you think John Graunt huddled—to the extent that he dared get close—with the Searchers and asked them how they did their jobs? What did they really know about rickets versus consumption? Isn't it possible that John Tukey talked to soldiers and officers in the infantry when he helped create a new range finder? *When someone's trying to blow your ass up and you need to fire back, how can we help you judge the distance better?*

In wartime, and plague time, there wasn't time to wait for perfection. Data analysis—data science—had to be useful. This was Graunt's complaint: All the people reading the Bills of Mortality were not *making use of them*. And along came John Tukey, three hundred years later, working on spy planes, and said, *I know exactly what you mean. We need a new science to do this*. What was its mantra? Basically what Dave Miller said. Is whatever you have come up with, using judgment, using inadequate evidence, better than your next best alternative? Yes? Then that might be good enough. For a Londoner trying to avoid the plague or an infantry soldier shooting a shoulder rocket or the captain of a ship trying not to get sunk by a Nazi submarine, good enough meant everything.

I believe there might have been another reason for the urgent tone of Tukey's paper. I believe he saw the data revolution coming.

Four years later, Tukey published another paper. It wasn't as famous as FoDA. He listed "four major influences on data analysis today." Of the four, two were related to what we now call Big Data. There's been a library of books and articles written about Big Data, so I will stop capitalizing it and define it quickly as data where there is more than a sample—data in massive quantities on any subject.

The 1960s, when John Tukey wrote these papers, was not an era of big data. But Tukey saw "the challenge, in many fields, of more and ever larger bodies of data." And he foresaw "the emphasis on quantification in an ever-wider variety of disciplines."

"The need," he went on, "is to understand the similarities in data analysis in nuclear physics, in the physiology of cell nuclei, in antiviral agents, and in opinion polling."

Tukey saw a world where many disciplines—maybe all disciplines—were creating massive amounts of data. And demanding faster and more sophisticated analysis. The processing of data, Tukey foretold, would need to be "not only in some sort of real time" but also to "perform as well as current expert judgement."

Which led him to another major prediction:

"Accelerating developments in computers."

There was no way that the human mind could keep up with the data bursting out of the fields of biology and medicine and nuclear physics—and certainly not ever-changing human opinion. Out there, there was infinite volume. Infinite complexity. We would need help processing it all.

We would need help from machines.

And so, attempting to grapple with infinity forced data science to become a domain that was bionic. A collaboration of human and machine. A sport for cyborgs.

Tukey's vision would need help from one of the twentieth century's computing visionaries, Alan Turing.

JOHN TUKEY AND Alan Turing almost certainly met.

Princeton University was the connection point. Princeton was the nexus of advanced math during WWII. Tukey worked there. Turing visited. They both worked on Enigma. They were about the same age—Tukey was three years younger. But I can't see them being friends. Alan Turing was too odd. Set them side by side, Tukey and Turing are poignant counterparts:

Tukey: Burly, humble, hetero, homeschooled, American as they come.

Turing: Scrawny, scruffy, gay, Old Shirburnian and King's College Cambridge.

Tukey: Brave and forceful as an army.

Turing: Leaping galaxies like a laser.

Tukey: Living a full life, dying at eighty-eight among friends.

Turing: Dead of suicide at forty-one, ten years before Tukey named *accelerating developments in computers* as a major force in data science despite Turing having, basically, invented computers.

THE OLD DEFINITION of a computer is how, today, we think of a calculator. A device that takes a specific question (What is 147 times 29?) and returns an answer (4,263). Teams of humans were sometimes tasked with executing calculations. And they were called "computers." Turing himself—in addition to being a notoriously sloppy typist—was, ironically known to be a lousy computer.

At twenty-four, Turing brought everyone much closer to the idea of computing the way we think of it today. He grappled with a problem posed several years before by a German mathematician named David Hilbert. Hilbert posed the "problem of decidability." The idea was that, for any mathematical proposition, you had to be able to prove if it was true or false.

Turing's mentor and professor recalled how Turing got involved in the problem.

"I believe it all started because he attended a lecture of mine. I think I said that [of Hilbert's decidability problem] it's purely mechanical. I may even have said, a machine can do it. Turing took the notion and tried to follow it right up."

What Turing did was wrestle with how you could create a machine flexible enough to do what Hilbert (and Turing's professor) had suggested: Get the computer to prove any proposition.

That's what Turing wanted to understand when he came at the problem. But what he came away with was much more interesting.

Turing conjectured a computing machine that was flexible enough to handle any problem at all.

"We may compare a man in the process of computing a real number to a machine," he wrote. "[A machine] which is capable of a finite number of conditions, which will be called m-configurations. The m-configurations may be changed."

And after explaining how this might work, he concludes: "These operations will include all those which are used in the computation of a number."

All those.

Boring, small words. But they implied a previously unimaginable expansion, leaping from a world where a "computer" sat down and solved a multiplication problem (147 times 29) and instead encompassed *all those* operations used in the computation of a number.

Which is to say, the computation of any number.

Which is to say, applying computation to *any problem*.

His professor later explained the significance of Turing's work: "He produced this extraordinary definition of a 'computable function,' giving the first idea of a perfectly general computing machine."

Turing went on to build the famous Colossus computer at Bletchley Park and the first proper computer, by our modern definition, at the University of Manchester. But the *notion* itself of a general computer was not new. Ada Lovelace, the brilliant daughter of "mad, bad, and dangerous to know" Lord Byron and an accomplished mathematician, had expressed the idea much more elegantly and expansively nearly a hundred years before. Lovelace had been working on an "analytical engine."

"The operating mechanism might act upon things beside number," Lovelace wrote. "Supposing, for instance, that the fundamental relations of pitched sounds and of musical compositions were susceptible of such expression . . . the engine might compose elaborate and scientific pieces of music."

Music? A machine? I thought these machines were supposed to be calculating 147 times 29.

If the notion of a "perfectly general computing machine" can be extended to something as ephemeral and so essentially human as music, then perhaps there is no limit to the "use" of data (to echo Graunt's phrase). Between the four of them—Graunt, Lovelace, Turing, and Tukey—an astonishing picture emerges. A world where "ever larger bodies of data" can be "made use of" to affect an "ever-wider variety of disciplines."

And flexible, powerful machines, with m-configurations that swap and switch in whatever way we need, may munch this data. Machines that can do the work of legions of sweating, ink-stained human calculators. Algorithms, in effect, to answer any question.

Answers that are not mere proofs. Answers that are useful. Maybe more than useful.

Answers that are musical.

Answers—derived by a combination of man and machine—to interpret and to understand.

KEY POINTS IN CHAPTER 3

- There is something about epidemics and wartime—as we will see in a later chapter as well—that focuses the mind of data people. Thanks to John Graunt during the plague and John Tukey during World War II, we started to see data as a means to answer urgent questions, not perform mathematical proofs. Data had to be useful.

- My old friend Dave Miller had a definition for data's usefulness: *Is it better than your next best alternative?*

- But in a world where data assets grow larger, and our questions for it proliferate, we must harness data science to computing to keep up and to remain useful.

THOUGHT STARTERS FOR YOU

- Are there places in your domain today where you could use data to make a decision—but you're holding back because your information may not be completely accurate?

- Where are there places where a good enough answer can mean a better decision, even if it's not a great decision?

- Do you have access to incomplete, but potentially useful, data sources that you are not using?

WHERE DO WE GO NEXT?

If we're going to start talking about data science and computing, we're going to need to understand a little more about the wild bronco we are now riding as a civilization: Artificial intelligence. I won't try to summarize the whole concept in a single chapter but instead put AI into context and prompt us to think about its relationship to the data landscape.

CHAPTER 4

Artificial Intelligence

A Sport for Cyborgs

You are in Cambridge, England. It is 1948. You are pushing your baby in a pram. Your son is running around this little green park called Midsummer Common. Suddenly your boy sprints toward you, scarlet faced, terrified. You look up. A vast machine lumbers behind him. It's on tank tracks. It moves ominously. When you look at it more closely you realize why it has an uncanny vibe. It looks . . . kind of human. In place of eyes there is a camera. A loudspeaker juts out for a mouth. At its sides are two giant clamps for hands. A long cable trails it. It seems very interested in your son.

Alan Turing speculated about such a contraption as the first embodiment of artificial intelligence.

"Take a man as a whole and try and replace all the parts of him by machinery," he wrote. "He would include television cameras, microphones, loudspeakers. In order that the machine should have a chance of finding things out for itself, it should be allowed to roam the countryside."

Even so, Turing lamented, "The creature would still have no contact with food, sex, sport and many other things of interest to the human being." So Turing finally dismisses the ideas as "altogether too slow and impracticable."

Turing's robot is a melancholy creature because it has an impossible task. Its job is to wander until it observes enough of humanity to learn its ways.

The impossibility of the task comes from the vast imbalance between the complexity of real life—food, sex, and sport, for starters—and what a machine can process.

And if we take as a framework this weird relationship between the uncanny robot (the intelligent machine), your toddler son (some complex reality), the data about your son that the robot learns from, and the learning process that the robot performs, we can start a journey to explain the relationship between phenomena we've already discussed:

Reality.

Data.

Data science.

And now, artificial intelligence.

It's a journey that begins with a bonk on the head and finishes with a car crash.

"THE NIGHT WE were submitting, I pulled an all-nighter at Google," the intern later recalled. "I caught a couple hours sleep in one of the small conference rooms. I woke up just in time for the submission when someone coming in early to work opened the door and hit my head."

The intern was Aidan Gomez. The submission in question was a paper that described a "transformer model," a new type of algorithm that later became known as a "large language model." The paper, and the algorithm, changed everything.

Yet Alan Turing had anticipated it in 1948. At least in principle.

After dismissing the idea of a creepy roaming robot, Turing turned instead to describing the elements that would make a machine intelligent.

First, training. The machine would have to be able to be trained, like a college student is trained. "It would be quite unfair to expect a machine straight from the factory to compete on equal terms with a university graduate," Turing says. "The graduate has had contact with human beings for twenty years."

Second, nonlinear. To be trainable, the machine couldn't be a linear, one-trick calculator. It would have to be what Turing calls an "unorganized machine." It would have to possess a quality of malleability so when it received new information—like when your kid starts screaming because the robot is chasing him across Midsummer Common—such training could change the way the machine operates.

Third, the machine would need to make evaluations. That means it would need to be able to search back in its memory—*Remember last week, when I chased the little girl across Midsummer Common and her mother clocked me with a cricket bat?*—and have the ability to compare one data point to another, to learn from the comparison.

Fourth, for the training to stick, the machine would need to be provided with rewards and punishment. "Pleasure-Pain systems," Turing calls them. (Spicy!)

Finally, the machine would need to be able to "change its own instructions." It would need to be able to adapt. In other words, it would need to be able to make *decisions*.

But in 1948, these were just ideas "chiefly of interest when we consider what a machine could *in principle* be designed to do," Turing wrote (italics mine). "When," he qualified, "we allow it both unlimited time and unlimited storage capacity."

Well, in the seventy years that passed between Turing's paper and the Google intern getting bonked on the head, computers have gained these two powers—unlimited time and unlimited storage capacity.

Storage capacity, we have discussed previously. Storing *Antigone* for a lifetime, for the cost of a few pennies.

But unlimited time? Unlimited time *to make calculations* is what Turing meant. Computing power since 1948 has increased so dramatically that from Turing's perspective, the time computers have to make decisions might as well be unlimited.

For that, we have the *Asteroids* video game to thank.

IT IS 1980. I am sitting on a shag rug in the living room of my friend Steve Ludt. We are playing *Asteroids*.

Steve Ludt and I are in fifth grade. That year, my school decided that I would skip fourth grade and go directly to fifth. Which meant I passed from the total innocence of elementary school—lunch boxes and playdates—to the jungle warfare of middle school—cliques, parties, and spin-the-bottle—basically overnight. I am not handling it well. The invitation from Steve Ludt to play *Asteroids* and eat Doritos out of a bag is promising for my social life, which so far has been pathetic. But the fact that I am utterly gormless at controlling my spaceship is bumming me out. The asteroids keep closing in and smashing my ship with a doomy, bass-inflected *doozh!*

I am not the only one who struggled with *Asteroids*. So did its developers. The game is complex. It involves multiple spatial relationships, interacting simultaneously. The asteroid (moving shape) hurtles toward the spaceship (shape). The spaceship shoots laser bullet things (moving shapes) that hits the asteroid (shape) and splits it into multiple smaller asteroids (moving shapes), which, then, in turn, can be shot (more moving shapes) and destroyed (shape removed).

The game required so many calculations that the video game company, the legendary Atari, created a little piece of hardware to help things along, which they called the Alphanumeric Television Interface Controller, or ANTIC. The ANTIC allowed the Atari console to quickly perform the many calculations required to manage the relationships between hurtling asteroid and spaceship. When the coordinates of ship + asteroid, or laser bullet thing + asteroid, converged, there had to be an explosion. They called each object a "sprite," and they had to perform the calculations about the coordinates of sprites in real time. Or the game would seem slow and glitchy, and hence, not fun.

The ANTIC, in other words, was one of the first graphics processing units, or GPUs. A kind of silicon chip for computer processing.

If you contrast the structure of a GPU to the more familiar CPU, or central processing unit, it's different.

The CPU has a compact design. It makes decisions for the computer quickly. Information comes in, decisions go out. That's its main function: To sit in the center of the computer and help it do a variety of tasks swiftly. Perfect, in other words, for a PC.

The GPU has much more capacity to do math. Each GPU is heavied up with arithmetic logic units—units that do calculations, which can be distributed across multiple units—so that many, many calculations can be performed simultaneously. Perfect for a video game console juggling asteroids.

As video games evolved from *Asteroids* to *Assassin's Creed* and *FIFA*—games so beautifully rendered they look like movies or live TV—the GPU became powerful enough to be used not just to render and re-render what an empty warehouse might look like from the perspective of a first-person shooter, but to fuel artificial intelligence.

We could not quite give Alan Turing the "unlimited time" he desired for his intelligent machine. But we could compress the time required to do a calculation so much that it was almost the same thing.

THE ABILITY TO perform basically unlimited calculations was essential for the leap into proper artificial intelligence. It was all in that paper the Google team submitted the morning the sleeping intern, Aidan Gomez, was bonked on the head. The Google team called it the idea of *attention*.

Importantly, the Google transformer model worked on text.

The reason Alan Turing's robot scaring children in the park is so hopeless is that its task is impossible. There's too much complexity. Its camera eye watches a shape scamper across a field. Even if its computing system was sophisticated enough to label the shape as a "child" and see the larger shape standing near it and label it "parent," then notice a female-coded mode of dress for 1948 and refine that label as "mother," and so on, to truly understand all the relationships between spaces and objects and social norms and physics would be too much for it.

But in text . . . when Antigone says

O Love, no one can hide from you
You take gods who live forever
You take humans who die in a day,
And they take you and go mad.

. . . think about: All the relationships that are embedded within the words. There's vocabulary (all the objects) and grammar (all the relationships between the objects).

Admittedly, to understand all the relationships is the hard part. It's not just parts of speech—subject, verb, object. It's also the context. Is Midsummer Common a field as in an open space with grass? Or a field as in a topic for study? Am I the child's parent because I gave birth to him? Or his parent because I occupy a level above him in a conceptual taxonomy? That's what requires the *attention* in the attention model. You had to keep applying all the context and grammar you've already learned, to *every sentence*, heck, every word that you're reading and speaking. And to apply all that attention requires a ridiculous amount of computational power. Thank you, attention models. Thank you, GPUs.

So, yes, human language is an enormously complex game of *Asteroids*.

But it's still a game. With a finite number of objects. And a knowable set of rules.

And these rules and objects are based on observations from . . . data.

So if you had a computer with unlimited storage and unlimited time to perform calculations, you could stuff enough data into it so it could identify all the objects and understand the rules of the game. And thanks to the nature of text, all the objects and relationships are built into the data set. You just need to unpack it, and pay attention.

In other words, with enough data, you could teach your robot to read and write.

How much data do we need to teach the robot to read and write?

GPT 3.5, the predecessor of ChatGPT, trained on about a terabyte of data. That's the Bible, Shakespeare, Jane Austen, all fifty-two novels of Agatha Christie from *The Mysterious Affair at Styles* to *Curtain*, all three volumes of *The Lord of the Rings*, the works of Philip Roth . . .

. . . times twenty-three thousand.

So now, in text form, we have a robot who can stroll up to you—on paper, anyway—and say, "I'm frightfully sorry. I'm afraid I've rather given your boy a bit of a scare."

I mean *I* would never say that. But the robot knows that it's 1948, and it is speaking England-English, and it's addressing a lady—so it, in turn, needs to speak like a gentleman. And it knows it's a tense situation in which it needs to apologize and so use layers of tension-diffusing, self-deprecating phrases like "frightfully sorry" and "rather" and "a bit."

So we have taught a robot to roam the countryside of language.

And this one can do it well. The transformer model is a successful robot—a successful intelligent machine.

Our generation, in other words, has successfully completed the journey that Alan Turing set us on. We have reached the destination of true artificial intelligence.

What we do with that power now that we, as a species, have arrived is a big issue, larger than the scope of this, or any single, book.

What I am trying to do is help clarify how it works. And what it means. You can read all sorts of great writing—and clickbait drivel—about the tricks you can get AI to perform. But what these robots are showing us—Turing's lumbering humanoid and the Google transformer—is that we have beaten a path that turns reality into data, data into decisions (with data science), and, now, data science into artificial intelligence.

These robots touch the membrane between cyborg brains and reality.

They give us the power to speed up our understanding of our world.

So that passage from data to AI is critical to understand.

To do so, let's leave Alan Turing's England for a while—too gray and dingy anyway—and go someplace sunnier. Let's go to America! And do what Americans do—at least in the movies. Let's smash up a car.

On Valentine's Day. In California.

MOUNTAIN VIEW, CALIFORNIA, is in Northern California, the Bay Area—geographically. Yet its microclimate makes it feel more like Southern California. Dry gullies and dusty bike paths. Eucalyptus trees with fragrant peeling bark. Hot sunshine.

Despite all this sunny goodness, and being the heart of Silicon Valley and its billions, Mountain View strikes the New Yorker's heart with dread. Because it really is stucco suburban hell. And the restaurants are just okay.

Take this street corner—the intersection of Castro Street and El Camino Real. There is a print shop. Across the way, a Chase Bank. The streets are free of garbage and black gum stains. There is always parking.

Yawn.

Yet it is here, on this street corner, that we will truly understand the conceptual path leading from reality, through data, and data science, to artificial intelligence. Let's call this framework the Analytical Pyramid.

Here is the short version:

- In reality, things are and events happen.

- In data, people and machines locate, label, and count things.

- In machine learning, machines make narrow decisions.

- In AI, machines make humanlike decisions.

THE LONGER VERSION requires a closer look at this dull little Silicon Valley street corner.

There's an eight-foot-wide concrete sidewalk. And that print shop with a bunch of printed signs taped up in the window for FAX SERVICE and CAR MAGNETS (car magnets?). Trees grow out of the cut holes in the sidewalk concrete every twenty feet. And traffic inches by. Again, boring. A place to do an errand and get out of. But that's my cognitive filter. If I were to take a thousand-milligram dose of psilocybin, why, then, the pattern of the oak leaves overhead, the sandy stone of the print shop's wall, the musically pausing and advancing traffic would become a sensory nirvana, a mystical feast. Thanks to the drug, reality would be unfiltered. The multitude of namable and unnamable objects, all that complexity and change, would be revealed.

I would understand the first layer of the Analytical Pyramid. Things are. Events happen. Things are and events happen with infinite complexity, and endless change. And because—in this example—I am on a lot of drugs, I can say something like "that is deep."

Too deep, for data.

To turn reality into data, we need to apply a filter.

Let's go back to Herman Hollerith and our most essential act of data gathering: The census. Someone at the census bureau had to have invented a labeling scheme: White, Black. Children under eighteen, no children. Rich, poor. Renter, owner. Then, with the labeling system in hand, and embedded in punch cards, the census takers knock on doors. The census takers—the enumerators, if you remember that term Hollerith used—wait for the doors to open. Then, seeing before them White people and Black people, children and no children, the enumerators label the people inside, and then they count them.

Enumerators act as the bridge between an infinitely complex reality and something we can analyze. Something as infinitely complex as a town (Mountain View) can be enumerated (population 82,376, median age 35.9 years).

Obviously this is a filtered, incomplete view of reality. A person is much more than White + renter. A town is more than its population.

In *so* many ways, data is the opposite of tripping. It is reductive. It is inadequate. In this way, it is very human. "Through a glass darkly," data peers out into the world.

Yet data serves a critical purpose. It gazes out at unstructured things and, in its way, *perceives* them. (*I see a 35.9 year old!*) It records those perceptions in an internally coherent way. (There is much more to this 35.9 year old, of course. He's a failed violinist who binge eats in secret and volunteers at a homeless shelter on Wednesday nights. But his age really is 35.9, and if we look at his neighbor, and his other neighbor, we record them all in the same way. Ignoring their virtues, vices, and hobbies and only, accurately, recording their age. Incomplete but coherent.)

Data reduces that gorgeous passage from *Antigone* to a word vector.

A camera reduces the little boy running screaming from Turing's robot to edges and shapes.

Even though it is through a glass darkly, data perceives things and events. And it records those things for processing.

In other words, data acts as the five senses for us and for our machines.

And since our devices are now "smart," they, too, can be enumerators. So we can expand our description of the data layer in the Analytical Pyramid to say, "People and machines label, count, and locate things."

Consider the white Lexus RX450h approaching the print shop on El Camino Real on the afternoon of Valentine's Day.

• • •

THIS LEXUS IS a five-thousand-pound smart device. It's part of Google's self-driving vehicle program. It's using cameras, RADAR, and LIDAR ("light detection and ranging") to perceive the outside world of the car. This cluster of sensors sits on top of the car like a fez. The car's eyes.

For instance, the LIDAR on top of the Lexus is pinging away. It's perceiving three-dimensional space. It's assigning volumetric pixels, or "voxels," to the edges and peaks of three-dimensional spaces, assigning labels to these objects.

But having labels on its own is not useful. It doesn't pass the John Graunt test.

We must pass another level up in our pyramid, to the level of machine learning, or data science, to do that.

Machine learning must start making sense of the data. And in doing so, it must make sense of the world at the corner of El Camino Real and Castro Street. But it starts in small ways.

You could compare this to a familiar marketing scenario—when a direct marketing model, or a digital advertising model, scores one home address, or one cookie, as the one most likely to respond to an offer. You wouldn't say the model is taking over from a human by doing this. It's making a small decision that contributes to a whole advertising and marketing process. And the concept of scoring (discussed in depth in a later chapter) is a great one to focus on for this layer. Assigning a score is not really an imitation of a human function. It's narrow.

Like, today, Valentine's Day 2016. The self-driving Lexus is supposed to turn right on Castro Street. The map says this is an open traffic lane. But the LIDAR—pinging away and sketching three-dimensional voxels—is perceiving these weird oblong shapes. Uh-oh.

The system consults the RADAR and the cameras too. A new algorithm kicks in a process called *clustering*. Clustering uses incomplete information from different sources—LIDAR, RADAR, cameras—to make a small decision.

The clustering algorithm decides. The oblong objects are sandbags.
Sandbags are used in construction projects.

There is construction.

The lane is closed.

Yikes. Now what?

The machine learning or algorithmic layer has done its job. It has taken unstructured perceptual data and made an important observation: The lane is closed.

But that's a narrow observation. It's a score.

For this Lexus's self-driving systems to really make humanlike decisions, they need more.

The Lexus is ready to flex and show some artificial intelligence.

AN IDEA I'LL call *stacking* kicks in now. A computer science person would probably call it *abstraction*. But I like stacking better. It's why the pyramid shape is apt. The idea for stacking is, as you go higher in the pyramid, you need to rely on more information beneath you, aggregated together to create a single idea.

Stacking happens throughout our model.

For the Lexus's machine learning to accurately score the oblong object, it needed information from LIDAR, RADAR, and cameras. And it needed a previously loaded object classification database.

That's at least four data inputs to make one narrow scoring decision.

Now, to graduate up a level, the Lexus must stack a whole new layer of inputs. It needs more than "Hey, this is a sandbag." First, the Lexus needs to decide to stop. So it needs a decision matrix algorithm that predicts that if it drives into the sandbags, that's striking a solid object, and striking a solid object = bad (input 1).

Then it needs another input—namely, a destination. Otherwise it might just say, "You know, this print shop is great. Maybe I'll just stop here. I mean it's seventy-three degrees and sunny. Plenty of parking. Why not?" Its destination (input 2), combined with a map that tells it that reaching its destination requires making a right on Castro Street (input 3), prevents the Lexus from surrendering to lethargy. Then, of course, input 4, which is a consultation with GPS to remind it that it has not yet made this right; it is still at the corner of Castro Street and El Camino Real.

It needs more perceptions and classifications from its LIDAR to tell it how to get around this darned sandbag and resume its journey. The Lexus needs to pull back into the left lane. It needs to keep going on El Camino Real for another thirty feet. And then, having passed the sandbags, complete the right turn onto Castro. (Let's call all this input 5.)

Finally it needs to engage the vehicle's "drive by wire" system, the tech that connects the decision matrix algorithms to the mechanics of the car.

Still stacking! Six inputs!

Object classification + decision matrix about not hitting solid objects + destination + route map + GPS + new route + "drive by wire" system—all this stacking, all these narrow decisions to sum up to something bigger, to sum up to the humanlike decision to . . .

. . . cue the Strauss . . .

. . . MERGE LEFT!

And this is where the Lexus crashes into a bus.

ONE OF THE Lexus's decision algorithms predicted that this giant Valley Transportation Authority bus over here on the left, heaving down the single open lane, would brake and let the Lexus go by. I mean, that's what the Lexus would have done. That was what's in its rule book. But the self-driving system was too idealistic. In Mountain View—just like Flatbush Avenue, Brooklyn—the buses don't stop for nothin'.

The Lexus pulls left. It smashes into the city bus—and creates the Valentine's Day fender bender, one of the first in the Google program.

No one was injured. The sun still shone in Mountain View. But even if it damaged city property, and even if it did so imperfectly, the Lexus had, indeed, reached the top of the AI pyramid.

• • •

THERE IS ONE more level of the Analytical Pyramid: Artificial General Intelligence, the idea that AI is human, even superhuman, because it can apply intelligence across a range of domains. AGI is at the top of the pyramid because—again, in theory—it spans different human activities. Driving in California. Teaching philosophy classes. Booking travel. Shopping for jeans. Diagnosing rare cancers. Anything we can do, it can do better. Because it doesn't need sleep or rest. And with the addition of any new data set, it can learn instantaneously. Read Mandarin overnight. Perform rhinoplasty. AGI stacks and stacks and stacks until it sees everything and learns exponentially.

Given that I can't get Google Bard to perform even the simplest web research for me, for this chapter, without bizarre errors and hallucinations—and that self-driving cars are still crashing—AGI seems a long way off. But it is the logical extension of the concepts we have explored.

A colossal, spooky descendant of Alan Turing's rickety robot wobbling around Midsummer Common. Emerging from the mists of our future.

KEY POINTS IN CHAPTER 4

- Alan Turing—and Ada Lovelace before him—foresaw the essence of artificial intelligence as a flexible machine that could learn and perform any cognitive task.

- Performing any task requires information from mountains of data about human experience. So, if there is enough data, and a computer fast enough to process it, computers in theory should be able to learn anything.

- That creates a very important hierarchy, where we change reality to data, data to analytics (to interpret reality as scores), and AI to synthesize all the scores into humanlike decisions.

- Leaps in computing (GPUs) and modeling (transformers) have made this possible and landed us squarely in an AI universe.

THOUGHT STARTERS FOR YOU

- Turning specific domain knowledge into data, and that data into an AI machine that can fulfill tasks tirelessly, is juicy and will be *the* business question for the near future.

- For most of us, it will go back to the question of data: What data do you have that is specific to your domain, that you could use to train an AI machine?

- What decisions do you want the AI to make? What task? If you wanted to extend your expertise into some narrow task (recommend faster driving routes) or broad task (drive a car), what would it be?

WHERE DO WE GO NEXT?

We have oriented ourselves in our data-stuffed world: What it looks like now, and how we got here. We have understood how a preponderance of data led us to make decisions with that data, then train computers to make humanlike decisions with that data. Before we go on, together, to learn about the superpowers data confers on us, let's take a quick tour into how we should, and shouldn't, act when it comes to data.

PART TWO

Good and Bad
Data People

If a person has ugly thoughts, it begins to show on the face. And when that person has ugly thoughts every day, every week, every year, the face gets uglier and uglier until it gets so ugly you can hardly bear to look at it. A person who has good thoughts cannot ever be ugly. You can have a wonky nose and a crooked mouth and a double chin and stick-out teeth, but if you have good thoughts they will shine out of your face like sunbeams and you will always look lovely.

—ROALD DAHL, *The Twits*

CHAPTER 5

Data Bullies

A Story Where Bankers
Are the Heroes (No, Really)

They called it "Project Atlas."

It is so cheesy when grown men in corporations give projects code names. It's like wrapping your towel around your neck when you are five and calling yourself Superman. Yet it is irresistible. Project Atlas—you practically have to say it like a World Wrestling announcer— "Project! Atlas!" It was global in scope. Monumental in its intended impact. It was going to fix data production for Nielsen's grocery data business.

What seemed to be its chief requirement was to get a bunch of executives into a boardroom several times a week so they could argue with a bunch of consultants.

For those of you who have not had the pleasure of participating in a major consulting project, there is a predictable approach. The consultants just want to create a PowerPoint, send you a huge bill, then sign you up for another project, so they can create another PowerPoint and send you another huge bill. They must pretend that this is all, like, super organic to the needs and desires of the company, so instead of just tramping in with the PowerPoint, they wrangle a whole bunch of the company's own executives and analysts to be part of the project team. Soak them for information, then put at least some of what the employees contribute into the PowerPoint. I was part of the project team. I didn't know much yet, which meant my job was to watch the data executives and the consultants argue and pretend like I understood what was going on.

I would call this the Confusion era of my data career.

I would usually settle in, not at the big conference table, but in a back bench, one of the rows of seats set up behind the conference table against the wall.

At the table were the consultants. They were all men. Under forty. In gleaming, creamy dress shirts and silk ties. The consultants were all slim. Angular faces. Global. Some Indian, some Brits, some Aussies. They looked like they lived on Soylent. Whenever any of them spoke, they included (1) a list of the three topics they wanted to address, (2) paragraphs elucidating each of their three points, and (3) the inclusion of the word *right* as a kind of punctuation. "So you have a cost structure that's increasing, right, and a revenue environment that's challenging." I always felt this was a kind of subliminal messaging. So the listener, unconsciously, would say to themselves, *Yes, that is right!* I am now allergic to speakers punctuating with "right," and when I hear it, I want to bite the speaker's face.

On the other side of the table were the data executives. Nielsen men. (Almost always men as well.) The Nielsen men were over forty. More like fifty as the median age. They all wore pleated slacks. I cannot explain this phenomenon. Why so many pleats among so few people? Pleated slacks—mainly khakis—held up by braided belts. Most, thirty pounds overweight. Some with mustaches.

It was like watching two groups of sports fans—for the English National Cricket Club and the Chicago Bears—face off across a board-room table over muffins and coffee.

And what were they arguing about? The facts of the case seemed straightforward. Here is my simple summary . . .

Nielsen had come together through acquisition. Its largest division at that time performed data services, like market share metrics, for the massive global grocery industry. The customers were corporate giants like Procter & Gamble, Unilever, Kraft, and Coca-Cola. The way all Nielsen's different divisions produced data, however, was different. (Why? Because Nielsen acquired many of the divisions as independent companies, and each had their own ways of making data. And no one, yet, had forced them to pick a *single* way of producing data.) So it wasn't very efficient. Nielsen needed to consolidate and modernize its data production so it could be more profitable.

That's pretty much it. No need for a Harvard Business School case for this one.

And I don't think anyone in the room—Cricket or Chicago Bears— disagreed with that.

So why did the room get so argumentative? Why did the Nielsen executives sound so defensive? Why did it always sound, from where I sat, like they were kind of, on one level, telling the consultants to go screw themselves?

Their language was full of phrases like:

"The reality is . . ."

"At the end of the day . . ."

"This business . . ."

"When you know this business . . ."

"What this business really is, is . . ."

And then jargon, which I had to piece together from the sidelines like a foreigner learning a new language. "Trade," I learned, meant "trade promotions," which means coupons and discounts offered in a grocery store. "Skew" was SKU, or stock-keeping-unit, which meant an individual grocery item for sale. "Entanglement" was Nielsen language for a program to keep retailers happy so they would continue to offer their data to Nielsen. And so on.

The chest-pounding verbiage, the jargon meant to confuse—Project Atlas was, really, a long, highly expensive exercise designed to get these executives to admit that they had overlooked something important—namely, to consolidate data production—and now needed to do something about it.

And what do people do, if you corner them, and they know more than you about a complex subject?

They dazzle you with jargon.

They intimidate you.

They keep you out.

And it worked. Project Atlas was a failure. The executives deflected. The consultants slunk away. Nielsen's grocery data business did not change. The results never improved. Because, at the end of the day, the reality was, the executives knew this business. And the McKinsey consultants, and the flustered new corporate strategy kid on the back bench, did not.

Did it occur to the Nielsen executives to share information, to instruct these newcomers in the ways of data? Did, like, one of the pleated VPs jump up to the whiteboard and draw a diagram, for mercy's sake? So everyone else could understand?

Not a chance. That would mean that, at the end of the day, *everyone* would know this business. That would mean: Humility. Vulnerability. Sharing power.

I ONCE WENT on a business trip to Israel. The start-up I worked for had just raised $50 million in a round of funding. We were on a shopping spree. We drank beer in the Tel Aviv cafés. Ate hummus. Listened to the *poc-poc* of Kadima paddles on the beach. We piled into cars driven by Gett (the Israeli Uber). We drove to Herzliya to meet venture capitalists in their sunny offices. We drove to shabby digs to bro-hug with tech entrepreneurs.

There were five of us. Every meeting began with pleasantries. The start-up team described their business, their intellectual property. Then at last came a discussion about how it all worked. This last part of the discussion would be a verbal Ping-Pong match between their chief technical officer and our chief technical officer. The rest of us—the four nontechnical guys on our side, the four nontechnical guys on their side—would sit on the sidelines and watch, back and forth, back and forth. At the end, we grinned and shook hands and bro-hugged and tumbled into the Gett. And I would ask our CTO:

"Anything?"

"Not really," he would say.

And the driver would take us to the next meeting.

Our start-up failed. For many reasons. But one reason was that I—and the other three guys on our team—did not grill our CTO. And he did not offer any more information. He was a pompous ass who loved the power of holding, and withholding, information. His software balderdash and his condescending tone cowed us.

In an alternate universe, would we have bought a plucky young Israeli start-up for $50 million and changed the world? Maybe. Maybe not.

But in those sweaty little Gett rides—all of us in our blue blazers with our phones and our Filson bags—we manifested an unhealthy society, where one-fifth of the population hoarded the knowledge, and four-fifths let it happen.

And everybody lost.

A COUPLE OF years later, that same unhealthy dynamic played itself out at Nielsen. Too many executives in pleated pants had said no to too many decent ideas. Our stock price tumbled. And we, as a public company, were chum in the water. We were a takeover target. The sharks—also known as private equity firms—were circling.

And not just any sharks. All the damn sharks.

A consortium of private equity funds from the famous KKR (Kohlberg Kravis Roberts, featured in the book and movie *Barbarians at the Gate*), Blackstone (which sounds like the wicked "Treadstone" of the *Bourne Identity* movies and whose lead partner in our deal looked like Dracula), the Carlyle Group, and T. H. Lee all came together to write a $10 billion check to buy the Nielsen Company and turn us around.

But first they needed to understand the business.

So up we go, back to the boardroom.

It was a nice boardroom. It had softer carpeting than the rest of the office. The table was broad and generous, beveled on the edges like it had been hacked from the wing of a spy plane. Big paintings.

But the private equity guys were smarter than the consultants.

They brought the executives up to speak, not in a pack, but one by one.

And the private equity guys? They rolled deep. They had to. Each of those fancy firms had to be represented at each meeting. So the meetings felt like a PhD candidate defending a dissertation. If, that is, the professors doing the interviewing wore $2,000 suits and ran five miles every morning.

The interviews would begin the way you would have expected them to. The private equity guys would say, "Hi, John, thanks for making the time. We want to get to know your division of the business. Can you start with the big picture?"

And the executive would start trotting out the balderdash because the Nielsen executives knew how private equity takeovers worked. The employees got fired, especially the executives at the top with the big fat salaries. So the more the executive could convince the bankers, the private equity guys, that *no one can understand his business but him*, well then, they can't fire him. Who else could they find to run the business if no one else could understand it?

"At the end of the day, we're integrating data from multiple sources. Including the client data. Then the model we've developed creates a sixty-four-grid schema. And that's [insert silly B2B product name here]. It generates $50 million, twenty is profit."

But these private equity guys, as I said, were not idiots.

One of them, I recognized. We had gone to the same high school. He had been a senior when I was a freshman. What had he been up to since high school? Ivy League University. Top Honors. Then, a Marshall Scholarship. So a degree from Oxford. Then a stint at Goldman. Then a Harvard MBA. Then his current role at Blackstone. Not everybody loves bankers. But if you're going to be one, there was no better résumé than this guy's. I got curious about the other bankers in the room. I looked them up too. Oh, yeah. Fulbright and Rhodes Scholarships. Harvard. Harvard. Princeton. Goldman. Goldman. MBAs. JDs. I was sitting in a room with, as they say, the sharpest knives in the drawer.

And the data balderdash? Not having it.

BANKER:
You say you integrate data from multiple sources.
Which sources?

EXECUTIVE:
Oh . . . multiple. We've been doing this for twenty years. We keep adding sources to make the models more accurate.

BANKER:
(Politely)
Got it. So, how many data sources? Roughly?

EXECUTIVE:
I mean, I'd have to check.

BANKER:

Just estimate. We won't hold you to it.
[Smiles and chuckles around the table.]

EXECUTIVE:

Maybe twenty.

BANKER:

Got it. And which source, would you say, was the most
important?

EXECUTIVE:

Well, on the consumer side, our demographic data from
Experian. And on the client side, the impact data.

BANKER:

Impact data?

EXECUTIVE:

The sales data. From the store.

BANKER:

So, sales data, from the store, in the location where you create the sixty-four-cell grid?

EXECUTIVE:

Exactly.

BANKER:

Great. Let's start with that sales data. Tell me about that.

So the executive would explain the sales data. And then the
demographic data. And on it went. The banker asked him to explain

the other eighteen data sources too. The meeting had been scheduled for two hours. The executive thought he only had to dance for 120 minutes, run out the clock, and go back to his desk with job security. Nuh-uh. The banker leaned back in his chair, to address the admin who was in the room. "Can we push back our 1:00 p.m.? And maybe get a lunch order going?" The executive would gulp. Lunch? The banker would turn back to the executive, unfailingly polite: "You can go a little long, can't you?"

They could always go long.

They went for as long as it took. The private equity firms were about to spend $10 billion. They picked apart all twenty data sources. They learned about the modeling, the sixty-four-cell grid. They learned how much each customer paid, how often, and how profitably.

And what I learned in that room was: Balderdash does not survive scrutiny.

You *can* isolate every component of any data contraption there is. And having isolated each component, you have exposed it. The whirring and whizzing and banging and smoke coming out of the machine no longer distracts you. You only have to ask yourself: *Can it be understood by someone as smart as me?* If the answer is yes, then all you need is determination.

It helps to have $10 billion, four degrees from Harvard, a Rhodes Scholarship, and to have the person across the table owe you their job. That's a lot of leverage.

It helps. But believe me: It's not necessary. The only thing stopping you from saying, "Hold on. Explain that." "Okay, and now explain the next thing too," is the little voice in your head that is shamed by the pomposity and swagger and arrogance of the person across the table. And the fatal, *fatal*, assumption that everyone else gets it except you. (This is almost never true.) And this comes with its devious, undermining henchman: The idea that you're wasting everybody's time by trying to understand something clearly and learning the truth.

You are not.

And what if, sometimes, you don't, or can't, get a clear answer? You have learned something. You have learned that the person you are dealing with has something to hide or is lazy or doesn't value you. In other words: They are not trustworthy.

And what information could be more valuable than that?

KEY POINTS IN CHAPTER 5

- Data bullies are a breed of data person who understands data but who won't share that knowledge. In fact, they like to lord it over others.

- Withholding information confers power on the data bully. By condescending to you, they will prevent you from asking questions. Once asked, they will dance or dazzle to avoid truly educating you. They will avoid this for the same reasons powerful people throughout history have kept the masses illiterate.

- What separates you from knowledge is your courage to ask totally idiotic, elementary questions, without fear, and the fortitude to keep demanding answers you understand.

THOUGHT STARTERS FOR YOU

- Conduct a private lab. Approach an analytics or machine learning specialist in your office. Better yet: Buy them lunch. Do they have a thick accent? Good. Now: Ask them about one thing they do.

- Politely ask them to break it down for you, step-by-step. Still not following? Break it down to even smaller pieces. Acronyms or terms of art tripping you up? Ask them to explain every term you don't understand. Maybe whip out a napkin and draw a diagram. See how far you get to wrapping your head around it.

- This is practice. Just like the bankers, if you break it into small enough chunks, eventually, you can get it all.

WHERE DO WE GO NEXT?

Okay, so if the data bully is an example of how *not* to act as a data person, what is the model? How should a data person act?

CHAPTER 6

Data People
and Why I Love Them

The Day Priya Saw the Line

P riya had just relocated to the thriving, up-and-coming city of Pune, India, the day she saw the line.

Priya was running late to her job as a recently promoted team leader in accounting for one of the giant multinational corporations situated in the office park. Because she was late, and stressed, her husband offered to drive her. But then the traffic was bad, and Priya felt guilty about making *him* late. So she instructed her husband to drop her at the turnoff.

It should have been safe. She could see her office from the car. But Pune then wasn't what it is now—a gleaming office park. Then, the jungle came right up to it. Not just ecologically. Human predators were there too. Men lurked in cars outside the Pune offices, attracted to the flow of young female workers. The men would sit in cars, show their junk, and hope that women would get curious, wander over, accept their implicit (and totally blatant) invitation: Service me sexually. Make a few bucks. The workers were from all over India, all over Asia, and maybe some were poor enough or maybe addicted to drugs and desperate for cash, or, who knows, just curious or naive enough to get close. To say yes. To get in the men's cars.

And sure enough, that day Priya was late, two men were waiting. One, sitting in the car, shirt only, no pants or underwear. And standing next to the car, his associate. What was his job? To stop the women if they ran away? Priya saw them. The two men saw her. Priya realized how stupid it was to have stopped so far from the entrance, how risky it was. These men might physically force her into the car. After the eye contact, Priya ran. Holding her company laptop stuffed with all the company's Excel spreadsheets, in the Pune heat, she ran for her life. And when she reached the lobby, sweating, and caught her breath, she wondered one thing . . .

What would have happened if the men had caught her? More chillingly—what happened to the women who *did* get in the car?

Is that how thin the line was? How fast you can run while holding a laptop?

Priya never forgot that moment. Years later, when Priya turned her skills with numbers into a career in data science in the United States and a nonprofit offered her a job to hunt human traffickers using analytics, she remembered that terrifying morning in Pune. And she accepted the nonprofit's job offer.

She had seen the line for herself. How anyone can end up on the wrong side of it.

I STARTED USING the term *data person* when I was about fifteen years into my career.

I started using it to describe people I had a shorthand with. All the ideas about data in this book? With another "data person," it's all understood. You jabber away like you went to the same high school.

When I was leading data for a division of Comcast, we were transforming the business. We were switching from the traditional TV business of broadcast and cable to one that needed people who understood big data and analytics. I had to build a team—a large one; I had a hundred people in my org chart—with new skills and do it quickly. I needed a certain kind of person.

It was the *character* part I grew more aware of as I built the Comcast team. Why would I hire Greg but not Susie? Jenny but not Sam? Of course, there were skills and experience to consider. But the crew we hired had something intangible in common with one another.

Why were members of my team (at Comcast, and later at Samsung) always on the verge of burning themselves out? You would have to *order* them to stop working on a project. To go home. To sleep, even. Freddy Hewlett was a "best of the best" leader I worked with. During the COVID pandemic, when no one was in the office, he started writing a perky "good morning" Slack every morning, with a goofy GIF. He wanted to monitor who would react (with a thumbs-up sign, or whatever) before 9:30 a.m. because he wanted to check that the analysts were getting normal sleep and not staying up all night working.

Why were these people so committed that you couldn't get them to stop?

If *data person* were an astrological sign, the profile would read something like this:

SIGN: Data Person

ELEMENT: Air

POLARITY: Positive

LUCKY GEM: Nuggets of insight

STRENGTHS OF THE DATA PERSON: The data person is not just analytical. They are this weird combination of analytical and creative. They love to chop up numbers, write queries. But they are also inventive. Their minds move laterally, leaping from one data set to another, looking for ways to join data sets together, scanning them and turning them upside down for answers like the sci-fi movie sleuth spinning around the hologram looking for clues.

WEAKNESSES: Data people can be childish. When you take them out of the reverie and play of data, they can feel let down to be out of that "air element" and back on earth. Few of them become successful corporate leaders because of their excitability over ideas versus practicality, and their discomfort around money. Unlike data—which is ethereal and can always be copied over and revised, manipulated and deleted—money has a finality to it that makes a data person nervous.

CHARACTER: The data person is a truth seeker. The reason they like delving into data is because they believe it holds an answer. And they believe that they are the only people in the world who can find it. Plus, there's usually a client on the other end. And to that client, the data person has made a promise: That they will find the answer. And so the relationship becomes not about the client and the data person, but about the data person and the answer they promised to get. Even if that answer is some boring-ass topic, or something just designed to make the client a buck, the data person feels the nobility of their promise. And that drives them to work all night even if you didn't ask them to.

Later in the book, you will meet all sorts of data people. An epidemiologist who uses analytics to stop outbreaks. A nineteenth-century railroad fanatic who tamed the Wild West with numbers.

Each of their stories starts with a childish what-if question.

What if I could identify disease clusters as they are happening?

What if I could force railroad corporations to be honest about their business?

That what-if question is a turning point for every data person. It's the clue to their commitment. It's the weird bridge between the analytical (*I have the skills to get an answer*), the creative (*I can feel and taste the answer I might get*), and the truth seeker (*it's my mission to get an answer*).

The instant you conceive the question, you conjure another reality. A reality where you can answer that question in the positive: *Yes, I can identify disease clusters as they are happening.*

Now the pressure is on. Now, the data person must go find that reality. Or create it.

They must ride off, alone, into the zettabytes. And not come back until they have found their what-if or declared it lost.

That, back at Comcast, was what we were hiring for: People who had that sense of mission, who could feel the existence of the what-if world in their guts, and understand how important it is. People who would accept the mission.

People like Priya.

THERE WAS THIS horrible dynamic in Priya's work combating human trafficking—namely, that when the girls turned eighteen, all bets were off when it came to rescuing them. Some of the girls were trafficked as young as fourteen or twelve or even nine or ten. They were runaways or fleeing abusive homes. And the traffickers would scoop them up in train stations or bus stations and offer them food and companionship, and offer to be their boyfriends, and the girls would gladly accept a roof and a meal and a friend, until they learned the horrible consequences.

And for Priya and the small team she worked with, if they identified a girl to rescue, and the girl turned eighteen, then, according to the law, that girl was an adult, and any life she was leading, well, it was her choice. That made it much harder to get convictions. Which was the case with the girl we'll call G. Priya zeroed in on G when G was seventeen. So the clock was ticking.

Priya's work at the nonprofit was intense and difficult. She would go into the open plan workspace at 9:00 a.m., and the first thing she would do would be to go to websites where men went to find sex for pay.

Priya asked me not to reveal the techniques she used to identify trafficked women. But the analysis involved a lot of time on these sites, looking at "women posing without their face, flashing their objects"—Priya's strangely flat word for showing themselves suggestively, naked. "'What services do I offer? How much do I charge? What is my specialty?' These are all the things for someone to look at when they're buying the service." And over time, as you can imagine, the work desensitized her. "You go numb. It affects you."

When Priya identified G, the tension ratcheted up. Slowly: They built their case over months.

"I gave my analysis to the CTO," she said. "Then we all had this meeting. 'Are we sure? Are we sure?' Because we had to verify with multiple data points that what I'm seeing is right."

"I worked weekends," Priya admits. "Every day I used to feel like I needed to make progress. I cannot be slow on this. I cannot be wrong. You have this conscious guilt every day, like, biting you in small pieces. That if you don't do this, someone is not going to see the daylight. So: Why don't I work more? And I used to work, like, around the clock."

Soon, Priya and her colleagues brought her analysis to law enforcement.

Priya was not wrong. They rescued the girl, G. But it was three months after her eighteenth birthday. Priya had missed the window. They convicted the trafficker, yes, but of a lesser charge.

And Priya went back to the websites, to start again.

• • •

THESE ARE THE good data people we are talking about.

Not all of them are good.

There are several ways a data person can be bad. First, as described earlier, they can be opaque and use their technical knowledge to gain power in a relationship.

Another is that they can display the opposite of a data person's virtues. A data person believes they can find answers in data. They believe they have a responsibility to the client—whoever that is.

But I also believe a data person is not a mercenary. They don't point these skills at any problem, good or evil. Their responsibility involves an ethical filter.

IT WAS NINETY degrees in New York City. We were working at a venture-funded start-up, Bill Lyman and I. Bill and I were going to a meeting with another start-up, like, a teeny one.

The start-up was situated in one of those converted warehouse buildings in Lower Manhattan. Where the sheetrock and the white-wash and the carpet were new but cheap and looked like they had been finished twenty minutes ago. And there were giant steel-framed windows to let in the baking sun.

Bill and I go into the office, and it's just this one room. In the room are the three guys who make up the entire staff of the start-up. We are there to talk about a partnership about data. This start-up claimed to have data from social networks. Bill and I weren't sure what to expect.

And what happens is the three dudes tell us they have profiles on 250 million Facebook users that they can sell us.

"No, you don't," I say. How could anyone have sucked up 250 million records of another company's data? How could this teeny start-up—three dudes, literally—get data from Facebook? It didn't make any sense.

"Yes, we do," one counters. "We have an app. We launched it on Facebook. And when people opt in to our app, they also push a button that says they give us permission to get data about all their friends on Facebook."

"Two hundred and fifty million people did this?" I ask.

Another of the dudes jumps in. "No. Each person gives us permission to access the data of all their friends. So it's exponential. We just need enough people to opt in who have enough friends until we get . . ."

"All of it," I finish for him.

Bill Lyman has been sitting quietly. He studied software engineering at Harvard. He was already a successful entrepreneur when we met, the kind of technical badass who you would wave goodbye to on your way out the door at night and who when you came back in the morning would still be at his desk, only now, with glassy eyes—and a working prototype.

I like Bill. He has never been anything less than supportive and friendly to me. But he has, like, this evil side. And it comes out when someone tries to bullshit him.

"The user on your app," Bill says, his soft voice dangerous, "does not have the authority to opt in all those other users."

The three dudes sputter.

Bill went on—completely inappropriately, according to the rules of etiquette, anyway—to use the remaining hour to rip those boys a new one. The app user didn't have the rights to opt in their friends, he repeated. There was no way. This would have had to have happened millions of times. And anyway, where would these three random dudes in a single-room start-up have the capacity to store data on essentially every single user on Facebook? And given that Facebook had such high enrollment, we were basically talking about every single person in the United States.

The boys just sat there and took it. In the heat, everybody sweating. Bill was calling them liars. He was calling them jerks for being liars.

We walked out shortly thereafter, believing we had wasted our time, with yet another group of over-claiming, exaggerating, start-up bullshit artists.

Only here's the thing.

They weren't lying.

It was another five years before the Cambridge Analytica scandal broke.

A UK consulting firm, Cambridge Analytica, had used an app to pull data out of Facebook and then use it for profiling and election manipulation. Cambridge Analytica was investigated. Went bankrupt. Facebook paid a $725 million fine. The press treated it like it was this anomaly. Like somehow Cambridge Analytica had outsmarted the system and, with their wiles, tricked the data out of Facebook.

When seemingly—according to the Three Shmucks in the Hot Room—anybody with an app could just walk away with the data like a drunk at an honor bar.

If the government wanted to, they could probably find a hundred more Cambridge Analyticas.

We never heard from those boys again. But I do, now, wonder what they were thinking when Bill scolded them. He was calling them liars. *They knew they were telling the truth.* Yet the expression on their faces—they didn't look arrogant or aggrieved or annoyed.

They looked . . . guilty.

And this was not my only encounter with Facebook as the epitome of the anti–data person.

I AM WORKING for Nielsen. Nielsen is doing a deal with Facebook. We fly out to Silicon Valley. We have an all-day meeting. Then we go out for beers. We are at a place with picnic tables. The Facebook fellas—and they were fellas, all guys in their thirties, with tech bro energy—are all buzzing about how Facebook Beacon had been killed because everybody was *whining about the privacy implications.*

(Facebook Beacon, for those who don't recall, was this weird feature where it told everybody on your network what you were doing online. Without your permission. So one day you would log in and it would be trumpeting "Justin just bought hemorrhoid medication at CVS.com!")

Then one of the bros said, "But Mark will think of a way out of it."

I asked what he meant.

He said that Facebook Beacon was an in-your-face violation of privacy, that it might sink the company. But Mark "has a way," he said, of coming up with new ways of getting to the same destination, only with a more palatable approach: "Facebook Connect," he said, and grinned. Facebook Connect, he went on to explain, would collect the same data about users that Facebook Beacon had. Only it would be less in your face. No one would complain. And Mark would have done it again.

The bro crossed the fingers of both hands and scrunched up his face in an expression of urgent hope. He raised his face to the heavens, like you would just before your soccer team makes a penalty shot in a tie game.

If only Mark Zuckerberg can pull the wool over everyone's eyes!

Later, I saw that bro in a documentary about the evils of social media. He was making a sanctimonious commentary about how social media might push the United States to the brink of civil war. He was tan. His clothes were expensive. Clearly, he had made millions.

Integrity pays, I guess—just at a lower rate.

THERE IS THIS term that sounds so boring. But I have come to love it. The word is *fiduciary*. And oh my gosh, it's just the most boring-sounding word in the world. It's like having a crush on a fat guy in a plaid sports jacket. But I, and maybe a few law professors somewhere, we swoon over the word *fiduciary*. It means "in trust." When you have a fiduciary duty, you have a duty of trust. It's got that Latin root *fidere*.

The same root that's in calling a dog Fido; or in the amazing Beethoven opera *Fidelio*; or in *confiding* to someone you trust; or having *confidence* in them.

Because when someone places their business in your hands—or even a single query or their hypothesis about how they can change the world—they are placing that idea with you in trust. They are saying, go off into the zettabytes to help me with my mission. Come back with medicine. Come back with what I need.

The data person is in a position of service. They are entrusted.

Priya understood that.

I met Priya later in her career when she had become a success in the for-profit sector.

Did she burn out? Is that why she left the human trafficking nonprofit?

"No," she said. "I didn't want to leave." There were visa challenges, she explains.

I'm about to take the conversation in a different direction, but Priya stops me.

"The world you see is different from the world I saw" while she was working for the nonprofit, she tells me. "In your world there is happiness, security. You have money, a job, everything. But the world I saw, what I started feeling was, it's lucky to be alive. Because there are other people that are not able to see daylight. They don't know what's going to happen with them next. Whether they are going to be sold—here or international. They can be killed, or they might have already caught an STD or HIV."

After the experience she had rescuing G, Priya says, "I have started becoming more grateful of what I have in my life. Because you should be, after you see this darkness in the world. There is a totally different world out there, which you have not seen. Which no one should see. It's not good. But then, we should be grateful about what we have."

She adds: "I think so."

KEY POINTS IN CHAPTER 6

- Data people have skills that are both analytical (they break things down) and creative (they make lateral connections to generate something new).

- Data people are driven by a relationship of trust with their client (or customer or boss or whomever) who has asked them to work with data. The data person has a sense of mission that they owe the client an accurate answer.

- Ethics inform the work. The data person should act with the assumption that no one will take the data improperly or use it for an improper purpose. What is proper? Subject of another book perhaps. In the best case, the data, once it has yielded up its answer, will make the world a better place.

THOUGHT STARTERS FOR YOU

- What is a nonquantitative question you might be able to answer with data? Priya and her start-up asked themselves, "Can we use analytics to catch human traffickers?"

- Assume that there is no question too nonnumerical that you can't use data to answer it. ("How do I measure the feeling of fellowship in my neighborhood?") Make it a question that, when answered, you could use to improve everyone's lives.

- Now entertain ideas about how you might go about measuring it.

WHERE DO WE GO NEXT?

Now that we have laid the groundwork about how prevalent data is in our lives, how we got here, and what our mindset should be, it's time to talk about what data can do.

PART THREE

Superpowers

"I would even tear one eye out of my head if it would buy me the right to drink of this water and acquire such depths of wisdom that I might thereby save those who dwell in Asgard and Midgard!"

—ROGER LANCELYN GREEN, *Myths of the Norsemen*

CHAPTER 7

Omniscience: Solving One Big Problem

Skate the Lake

F rom the time Christy Lewis was five years old, there was this thing in her hometown of Evergreen, Colorado, called "Skate the Lake." It was a New Year's celebration. Evergreen Lake would freeze. All the kids would go to the lake house. They would sit with their moms and dads and tie their skates, then do that awkward skates-on-land duck walk out to the frozen water and skate in circles and figure eights and see their friends, and because it was New Year's Eve, their parents let them stay up until midnight. Grown-ups would have fires going in barrels for roasting marshmallows, and there was hot chocolate at the lake house, and at the stroke of midnight there would be fireworks. This happened every year. That is, until Christy reached high school. That year, the December temperatures in Evergreen, Colorado, had risen, and for the first time she could remember, the lake didn't freeze. "Skate the Lake" was canceled. Even a teenaged Christy Lewis knew something serious was happening.

Ten years later, with a degree in environmental engineering, Christy found herself at an entity that could maybe only exist in America in the twenty-first century, and in the Bay Area. And that is a tech non-profit start-up. With a few hundred grand from a foundation and the requisite nerdy impassioned founder—Gavin McCormick, a Berkeley-trained PhD so jumpy and skinny and fast talking he makes Zuckerberg and Jobs look like starting D for the San Jose Sharks—they called the start-up WattTime. They were determined, once and for all, to track the emissions from power plants. Christy joined WattTime as an analyst. Within a few years, she rose to director of analysis.

But why power plants?

Christy and the team knew that power plants—the way we create our electricity, from coal, hydroelectric, nuclear, and other fuel sources—are the single biggest producer of emissions in the world. Ninety billion tons of CO_2 equivalent per year. More than transportation. More than fossil fuels even. These are electricity *factories*. And Christy and WattTime knew that, globally, most of the information we have about emissions is self-reported . . . by the power companies themselves.

Want to know if PG&E is a polluter?

Just ask them!

They also knew that self-reporting is actually a legal obligation only in some places, like the US and the EU and Australia. In other countries? Those inconsequential little landmasses like China and India and Russia? No obligation. Nothing about power plant emissions has to be written down, much less reported to the government.

So the idea was: What if instead of politely asking power plants all over the world for data about their emissions—which, let's face it, they have an interest in minimizing—what if Christy and the WattTime team just watched them? Monitored them. From the sky.

From satellites.

IN THE 1800S, it's easy to forget, some of the world's biggest bad-asses were mapmakers. Because in those days, if you wanted to make a map, you had to *go there*. If someone had already been there, there was already a map, so you had to go where no one had been.

In 1869, thirty-five-year-old John Wesley Powell led a nine-hundred-mile exploration of the Colorado River. He returned with mind-bending descriptions—"carved walls!" "royal arches!"—of what we now know as the Grand Canyon. It was also a great story. Powell was an amputee from wounds at the Battle of Shiloh, and he had led the Colorado River expedition with one arm. This was such a great story that Powell wrote a bestseller and got himself named the head of the fledgling US Geological Survey (USGS), putting the stamp of his twin obsessions—maps and climate research—on that organization. For Powell, it was all about the arid West, watersheds, and agricultural development. And the pictures you make about them: Cartography, hydrography.

In retrospect, it makes sense how those two things go together: To manage, steward, support, expand into, and generally not screw up your land, you need to have information about it.

Powell's successors held fast to that mission. And a hundred years later, no one had to paddle the Grand Canyon or get attacked by grizzlies to make a map for the USGS.

Because the USGS started launching satellites.

WHEN YOU LOOK at the orbit of the Landsat 8—one of the latest USGS satellites—it's almost . . . beautiful.

Its goal is to take pictures of the earth's surface. So its journey needs to remain in sunlight. It travels from the North Pole to the South Pole with one-half its journey in sun, the other half in darkness. It makes a single circuit of the planet every ninety-nine minutes, which is sort of insane. It needs to travel at seventeen thousand miles per hour to do this. But the beautiful part is the pattern.

Landsat 8 kind of stays in place with its sun-facing orbit. But the Earth spins under it. So, together, satellite and planet—recorder and object—do this kind of dance. Landsat 8 in place, Earth spinning beneath. As a result, Landsat 8 makes a kind of corkscrew weave around the planet, a loop-the-loop—like the ribbon flung around by one of those corny Olympics rhythmic gymnasts. Only the ribbon is a hundred-mile-wide swath that images the entire planet every sixteen days.

The Landsat program is run and funded by the USGS. The European Union has a similar program, with satellites called Sentinels. Both programs are government-run, so the data is public. You can download it for free.

Then there's another organization, a company called Planet—what you'd call in business jargon a disruptor—who decided to make smaller, lighter satellites. (They make you pay for the data.) A Landsat 8 satellite is the size and weight of a Chevy Silverado. Planet started launching satellites about the size and weight of a clarinet case. They called each satellite, a small, fragile-looking plastic box, a Dove, and they launch them with wacky patterns and sayings etched on the sides—more only-in-Silicon-Valley culture—like "Who Let the Doves Out?" These satellites travel in multiples, which Planet calls Flocks. With their solar panel wings, they whip around the planet getting a full picture of the Earth not every sixteen days, but *every day*, and with a much finer resolution. They can recognize objects not a hundred feet wide, like the Landsat can, but *ten* feet wide. When you look at pictures taken by a Dove, compared to pictures taken by Sentinel and Landsat, it's like you put your glasses on.

WITH SUCH INCREDIBLE technology at their disposal, you would think Christy Lewis and the WattTime team would just need to download a bunch of information from the USGS website to answer whatever question they had about emissions or anything else happening on the planet.

But of course it was far from that simple.

First, their effort really needed to be global. You can track emissions of US and European power plants, where you have a lot of data. And that would be meaningful. Those countries make up a big portion of the global total. But what about the rest? Even if you could hold US power companies accountable—a big if—you have that problem where one group of people can be good actors and everybody else is polluting and nothing improves. Evergreen Lake will still melt in January because of emissions halfway around the world.

So Christy needed a list of the largest power plants in every country in the world, to start.

And that was the easy part.

Then she would need each plant's location.

Then she would need *satellite imagery* of each power plant, down to the ten-foot level.

Because she knew something about power plants.

She knew that every power plant must pump out vapor. Exhaust, basically. And that there are two kinds. Cooling towers, the fat-bottomed concrete tubes like you see in the nuclear plant in *The Simpsons*. And stacks—the tall skinny ones that are kind of synonymous with industrial landscapes, like the ones from the Pink Floyd album cover *Animals*.

And she knew that the towers and the stacks all emit vapor in the form of plumes.

And the plumes could be seen from space.

So what Christy and her team do is, they gather a list of power plants. And for each one (say, Alabama Power), they link the address (Gadsden, Alabama) to a latitude and longitude coordinate (34.0128, -85.9708) so they can map it for the satellite to find. Then they determine what kind of fuel it burns (coal) and download the pictures from the satellites to see *how big the plumes are*.

Then comes the fun part.

They access data from the Environmental Protection Agency to see *when* the plant in Gadsden was running—what days and times it was functional—and at what capacity. Was it at full capacity? Or, like, 40 percent on a particular Tuesday?

Do you see where this is going?

Then Christy's team joins all this data.

If they have a time stamp, which they do, for all the photos taken by the Landsat and Sentinel and Dove satellites, they can associate those photos of plumes with the times the plant was running, when it wasn't running, and when it was running at partial capacity. So then Christy knows what the plume looks like for a coal plant running at 40 percent capacity, what the plume looks like at 100 percent capacity, and, of course, what it looks like when it's not running. (Even I can tell you that. The stacks and tubes are black. No plume.)

And from there it's all downhill.

Now they know what the plume of a plant looks like when it's running at full tilt—every power plant type, coal, nuclear, and hydro-electric, and so on.

Next they go back to the database of all the power plants. And they look up all the lat/longs of all the plants, and look at all the Landsat and Sentinel and Dove pictures of all the plumes.

They train an AI model to review all the pictures of all the power plant plumes and, based on those pictures, to calculate the capacity that *each* power plant was running at, for all the months they were being photographed (which was every month).

Then Christy's team uses data about how much CO_2 equivalent output—emissions—a power plant, of that type, generates, when they are running at what capacity.

Then . . . well, it's easy.

They multiply each power plant x the average capacity for each month x the CO_2 equivalent emissions for that level of capacity, per month, per fuel type . . . and they do that for hundreds of power plants all over the world. Then they put it in a table. They're Slacking each other and holding videoconferences, with things getting frantic around

July, because they need to quality check the data in October to publish in November . . . and then it all goes up on the website.

And then you and I know something.

Something that is freakishly impossible to know.

Impossible, because it's just too broad, too detailed, too esoteric, too spread around the world, too hidden, in plumes rising from the Naghlu Dam Hydroelectric Power Plant in Afghanistan, the Bayanhua Jinshan power station in China, the Simhadri Coal Plant in India. Hundreds of power plants. Thousands of them.

Impossible because, arguably, many people don't want us to know it.

And that thing we know is: Which power plants are polluting and how much.

Everywhere on the planet.

WHEN I WAS a kid my dad read me *The Myths of the Norsemen*, a story book about the gods and dwarves and dragons of Scandinavian legend. When we got to the part about Odin gaining wisdom, it was like a horror movie to me.

The giant Mimir offered Odin wisdom. The ability to see anything, anywhere. But Odin had to offer a sacrifice. Odin ripped his own eyeball out (in my version, with the tendons and nerves and blood vessels dangling). Then he threw his eye into Mimir's well, where (my version again) it landed with a squelch, like a poached egg in a mud puddle. Now Odin had one eye, in exchange for wisdom.

Part of the horror I perceived, hearing the story, was what a torment Odin's life would be after that. With his omniscience, he understood that Ragnarok was coming. The end of the world. The end of his world, anyway. The end of the gods.

"The gods were sorely troubled . . . and wise Odin who had drunk of Mimir's Well grew sad. But he did not believe the day of doom would come for many a long age."

• • •

IS OUR SITUATION more hopeful? I am not a climate scientist. I cannot tell what all Christy Lewis's data means for us and for our world, how close to Ragnarok ninety billion tons of CO_2 equivalent annual emissions pushes us. But as I write this in summertime, newspapers carry stories every day about hundred-degree heat all over the world. Phoenix, Arizona, is reportedly so hot that when seniors trip and fall on the pavement and can't get up for a few minutes, they not only need treatment for their fall but also for the sunbaked asphalt burning their skin.

Our world-tree is withering. No problem seems bigger, more overwhelming, and threatening than climate change.

Yet, faced with this monumental problem, we should also acknowledge how extraordinary WattTime's achievement in data is. Especially given what came next.

WattTime's founder, Gavin McCormick, realized that the approach Christy's team took to power plant emissions could be replicated across other areas of environmental data. They joined up with other climate groups. They got funding. They created a bigger, global organization they call Climate TRACE—yet another tech nonprofit start-up, with a mission.

This time, with variations on the methodology Christy uses, they started measuring emissions from everything you can possibly think of:

manufacturing (steel, chemicals, aluminum, cement, paper)

fossil fuels (coal, oil, and gas)

transportation (air, road, rail, shipping)

agriculture (crop burning, synthetic fertilizers, cow farts—I mean methane)

buildings

garbage and waste

mineral mining

forestry

All of it. By country. By CO_2 equivalent.

Their models and their data give us an Odin's eye. The superpower of omniscience to see the hidden cause of climate change across many countries and across a multitude of sources. The data Climate TRACE gathers and calculates allows us to see the problem everywhere. It allows us to aggregate and simplify the data to a single metric (CO_2 equivalent tons).

This gives us the power to take action. And specific action. Because the data is, what we call in the biz, *granular*. It takes us down to the site level—each power plant, where something can be done. Data has given us the superpower to tackle our biggest problem, climate change.

Will we do so?

With the superpower of omniscience comes the melancholy of the data person: Lots of knowledge, not necessarily the superpower to force people to do something about it. Data is information, not action. Odin knew this too.

At the end of the story, Odin has a vision:

At first he saw only a great waste of water, tossing and tumbling over all the world.

But as he watched, a new earth rose out of the sea, green and fruitful, with unfading forests and pleasant meadows smiling in the light of a new sun.

Then Odin wept with joy, and as the tears coursed down his face, the vision faded . . .

. . . into the grayness of the cold northern world where Ragnarok is yet to come.

KEY POINTS IN CHAPTER 7

- Data confers on humanity the power of omniscience. Obviously this is a metaphor. Omniscience means knowing everything happening everywhere. Data does not literally provide this, but it provides the ability to gather information on far-flung events and therefore gives us the ability to act on that information.

- Satellites are a great example of this. From government Landsat satellites to commercial Planet satellites, they gather data from every nook and cranny of the planet and bring that data back to us.

- Then we can apply the data to important problems, like climate change. In the case of Climate TRACE, they apply the data to the root cause of climate change—namely, detecting who is polluting.

THOUGHT STARTERS FOR YOU

- Where is there a "zone of ignorance" (I am coining this term) in your business or organization?

- Maybe you perform a function—say, a public service—but you don't know what impact it has. Or maybe you're a manufacturer, but you have no idea how customers interact with your product on the shelf.

- Now brainstorm what you could do to bridge that knowledge gap. How could you gain some omniscience about that zone? (I recognize that "some" omniscience is a contradiction. Fine.) How can you use data to project yourself into that zone and bring back useful information?

WHERE DO WE GO NEXT?

Using climate change as an example implies that omniscience is some mighty power that we can apply only to massive challenges. But that's not quite right. We can apply it to small challenges too.

CHAPTER 8

Omniscience: Solving Many Small Problems

"But It's a Map!"

A little boy sits in a classroom holding a sharp metal spike.

It's, like, this six-inch metal skewer. With a wicked sharp point. The spike is the end of a compass, a tool used to draw circles in geometry, where the sharp end plants in the center—the vertex—and the other end holds a stubby pencil, which swings around and draws arcs on paper. But that's not how he's using it. The little boy is using the sharp point to etch lines in the wood of his wooden desk.

The lines he etches—does the little boy even know this yet?—are vector lines. Vector lines connect one point to another.

"What are you doing!"

An adult voice interrupts the etching.

"You're destroying the desk!" The boy's teacher is outraged. "Look at this mess!"

The little boy is hauled to the principal's office.

"But it's a map!" the little boy protests.

As if this makes a difference.

The boy is suspended for destroying school property.

• • •

MEET BARRY GLICK.

I meet Barry as an adult. He is a legendary tech entrepreneur, generous with his time on boards and his investments. But what I love about Barry Glick is that, in a way, he is not obviously lovable. He's the colleague at the company off-site with whom you know you're going to end up working for it when you get paired with them on the bus to the ballgame. Because Barry Glick is deliberate. He listens carefully to you—even when you're not speaking carefully. He has a large, oval head whose ovalness is accentuated by receding black hair, and he wears dark-framed round glasses and a goatee, as if he is, above the neck, all ovals. Maybe we should call them spheroids. Because Barry Glick is an expert in geography. And it was Barry Glick—deliberate, careful, precise Barry Glick—who helped change the way everyone on Earth uses maps. And he pulled off what, a hundred years ago, might have seemed like a miracle, a flourish of beneficent magic.

Let no one, Barry Glick said, like a fairy godmother in *Cinderella*, *ever get lost again.*

BARRY RECEIVED HIS degree from Cornell University, studying geographic information systems. Cornell is frigid in the winters with a jet stream blowing down from Ontario and the Great Lakes. And Barry wasn't happy. Even though he was studying what he loved—maps— the courses he took focused on city planning. And Barry did not like city planning. He liked the computer science courses he took. So, after graduating and working for government vendors making maps, Barry started his own company, where he could put his two passions together: Mapmaking and digital technology. He called his firm Spatial Data Sciences—which is such a generic, Barry Glick name—and this business was going very well until 1989 when one of Barry's employees showed him a portable computer.

"Or what passed for a portable computer," Barry adds, remembering the incident. "It was really something . . . luggable."

The employee wanted to show Barry a driving route, generated by software.

It was the first time Barry had seen a digital driving route. "It looked like a bunch of squiggly spaghetti on the screen," he remembers.

There was a reason for that.

Barry's associate was dealing with what geographical information people call vector data. Vectors consist of three types of data: Points, lines, and polygons.

When Little Barry was etching a map into a wooden desk at school, that first plunge of the protractor spike was making a point. One point, one little place on the border of that map. When Little Barry dragged the spike an inch to the north, that was a line.

Sure, it comprised a lot of individual points. But that's what a line is. Then, when he really made a mess and scraped the line *alllll* the way around his desk, and closed the line to complete the map—that was a polygon. A shape. Made up of a closed line. Which was in turn made of joined points.

On the actual planet, data can describe each point on a map. A point of latitude and longitude. Then a *line* would be a string of latitude and longitude points. And driving directions, well, they are a line too. Following all the points that make up the lines of one road leading to another. Hooking left on Route 11 to Big Spring Drive, merging right to Low Bridge Lane, then a left on Bethany Drive.

But you can't just look at a line, in isolation, and learn much of anything, certainly not enough to know when to turn left and when to turn right. Or how to get to grandma's house. The technology on that luggable computer with its squiggly lines, revelatory as it was, was missing something. Something crucial.

And that's when Barry understood what he needed to do.

So Barry put on a suit.

. . .

THE BOARDROOM WAS in the company headquarters in Chicago, Illinois. Barry stood outside its closed doors. He was standing next to his pal, who was an executive vice president of the RR Donnelley Corporation.

Donnelley, now known as RRD, is a giant printing company. Its roots go so far deep into Americana that it used to print manuals for managing mules. It printed the *Encyclopedia Britannica*. The Montgomery Ward catalog. Since those days it had bloomed into a sprawling global print empire.

And just then, when Barry was standing outside the Donnelley boardroom, the company had a semi-moribund division that no one knew what to do with. This division made maps. It was known by the cheery name of MapQuest.

They distributed their maps to gas stations. The kind where, when you were driving along a twisty highway in the Blue Ridge Mountains and all the creeks and hairpin turns started looking the same, you would pull into a gas station reeking of motor oil, with a humming red Coca-Cola machine and a glass candy jar full of jawbreakers. And on the counter would be a rack holding road maps for lost people like you, maps Exxon or Texaco sponsored. And the RR Donnelley Corporation would have printed that map.

What Barry had figured out was that the vector data—the squiggly spaghetti—of driving directions needed to join with another form of data.

And that data is what is known as *raster data*.

Raster data is the other main type of data used in geographic information systems. The easiest way to understand what raster data is, is to think of that time you zoomed way in on a satellite image. When you did, all the treetops turned to green blocks. And the sand of the beach turned to beige blocks. Those blocks you were looking at were the cells that make up a raster image. Each cell is assigned a value—a color, in this example—beige for sand, green for treetops.

Raster data is data for making *visual* maps.

Barry's breakthrough was that squiggly spaghetti lines of the lat/long data mean nothing to us because we have been trained, as a species, since the beginning of our time as *Homo sapiens*—or at least, from the beginning of our time as consumers of information communicated on parchment—to think of geography in terms of *printed maps*.

Marco Polo. Henry Hudson. Christopher Columbus. Sure, their maps were made of pen and ink.

Those boys loved their raster data.

So Barry had reasoned: Spatial Data Systems had the *vector* data for the driving directions. But who owns a lot of *raster* data? Maybe someone who owned raster data but wasn't getting a lot of value from it. Because let's face it. Shipping a bunch of maps to Mr. Hart's filling station to give away for free is not exactly a formula for runaway business success—even if Exxon was paying for it.

Wouldn't it be better for a giant printing company with a boring, declining map business to do something with those maps, *digitally*?

Barry was about to enter the boardroom to make his pitch to the executives of RR Donnelley. He was a tech entrepreneur. A PhD. All substance and no swagger. But for this occasion, he wore a crisp white shirt. A suit and tie. He carried a briefcase full of printed presentations to review with the Donnelley team.

His pal, the EVP, stopped him.

"What is it?" Barry asked.

"Don't carry your briefcase," he said.

Barry was confused. "Leave it out here? It's got all my presentations . . ."

The EVP cut him off. "No. Don't carry your *own* briefcase."

Barry blinked.

The EVP smiled. "That's how you show you're the big boss."

A little dazed, Barry turned and handed his briefcase to his associate. Then he pushed open the door and entered the room, empty-handed.

When he came out again, he had a deal. RR Donnelley was an investor in Spatial Data Systems.

TODAY, GOOGLE DOMINATES the road map business. Only it's weird even to call them road maps anymore. Because it's just Google Maps. Google uses modern magic to offer this service. In 2006, they invented the cameras that go on top of cars. Since then they claim to have snapped eight billion pics on ten million miles of road. They've mapped the Arabian Desert using cameras on camelback. They use AI—convolutional neural networks!—to read road signs to make sure all the street names are accurate and up to date.

But Google didn't invent it.

It all started as a result of that Chicago meeting in the Donnelley boardroom. And it kind of happened by accident.

Barry had figured out the most important thing. He and his team had figured out how to *overlay* the vector data *on top* of the raster data. In other words, they didn't bother trying to bridge the two types of data. (They would have liked to, but the computing power wasn't there in the 1990s.) They just *drew* the squiggly lines they calculated themselves *on top* of the beautiful maps they received from Donnelley and which they had digitized into raster data. Doing this wasn't easy or clean. Nobody had latitude and longitude data for street addresses back then. "All the databases had the lat/longs only for the street intersections," Barry remembers. They just had to do their best with whatever wasn't an intersection. "You had to estimate."

And here's where the accident came in . . .

As a business, the cartographic services division of Donnelley, a.k.a. MapQuest, was still sweating it out doing custom data work for clients making custom digital maps.

They had all these salespeople out on the road who would show—demonstrate, or "demo"—the digital maps for the clients.

Here's how Barry remembers what happened next.

"Someone suggested, is it possible for us to do our sales demos on the internet? And the technical people said, 'Yeah. Great. We'll stand up a website. Anyone who's connected to the internet can access the demo.'"

So MapQuest put their sales demo of digital maps and driving directions online. It was a novelty. The salespeople liked the digital demos. The clients liked them too. Barry was happy.

Then, in the frenzy around new internet applications characteristic of the time, the mid-'90s, a couple of journalists wrote about MapQuest and its digital demos.

"And the next thing we knew, all our servers went down," Barry recalls. The site was buried in an avalanche of traffic. Millions and millions of hits. "We were gobsmacked."

It turned out vector data overlaid on raster data, downloaded to a personal computer, was something people really liked.

And in that moment, MapQuest.com was born.

Three years later, AOL purchased MapQuest for $1.1 billion.

Two decades, a Google, and a Waze later, no one on the planet Earth with an internet connection and a phone would ever get lost again.

Barry Glick had discovered a way to solve millions, even billions of people's small problems, using data. Going to a new city, or taking a wrong turn, was no longer a source of anxiety. Taking a foreign vacation didn't have to be a matter of deep research and preparation. A happy accident—set up by a lifetime of passionate obsession—had made Barry Glick a demigod for wanderers.

• • •

I WAS A teenager in Lexington, Virginia. Lexington is a small, pretty town in the Blue Ridge Mountains. Our family wasn't happy then. My mother wanted to be off teaching in a big city, Paris or New York. But she and my father ended up where my father got tenure: Lexington, population six thousand, with two grocery stores and one movie theater. So my sister came up with this thing she called *taking a drive*.

What my sister would do was get in my mom's car—a little Toyota station wagon, rust-colored, stick shift, which my mother had bought to commute to her teaching job—and drive off. Just, drive off. Into the country. Into the Blue Ridge Mountains. She would be gone for hours.

And when I turned sixteen, I would take a drive too.

"What do you do when you get out of town?" I asked her, before starting my first one.

"You go out Route 11. Across the bridge. But before you get to Kroger. And take that turn."

"And then what?"

"You just go."

So I would go. I would pull the Toyota out of the drive, past the Exxon station where Mr. Hart might wave to me. And I would drive out Route 11. Then hook that left. The road would slither alongside the Maury River. Past the spot with the rope swing hanging from a giant maple. Past the mill. Then veer off onto Low Bridge Lane.

And then, the landscape would soar.

Anybody who has driven in the Blue Ridge Mountains knows that the landscape is so gorgeous you want to be driving with a canvas, easel, and a palette of oil paints alongside you at every moment. On the uphill, you see green meadows alongside, spotted with limestone slabs surfacing likes the backs of leaping dolphins. Cows lazily munching. Up ahead, as you shift into second to climb the hill, you see tufty clouds catching pink sunlight. (*Taking a drive* was an afternoon affair, always.)

Then on the way down—vistas. Pastures and creeks and the far mountain bank all scrimmed with Virginia humidity, the bluish haze of pines. Fifteen shades of green and five of blue, all arranged there for you, your own private Cézanne. And over every ridge you crested there would be another one. And each time it felt like you were the first person ever to find it.

And sometimes—off in that Toyota, the symbol of my mother's frustrated wanderlust, her unpunched ticket to freedom—I'd pull over onto a gravel shoulder and have to get out and just stare at the valley before me. Not believing the beauty.

And there would be, in my chest, a ball of suppressed fear.

I was lost.

Definitely lost.

No road signs out here, no markers.

Somewhere two hundred miles to the north, in Washington, DC, Barry Glick was still pounding it out at a day job. He hadn't discovered how to merge vector data and raster data yet. He hadn't learned how to have someone else carry his briefcase to the big meeting. Barry had not played fairy godmother to humanity then and given us a gift. A superpower. A small problem to be solved millions of times a day, where everybody, armed with his data, could always find their way home.

KEY POINTS IN CHAPTER 8

- Barry Glick's version of the omniscience superpower is to provide not some sweeping Odin-like vision of Ragnarok, or of the solution to climate change but a small convenience, billions of times.

- It's more what you would call a "nudge." You could also call it "optimization" in the sense that it makes an existing experience (driving) ever so slightly better versus offering a new experience.

Or put another way, it improves the knowledge we have of our driving route (where do I turn now) versus offering a new set of knowledge. The maps, after all, already exist.

THOUGHT STARTERS FOR YOU

- I'm setting up optimization to sound small, but it can be a wildly powerful concept. If you notch a small gain every time you do something—and let's say you do it often—the results mount, and meaningfully. Just ask high-speed traders on Wall Street or direct response advertisers.

- What's an area of your life or work you could optimize with data that provides you just this little information edge every time you do it? And maybe do so because you've built an "omniscient" database that can guide you to a better decision?

- Maybe you have a lot of projects, and you could compare them to a high-performing benchmark to know how good they can be. Maybe it's about knowing the highest price the market could bear in many transactions, and adjusting your price upward every time you can.

WHERE DO WE GO NEXT?

The next data superpower is also about making better decisions. Only, in this case, it's about resources. When you have multiple places that urgently need resources, and your resources are limited, what choice do you make?

CHAPTER 9

Data Directs Resources to Where They Are Needed

A True Spartan

I t was around 2005 when Sharon Greene visited the Humane Society near Ann Arbor, Michigan, where she was a graduate student. Sharon peered through the bars of the cages. She picked out the tortoiseshell cat with the sweetest face. She named the cat Hallie. Sharon soon earned her PhD, got married, got a new job in Boston, then New York. She brought Hallie, the sweet tortoiseshell cat, along for every step of the journey.

Now, years later, Hallie was dying. Kidney failure. This happens with older cats. They can't process the toxins in the body. They need intravenous fluids to help clear their system. But this was during the COVID-19 lockdown. The veterinarian discontinued in-person visits. If Sharon wanted Hallie to live, she had to inject Hallie herself. So Sharon did. A loving but painful process where Sharon and her husband had to sanitize a site on Hallie's fur with a cotton ball, hold Hallie down, inject a needle, and squeeze fluids into Hallie's body with a plunger syringe or an IV.

It was a small sadness. But at this time and place, it seemed like an insult. Outside Sharon's apartment in New York City, the COVID-19 pandemic raged. Schools had closed. Streets lay silent. Refrigerator trucks parked outside hospitals to store the bodies.

Sharon Greene knew this because she is an epidemiologist. And it was her job to protect the city.

THE WARNING SHOT came in December 2019.

The Bureau of Communicable Diseases' Gotham Center sits in one of those tangled areas of the borough of Queens in New York City, where the J, Z, N, and W subway trains clatter above your head on a giant elevated steel track. Below, traffic has to wiggle through complex service roads. The Walgreens and the Lucky Pizzeria fight for space. Gotham Center rises above the urban chaos, a glass building, blue in the reflected sky.

At the BCD they have this thing called the "weekly outbreak meeting." A doctor or a veterinarian or a member of the Epidemiological Intelligence Services—yes, they call it that—stands up and runs a meeting about new threats. They call that person the "doc of the week." The doc of the week will describe outbreaks in any of the seventy or so communicable diseases that the BCD regularly tracks. From anthrax (there were bioterrorism incidents in 2001) to malaria (spread by the bite of an infected female *Anopheles* mosquito) to dengue fever, cholera, botulism, *E. coli*, Legionnaires' disease, smallpox, HIV/AIDS, ricin poisoning, even leprosy . . . all the way down to chlamydia and the clap.

That week in December, the doc of the week stood up and spoke to the group about an outbreak in China. This new disease was sometimes fatal. There was no cure. There wasn't even a test for it. And what made this disease most insidious is that it was often asymptomatic, which meant that someone—many people—could host it and spread it undetectably. And it was spreading.

Rapidly.

"We felt a sense of deep dread," Sharon remembers.

A New Yorker's pride is an epidemiologist's nightmare. New York City is the largest city in the United States, with more than eight million inhabitants. It is the most visited city in the country. Over the course of a year, tourists outnumber residents by seven times. Foreign visitors outnumber residents by one and a half times. And in 2019, close to a million of those foreign visitors were from China.

Whatever this new disease was, was coming.

DESPITE NEW YORK'S vulnerability to outbreaks, it also has advantages. It is a rich city. And big challenges, combined with vast resources, attract sophisticated talent like Sharon Greene. The Department of Health and Mental Hygiene (the parent organization of the BCD) had an epidemiology budget of $16 million in 2019. The apparatus for tracking and stamping out disease had grown vastly more sophisticated.

A pillar of this effort is a database. Mandated by the city, it pulls all hospital lab test data into a single place. The database is secure, with only qualified city employees given passwords. It tracks all seventy communicable diseases.

So, for instance, if one person gets salmonella, the database—called the Electronic Clinical Laboratory System, or ECLS—generates a report. The system tags that one person getting salmonella as an "event." The system includes the person's contact information so that, if necessary, city workers can follow up with the patient and understand how they contracted the disease.

The theory was that if another person then gets salmonella and another and another—let's say five people get it in a short period—the group of salmonella events might be a related cluster.

But detecting the cluster, and understanding if it *is* a cluster, is the tricky part.

New York City is enormous. It encompasses five boroughs—Manhattan, Brooklyn, Queens, the Bronx, Staten Island—and more than three thousand square miles, divided into almost five hundred ZIP codes. How could they detect those clusters?

They needed to test the system.

In the case of the five-person salmonella outbreak—which is a real example, from 2014—the analysts used a tool called SatScan. SatScan looks at historical data and allows the analyst to ask it questions. How close, or spread out, geographically were the five salmonella cases? Answer: The home addresses of the sick people were within 0.3 miles of each other. So basically all in the same neighborhood. That sounds pretty telling. But it's not definitive.

Next, they can set up an analysis to determine how long it would *normally* take for five people to get salmonella in a 0.3-mile radius of New York City. The answer is it would take 2.3 *years* for five people to randomly get salmonella in one neighborhood. These five people in 2014 got it from May 11 to May 17—so 2.3 years of disease in just seven days.

Cluster.

Now comes the second phase—the outreach and investigation. Within twenty-four hours, all five patients had been contacted by investigators, who in this case—because the system was still being tested—were a bunch of graduate student interns from the CDC.

The graduate students started contacting the victims.

Three of the five patients, the investigators learned, had eaten chicken at the same restaurant. Let's call it Restaurant A. The next day, the New York State Department of Agriculture and Markets had sent a case worker to Restaurant A. They tested all eighteen food preparers there—stool samples—and examined the food preparation area. In the meantime, more cases were springing up. Ten more. One was a food worker. All had eaten some form of the chicken—rotisserie chicken, chicken salad, chicken soup—from Restaurant A. One unlucky patron had even saved their leftovers. The investigators zoomed in on the leftovers. They tested the Tupperware full of chicken. All the patients, and the leftover rotisserie chicken, contained the same genetic strain of salmonella—*Salmonella blockley*, first detected in the United States in 1955—and the investigators also found the restaurant stored its food at temperatures ten degrees warmer than required.

Yuck.

Antibiotics like Cipro and Zithromax could treat the fifteen patients—experiencing the classic salmonella symptoms of vomiting, diarrhea (sometimes bloody), fever, and chills.

But the question wasn't only whether the BCD could detect an outbreak, confirm it, and help treat the victims. The question was also how much *faster* the BCD could respond when they used these techniques.

In the 2014 salmonella case, the analysts caught the disease within two days using the ECLS and SatScan. The graduate student interns visited Restaurant A and investigated the outbreak within another two days. So four days total.

The historical average for similar cases could take up to five and a half *months*.

And why was this significant? In *The Case of Restaurant A and the Disgusting Rotisserie Chicken*, it meant that they could label the whole affair with an "Outbreak ID." It meant that they caught the outbreak and stamped it out early. Maybe as much as five months early, statistically speaking. Think of all those customers and neighbors, over those four months, who were saved from bloody diarrhea and vomiting, and popping Zithromax with their sweating, feverish fingers, due to that early intervention.

"I was always very interested in the first step," says Sharon Greene, who had helped direct the system's creation. "The earlier you can detect, the more likely you are to stop the chain of transmission. Actually prevent people from getting sick in the first place."

The Bureau of Communicable Diseases was ready for bigger challenges. And those challenges were coming.

• • •

THE PELOPONNESE REGION of Greece, like many places in Greece, is glorious. Craggy tree-furred mountains climb to the sky and then plunge to the blue waters of the Mediterranean. But when you drive into the city of Sparta, it is, surprisingly, a little shabby. Auto repair joints pile their old tires out front. The sidewalks are just cement slabs with grass tufting up in the cracks. There's not much to make you remember the proud city-state of ancient Sparta, whose culture was so strong, whose warriors were so tough, they fended off a massive Persian army at the Battle of Thermopylae in *the* classic example of one of the principles of war that is still taught in military classrooms today: The principle of *mass*.

In 480 BCE, the Persian king Xerxes arrived to smash mainland Greece. Xerxes wasn't messing around. He brought a force of five hundred thousand men—including infantry, cavalry, and a navy—which was an enormous military force at the time. The Persians carried every conceivable type of military weapon. Bows, slings, spears, swords, javelins, and daggers. The Persian army's main move was mobility. They had light armor. Their tactics had been wildly successful. Their conquests included Egypt; what is now Afghanistan, Pakistan, and the Indus Valley; and Greek Asia Minor. They were experienced, skilled, with all the resources of empire at their disposal.

Xerxes marched this vast army toward Athens. To get there, he had to hook his army's path around the Malian Gulf and to pass through this one spot in the mountains known for its hot springs—Thermopylae.

And that's where the Spartans met him.

Greece at the time comprised city-states like Athens and Sparta and Corinth, with cross-alliances and nasty civil wars. So it's not like there was this unified Greek army waiting to take on Xerxes. King Leonidas of Sparta back home faced the equivalent of an "America first" campaign—Sparta first!—that opposed helping Athens fight the Persians. But King Leonidas showed up anyway with seven thousand men—only three hundred of whom were Spartans: The famous *300* from the movie and video game. King Leonidas chose Thermopylae as the spot to make his stand.

And this is the reason we remember the Battle of Thermopylae, and why it is a perfect illustration of the principle of mass.

"Synchronizing all the elements of combat power where they will have decisive effect on an enemy force in a short period of time is to achieve mass," is how the United States Military Academy describes it.

It's like King Leonidas had time traveled to West Point in the twentieth century, read the textbook, and then time traveled back to Greece to do everything perfectly.

First, he picked a narrow mountain pass, *only seventy feet wide*, where he could reduce the Persians' numerical advantage—five hundred thousand versus seven thousand.

There he planted his three hundred Spartan troops, who had been training together since they were seven years old. They could act in a coordinated force, taking shifts to maintain a twenty-four-hour defense.

The Spartans' offensive weapons were long spears—six feet long—so they could wound and kill their opponents before they even got close. Perfect for holding off an enemy in a confined space. The Persians' javelins, by contrast, were suited for throwing. For long-range battle.

Defensively, the Spartans were trained in the famous phalanx formation of overlapping shields, making them nearly impossible to penetrate, especially in a space as narrow as seventy feet. And if the enemy did get close enough to strike, the Spartan hoplite armor covered them head to toe in leather and brass, and included greaves to protect their shins.

And if that weren't enough, Leonidas had thought to arrive early and burn all the crops in the villages to the north of Thermopylae. So the Persians would have been hungry.

The long spears of the Spartans held back wave after wave of Persian warriors. The three hundred Spartans held out against the five-hundred-thousand-man Persian army for three days.

King Leonidas had *synchronized all the elements of combat power* to have a *decisive effect* in a *short period of time*.

King Leonidas died on the hill. But he had made himself into this singular—even sacrificial—example of the principle of mass. Of bringing what forces you have to a point of opposition that is as narrowly confined as possible to gain advantage.

Exactly the strategy employed by the Bureau of Communicable Diseases in the year 2020, fighting an invisible enemy against which there was—not yet anyway—any weapon.

When you are King Leonidas, you think in terms of mountain passes.

When you are Dr. Sharon Greene, you think in terms of *hot spots*.

WHY WAS THE COVID death rate so high in New York City? No one is sure. It was higher than London. It was higher than Delhi. And it happened right away. President Trump went on television on the night of Wednesday, March 11, 2020, to announce travel restrictions. That day the first victim died in New York City. By the next Wednesday, fifty-four people had died. A few weeks later, nearly three *thousand* people had died in New York City. By the end of April, *seventeen* thousand people had died, and the thirty-day trailing death rate in New York City hit an all-time spike of 197 people per hundred thousand. Sharon Greene and the team at the BCD had been assigned to COVID full-time. They were working from home.

"We were not sleeping," Sharon said. "It was all I did. It was in my head."

There was good news. The team had an approach to stamping out infectious diseases. They had constructed their early warning system, the system that helped them stamp out salmonella in Restaurant A.

More good news. The mayor created a Test and Trace medical corps that would "suppress outbreaks wherever they might arise." King Leonidas had gathered his Spartans. Instead of six-foot spears and greaves to protect their shins, New York had one of the most sophisticated medical establishments in the country, if not the world.

The problem was the sheer number of the enemy. Hundreds of thousands of COVID cases. If King Leonidas had taken on the Persian army in a full-frontal assault, he would have lost. And New York City was losing. Hospitals overflowed. They were converting lobbies into treatment areas. They rationed personal protective equipment—masks, gloves, face shields for medical workers. Ventilators for the sick and dying ran short.

Resources were in short supply—like the Greeks who were short on soldiers, there were simply not enough hospital beds, not enough PPE, not enough ventilators to treat all the people sick and dying of COVID. The Persians were trashing the place.

New York needed to find its Thermopylae, a place where it could send its well-armed medical troops to hold the line against the invaders. But where? COVID is invisible. It leaps from person to person in subway cars and elevators and in lines for coffee and on crowded sidewalks. All the places New Yorkers jostle and scrum every day. Where was the enemy army amassed? In the air!

And worst of all: Sharon's old system for detecting disease hot spots didn't work for COVID. Because COVID was new.

It sounds kind of basic. But it was a stumper. The way you detect communicable disease outbreaks normally is by comparing the rate of infection in a certain space, over time. You *know* how many cases of salmonella to expect per week in a 0.3-mile radius. And if the number is a lot higher than that—if you have 2.3 years' worth of salmonella in just one week—then you know you have an outbreak.

But what if the disease itself hasn't even *existed* for 2.3 years? What if there is no history? You have no trends. You can't compare the number of new cases to what's normally expected. There is no normal.

So Sharon and the BCD team made a slight but important adjustment to their model.

They would create a new normal. That new normal would be the rate at which New Yorkers, on average, in defined areas, tested positive for COVID.

If you detected people in a 0.3-mile radius testing positive for COVID at a 5 percent rate of positivity when in the preceding week you had seen only a 1 percent positivity rate, then you had a hot spot. An outbreak amid an outbreak.

And armed with this knowledge, they could deploy all the carefully prepared resources of the BCD and the city.

The BCD was using SatScan to do *daily* analysis now. The Electronic Clinical Laboratory System was in overdrive, reporting five thousand, six thousand COVID cases per day. Using their new method, they detected a hot spot on June 17. Investigators dove in. They discovered a superspreader event. People who had attended were tested, warned.

Then the system detected another hot spot on July 5, 2020.

The model was working.

Another hot spot on August 12.

Now the city was convinced by the BCD's new model, and they deployed the Test and Trace team in force—to Sunset Park, Brooklyn, a neighborhood with a namesake postage-stamp park that is also a microcosm of the city's entire history. Sunset Park was once on the travel paths of the Canarsee people. It was inhabited by Dutch colonists, then by slaveowners and slaves. Then by Polish and Italian immigrants. Finally by Chinese and Hispanic immigrants. The Test and Trace team, guided by the BCD's SatScan analysis, pumped out robocalls. Knocked on doors. They drove a bus with mobile testing equipment and parked it outside the Herald Gospel Center and shoved swabs up people's noses and told them how to get help.

It was Thermopylae on 44th and 6th.

The death rate dropped.

Six weeks after the testing bus heaved up to that street corner in Brooklyn, the thirty-day trailing death rate reached an all-time low.

From 197 deaths per hundred thousand . . . to 1.4.

For Sharon Greene, the victory was not sweet. She had been working seven days a week for months. Her office had been "pummeled" by reporting requests. The same burnout that affected nurses and other frontline workers affected the Bureau of Communicable Diseases. And Hallie, her beloved tortoiseshell cat who had accompanied her on her adult life journey from that day in the Michigan Humane Society, finally died.

So Sharon's husband rented them an Airbnb in the Catskills. At last, Sharon took a break.

She walked outside. She saw green. Green trees, green grass. Felt the sun on her face.

AT THERMOPYLAE, IN the end, all three hundred Spartans were killed. Not because the Persians broke the line. They didn't. But because a local turncoat tipped off the Persians to a way around. And the Spartans were surrounded. They fought to the last man. But the Greeks, strategically, benefited from the delay and, ultimately, won the war. Diverting resources to where they were most needed meant the difference between Greece surviving as a civilization, or not.

In New York City, forty-six thousand people died of COVID. That's eight times more than died in the Spanish flu epidemic of 1919, which is often compared to COVID. But if the city had not listened to Sharon Greene and her team and implemented a policy of detecting and defending based on hot spots—along with the other tactics they employed, including the citywide shutdown—the body count could have been higher. How much higher? If the infection rates and mortality rates of those first weeks of the pandemic had continued, based on some very simple math, *another three hundred thousand people* could have died.

"I consider it my wartime service," Sharon Greene says of her work in the pandemic.

"I hope I never have to do it again. But I will if I have to. It's what I trained for."

Spoken like a true Spartan.

KEY POINTS IN CHAPTER 9

- It is a given that we live in a world of scarce resources, which people in leadership positions who have to make choices always feel. Who gets the raise? What department gets the head count? What project gets the funding? In the crucible of wartime or a pandemic, the choices are vivid.

- The NYC Bureau of Communicable Diseases was able to use data to identify outbreak points where COVID was flashing up. Then they were able to bring testing and equipment to those hot spots, to keep the disease from spreading.

- This is comparable to the Greeks at Thermopylae, who were able to concentrate their combat zone from the width of an entire country down to a mountain pass seventy feet wide.

- In both examples, leaders are turning an overwhelming, open span of endeavor into a finite zone where they can win, or at least have a chance.

THOUGHT STARTERS FOR YOU

- Where can your data identify points of advantage in your or your organization's mission? Is it customers, some of whom will spend more money than others? Or is there a certain point in your relationship, or the buying journey, where you lose them?

Or maybe you have several activities or lines of business, and one of them has incredible potential, and the others are . . . fine.

- What analysis will identify this hot spot? What if, like Sharon Greene, you must identify the hot spot repeatedly, on an ongoing basis? How can you create an apparatus to do so?

- How can you deploy "mass" against that hot spot, stop the customer churn, or pump the new business line with resources?

WHERE DO WE GO NEXT?

In this chapter, we looked at data helping to decide among multiple, or innumerable, options. But what happens when a lack of information makes you want to avoid a situation altogether—out of fear? Conquering this fear is one of data's most fascinating superpowers.

CHAPTER 10

Data Is Light
in a Dark Room

Tiny Submarines

There's a Pixar film you haven't seen. It's called *Bottlenose*. It opens with a pod of bottlenose dolphins who dance and sing off the beaches of Pitimbu, Brazil. One dolphin, Schnozz, likes to race the human surfers. Schnozz has learned to understand the surfers' speech. One day, without warning, rolling, thunderous noise shocks the dolphins. Has a bomb dropped? Is it an earthquake? The dolphins panic. They cower. It's the end of the world!

Schnozz goes to find his surfer friends to find out what is happening. On the way, Schnozz sees a large ship, two hundred feet long, with churning diesel engines and a cannon-like contraption that's lowered into the water. On the ship's side is painted SEISMIC SURVEYS: OIL & GAS EXPLORATION. But before Schnozz can escape, the cannon fires! Bubbles smoking from its mouth! Schnozz reels and then returns to the pod to share what he has seen only to find he has lost the ability to communicate. His brain is a constant buzzing. Others suffered the same damage. In despair, the pod of bottlenose moves offshore where the waters are deeper, darker, scarier. Schnozz and his friends never recover their hearing. They are deaf and dumb forever. Life for the bottlenose dolphins of Pitimbu is now cold and silent.

The End.

OF COURSE YOU haven't seen the Pixar movie *Bottlenose*. It's such a downer! No one would ever produce it! I made the story up based on scientific research about the effect of seismic surveys on dolphins off the coast of Brazil (and way too many hours rewatching *Finding Nemo* with my kids). Those effects on dolphins include "diversion of migratory routes," "damage to the auditory system," and "an increase in stranding." It's an ugly story.

Seismic surveys are damaging to sea mammals. The reason we—our species, humans—are willing to do this damage to whales and dolphins is that seismic surveys are the only way we can understand the ocean floor.

Light travels poorly in water. You can't just take pictures and look for rock formations. You have to plumb the sea. You have to emit a sound powerful enough to penetrate ten thousand feet of sediment below the ocean floor and bounce back up so that sensors can capture it and piece together a picture of what's below. Trenches. Boulders.

Oil deposits.

And that's the key. Brazil has 104 offshore rigs. The North Sea has 184. Southeast Asia 173. Add them all together and offshore rigs globally generate about $560 billion worth of crude oil every year. That's a lot of black gold. Sorry, *Delphinus delphis*. We didn't mean to drive your species out to sea. We got bills to pay. Cities to heat.

The ocean floor, in other words, poses a massive information problem because (1) the ocean floor is difficult to understand and (2) beneath it lies massive economic opportunity.

And there is not just our oil-guzzling present to consider. There is our clean energy future. Ironically, companies place not just oil wells but wind farms offshore.

Wind farms, too, need ocean floor surveys. But being ecologically minded, wind farm builders are, in theory, keen to avoid damaging dolphins in the process.

They are also in a hurry. The United States is offering "production tax credits" for wind facilities—2.6 cents in credits per kilowatt hour. Given that *one* giant wind farm can create a million kilowatts *per hour*, that's a lot of incentive. But there's a catch. The facilities must be built before January 1, 2025.

So the wind industry must solve the ocean floor information problem—and not destroy dolphin habitats—and do it all before January 2025 or they miss the incentive deadlines, and fewer wind farms are built, and we burn more fossil fuel and accelerate the end of civilization as we know it.

This is a classic dark room problem.

THE IDEA OF the dark room problem occurred to me in 2020 when I was working for Samsung.

The COVID pandemic had forced everyone inside, and the only thing to do was drink, bake, and watch television. Every single major US entertainment company launched a streaming service. So television was in abundance. Disney+ and Apple TV+ launched in November 2019. Then followed HBO MAX, Paramount+, Discovery+, on top of the existing Netflix and Hulu. Everybody, it seemed, was watching streaming shows. *The Tiger King. The Mandalorian.* Within a few years there would be a million TV shows that you could stream, with billions of hours of shows.

Only no one was advertising.

I was in my living room on a conference call right after lockdown. That's right, a conference call. We weren't even Zooming yet—that's how fast the culture changed. I was having my team meeting. And Nelson Stone, who headed up our client research team, started speaking. Urgently.

Nelson is the kindest, most unflappable man you ever met, with a Midwestern baritone pure as corn silk. So when Nelson's voice skips a beat, a little stutter step, you know it's getting hot out there.

"We had about fifty requests this morning from clients," he said. "They all want to know what people are watching. *How* people are watching. Everyone's at home. They can't all be watching network. There's just"—stutter step—"not enough of it to go around."

What Nelson meant was that with traditional television—*linear* television it's sometimes called in the industry, because the shows play linearly from start to finish, like radio—the amount of programming you access is limited to the number of channels on air. Filter that by the number of shows you might want to watch, and there's a natural limit to how much TV you are likely to consume.

But with streaming TV, it's on demand. So there are massive libraries of TV shows to watch. A million shows. Not episodes. A million *titles*. Like, 156 episodes of *The Good Wife*. That's one title.

All the ad agencies, who were our clients, hadn't really thought that hard about streaming TV. Sure, Disney+ had just come out. Sure, streaming was a *trend*. It was a *thing*. But it was, like, a trend to *monitor*. Not a reality you're facing as you stand in your bare feet in your pajamas, in front of your smart TV, on the third day of the pandemic, suddenly realizing that the big black blank screen in front of you represents a paradigm shift of global proportions.

Before the pandemic was over, 1.1 billion people, all over the world—who, like the ad agencies, hadn't cared much about streaming TV—started watching it.

They were locked at home. And with those vast libraries of shows, they could watch as much TV as they wanted.

Now the advertising agencies cared. Even though there was a pandemic on, their clients still had products and services to sell. Okay, maybe not cruise vacations or concert tickets since no one was leaving the house, but new electronics, tools for home projects, brokerage services, food delivery apps, Pelotons . . .

Samsung, my employer, had just started offering what the ad agencies wanted: Ads on streaming TV. We had the smart TVs already. Now we could put ads on them. The new division was a scrappy little group based in New York City's Flatiron District in a dusty office above an event space where shoppers showed up in droves for the annual Jimmy Choo sample sale. There was a Samsung robotics team in the back. Sometimes on the way to the coffee machine, you'd accidentally kick a little pair of disembodied robot legs.

But now, a few days after the pandemic stay-at-home orders, I was in my living room, on a conference call, figuring out how to make fifty frantic clients happy.

"I'll make a dashboard," said Freddie H, our engineering lead. Freddie is an Aussie, with an accent like someone snapping a rubber band, as feisty as Nelson is smooth. You could walk up to Freddie and offer him twenty dollars for nothing, and he could make it into an argument. But when Fred's voice takes on a soft and almost melancholy tone—which is how it was at that moment—that's a signal to step back and let him work. It means he knows exactly what to do and is already dreaming of it.

So we made a dashboard. Nelson and Freddie spec'd it and built it. We started feeding clients data about what streaming TV was all about. How audiences watched it. How much time they spent. What they watched. When they watched.

And the money started to flow.

Because now the clients had information. Before, streaming was a mystery. Now it wasn't. Nelson's idea of what the client wanted, and Freddie's dashboard, told the clients exactly what was going on inside the mysterious world of streaming TV. Clients were accustomed to Nielsen ratings. Those weren't available yet for streaming TV and wouldn't be for several years. Our little dashboard proved to be enough.

Why? Why did the information we gave clients in those dark times work so well and, more to the point, persuade the ad agencies to spend money with us—hundreds of millions of dollars?

IN 1971, A young economist at UC Berkeley was having trouble getting a paper published. The paper was a bit light on econometric modeling, a bit heavy on anecdotes. It kept getting rejected. The editor of the *American Economic Review,* the author later recalled, told him they "did not publish papers on subjects of such triviality." Then—also because of triviality—the *Review of Economic Studies* rejected it. The *Journal of Political Economy* too.

At last he got it published. And the paper earned George Akerlof the Nobel Prize.

"The Market for 'Lemons': Quality Uncertainty and the Market Mechanism" was dismissed as trivial for one reason.

It focused on used cars.

Akerlof's idea was that if you own a car you want to sell, you, as the owner, know all about your vehicle. You know how well it runs, whether it gets good gas mileage. Whether you wrapped it around a telephone pole the night of your buddy's bachelor party and cracked the chassis. (We must take ourselves back to 1971, to a world before Kelley Blue Book and VIN, or vehicle identification number, lookups.)

But if you were to sell it, well, the prospective buyer would know nothing about the car. The buyer knows only what they can learn in half an hour appraising it in a used car lot or your driveway. The numbers of dents and scratches. The state of the upholstery. How it smells. How it runs in a test drive around the block.

"An asymmetry in available information has developed," Akerlof wrote, "for the sellers now have more knowledge about the quality of a car than the buyers."

So now a kind of game happens. An unfair game.

The buyer knows there is a *chance* the car is a lemon—for instance, that you cracked the chassis. But she doesn't know for *certain.* The seller, on the other hand, has perfect information.

This is *information asymmetry.*

You would think the seller might ask a lower price if the car was a lemon, since a car with a cracked chassis is worth less.

But why should he? The buyer won't know the difference until it's too late.

This seems like a game that would benefit the seller and rip off the buyer. But Akerlof points out that the real impact is to depress the market *as a whole*.

Without reliable information, the buyer will always assume there is a *chance* the car is a lemon and will therefore offer a lower price than she might have otherwise. So the market price for *all* used cars declines. They are all priced as if they might be lemons.

The impact? The sellers of *good* used cars can't sell them for their true value. And now only a seller of a lemon will sell his car. Because he, having perfect information, *knows* that the low price is what his car is worth.

Then a spiral begins, or so argues Akerlof. Buyer expectations decline. Prices decline. Until nothing but junk cars are available for sale, and the used car market becomes a cesspool of predatory salesmen and disappointed buyers, and ultimately winks out altogether.

Since 1971, this market problem has been cured. By data. You can go to CARFAX and get a VIN report for $44.99. And now the buyer and the seller both have perfect information. The accident history. The records of damage repair. Even whether the airbags had ever deployed.

But what I was witnessing at Samsung during the COVID pandemic streaming revolution—and what the wind power energy industry is experiencing now—is broader than what happens between a buyer and a seller. Because it's not strictly information asymmetry.

Asymmetry requires two parties, one with information, one without.

What happens when, strictly speaking, there is no buyer and seller? No single transaction? (Even single transactions, multiplied to the size of a market.) What if it's an industry that's stoppered by a lack of information?

There is a whole territory over here. In the spirit of economics jargon—we've come this far— let's call it a *potential market*. It could be streaming television advertising. It could be wind energy.

And there are people who want to do something in that space. Let's call them, still in the spirit of economics, *market explorers*. They might be individual buyers, sure, like Akerlof's car buyers. They can be companies. But more broadly they can be, say, investors who see market opportunity and want to make profits. Or workers at those companies who would benefit from new jobs. Even consumers of the potential venture, like the consumers who would want to watch free, ad-supported streaming TV, or energy consumers who want low-carbon electricity from wind farms. That's more than a buyer and seller. That's a slice of the economy.

And then, there is the big bummer. Something that holds back the market explorers from the potential market.

An information gap.

The streaming TV advertisers who *want* to reach audiences of streaming TV but have no ratings about streaming TV watching. Or the wind energy companies who *want* to build new offshore wind farms but have no information about the ocean floor, or at least can't get it in time to take advantage of the US government's production tax credits and not without destroying the lives of dolphin pods and becoming the villains of a Pixar movie.

I call this problem the dark room problem. Because your experience of that potential market is like your experience at the threshold of a dark room.

What do you want from that room? You want a comfortable chair and a place to do puzzles on your phone.

Fine. But the room is pitch dark. It's strange to you: You've never been inside it before. And human nature fills that void with terrors. Maybe the room has no floor, and you could fall twenty feet into a construction zone. Or maybe there's no fall, but there are snakes or killer clowns or hypnotizing whispering voices urging you to commit murder—or whatever fear jolts you awake from nightmares at 3:00 a.m.

As far as you know, standing at the threshold, all these things *might be* true of the dark room. You'd be crazy to set foot inside of it, much less fully commit and stride right in.

The darkness holds you back. The lack of data. It's not that there is information asymmetry and the market fails because no one knows who is ripping off whom and prices are spiraling. It's that the market has failed by not starting. Because no one has done the work to supply the information needed to make it *not dark*.

The flick of a light switch dispels it all. The room may or may not have the comfortable chair you wanted. Or that killer clown.

But now you know.

ANTHONY DIMARE THINKS he can perform undersea surveys better than the bad guys in my Pixar movie. Despite being named after the ocean (DiMare means "of the sea" in Italian), he claims that his heritage kept him away from the ocean. At least for a while.

"My great-great-grandfather ran a lobster fishing business in Boston," he says. "That business ended up going to zero. I grew up in the aftermath, learning that the maritime world is evil and, like, will destroy you."

Tempting fate, DiMare—a pleasant-faced young man in his thirties with an entrepreneurial twinkle in his brown eyes—became a naval engineer. Eventually, with Charles Chiau, a former SpaceX robotics engineer—tall, thin, surfer haircut, with the tendency to riff on "energy calcs" and "autonomous systems"—DiMare started a company to perform undersea surveys, called Bedrock. Their target clients are wind power companies you've never heard of like Orsted and Vattenfall and Iberdrola and Avangrid, many associated with European state energy utilities.

You can see why a nation-state is required to lead wind farm production. Sticking those giant-sized white pinwheels in the ocean—*wind turbines* is the official name—is a colossal undertaking.

The massive base of the turbine, called a monopile, is loaded onto a special ship by crane. The ship is special because it's the kind of ship that has legs that extend down to the ocean floor to create a solid, construction-worthy anchoring.

The monopile, which is ten stories high, is hammered into the ocean floor. Then a yellow "transition piece" is installed on top, like a cap. (It's got steel ladders that some poor engineer one day will have to climb up to make repairs and do maintenance.) Then the tower is installed: The turbine's stem. This rises six hundred feet in the air. The "nacelle" is then screwed on. If we're going with a plant-stem metaphor, the nacelle is the black center of the sunflower, the axle that the blades spin on.

Once the nacelle is on, you attach to it three of those spooky, whooshing, white blades, or rotors—each a little shorter than a football field. Then cables are laid, connecting each turbine to an offshore substation. The substation links the power from the turbines to the grid. And at last, you have wind energy in your home.

Each turbine costs about $4 million. The largest offshore wind farm has 175 turbines. So the largest farms would be a $700 million endeavor to install, and close to $9 million per year to maintain.

A massive effort, and a massive expense.

As a result, you must have a good survey. You can't go denting every other monopile on unseen boulders at the sea bottom. You'd endanger the whole delicate, expensive, high-tech endeavor.

Anthony DiMare and Charles Chiau think they can do it more quickly and more safely than the state of the art. Their first step is to stop performing the sonic booms from the surface. "It's not just extremely loud, it's dangerous," says DiMare. "We think it would be much more sensible to put that sensor closer to the sea floor." In other words, all that sonic noise that makes dolphins deaf doesn't have to be as loud if you put the boom close to the sea floor. Same principle as a silent disco. (Don't want to disturb the neighbors? Have everyone dance listening to the same music simultaneously in headphones. Bring the sound close to the source: Your ears.) That would argue not for a ship but a submersible. A vehicle to bring the sonar closer to the ocean floor.

Why not, then, DiMare suggests, use "an autonomous system that runs on a really small battery at the cheapest cost per nautical square mile."

And that's when they came up with the idea of an Autonomous Underwater Vehicle, or AUV. A little submarine that looks like the kind you take to the water park with your kid. Only this one is about the length of a surfboard.

Instead of booking a gas-guzzling trawler to perform surveys, DiMare and Chiau let the AUVs crawl along, close to the ocean floor where the sonar does not have to be deafening to sea mammals. They gather the data. Data to dispel the darkness of a fearful new space. Data to create opportunity. Which they then, simply, publish.

"A library," Anthony DiMare calls it, "of what the ocean is."

And the dark room is flooded with light.

KEY POINTS IN CHAPTER 10

- Market opportunities can be blocked by a lack of information. If you don't know how many people are watching streaming TV, why advertise there? If you don't know where to plant your wind turbine, why invest in wind energy?

- One way to sort the problem is to run around and peer in the windows of everyone watching TV and count how many are streaming. Or to strap on a wet suit and dive to the freezing ocean floor, yourself, to kick the boulders. But that's absurd.

- Instead, data will bring you back information about these "dark rooms." And while it's not quite as telling as kicking the undersea boulders yourself, it's the next best thing when you want reassurance about a good site for a turbine.

- And this clears a path for a whole market to spring up, with benefits for customers, employees, companies, investors, or other stakeholders.

THOUGHT STARTERS FOR YOU

- Oh, where to begin? Information gaps exist everywhere and represent massive opportunities.

- In your world, search your peripheral vision. Where are there intriguing opportunities but where you lacked information? Where could you get the information you need? Not to have full assurance, but to get enough information to feel safe. Enough for a first step.

- Think about used cars and how far we have come. All the information on Kelley Blue Book or Cars.com about VIN numbers and repairs and former owners and mileage. Now used cars are a safe market. Wine: It used to be a snob's hideout. Now anyone can get the secret scoop with apps where you photograph the label and get the reviews and the ratings.

- Therapist ratings. School system performance. Fair auto repair prices. Insurance company reimbursement rates. Government agency accountability. Good bosses / toxic bosses (or employees, for that matter). All these important areas of life remain opaque, ready for the bright light of data. Get on your wet suit and dive in.

WHERE DO WE GO NEXT?

Data performs this "light-shining" function by helping us to understand things that are opaque. Its next superpower is to reduce overwhelmingly complex problems into something the human brain can process.

CHAPTER 11

Data Crystallizes Complex Information

The Railroad Nerd

It was all about Carlene Balderrama's house.

Carlene shared the home with her husband, John, a plumber. The house was in a section of Taunton, Massachusetts, called Weir Village, after the low dams—the weirs—the original settlers used to dam up the Taunton River for fishing. Weir Village looks like a thousand other suburbs where the homes are reliable rectangles, where the lawns have a gradient down to the street. There's no hedge or privet. Maybe a few fences separating the properties. There's a sort of bareness to the sky.

Carlene managed the family finances. In retrospect this was a lousy job. John had filed for Chapter 13 bankruptcy three times and had been denied each time. Money was tight. In growing desperation, Carlene had taken to hiding the mortgage notices, ripping them up so John wouldn't see them. Also—an important detail—she wasn't paying them. Somehow she pulled this off for three years.

Finally, the day of reckoning. On Tuesday, July 22, at four in the afternoon, the house would be foreclosed.

At two thirty, ninety minutes before foreclosure, Carlene sent her mortgage company a fax: "By the time you foreclose on my house," she told them, "I'll be dead."

Carlene then took John's rifle and killed herself.

Carlene Balderrama was not alone.

This was 2008, the subprime mortgage crisis. By the time the crisis peaked, as many as 44,300 people per year were committing suicide because they were financially ruined. It wasn't just Carlene Balderrama with the rifle. It was people closing their garage doors and leaving the car running. It was people taking pills. It was people jumping.

Time magazine ran an article naming people responsible for the subprime mortgage crisis. One was an obscure corporate executive named Kathleen Corbet. Kathleen Corbet was president of a financial services company called Standard & Poor's, also known as the S&P, also known as the agency that provides the famous "triple-A" bond rating. The S&P's job is to be a neutral party between lenders and borrowers. Specifically, their job is to tell the lender just how risky it is to do business with this borrower.

But under Kathleen Corbet, the S&P was aiding and abetting the irresponsible lending so characteristic of the subprime crisis. S&P did this by providing good ratings on bundles of mortgages—making those loans seem secure. When they weren't.

With the S&P telling them *everything was just fine*, banks were lending money to people who had no business getting loans.

People like Carlene and John Balderrama.

How could Standard & Poor's get debt ratings so terribly, terribly wrong? It shouldn't be that complicated, should it? Hire a bunch of analysts, read the borrower's finances, rate the loan. How did S&P help turn what seems like a straightforward accounting exercise into a global crisis? How did they get debt ratings so wrong? They might have been partly responsible for thousands of people *committing suicide*.

The answer is that putting a value on a loan is not such a natural and simple thing to do. It's actually very complicated. It's easy to lose your way.

Someone must have done it the right way, originally.

That someone was the founder and namesake of the S&P, Henry Varnum Poor.

WHEN YOU TRAVEL to Maine, you see two versions. One, I call Stephen King Maine, after the horror author who lives and sets his books there. Twisty asphalt roads through raw woods, where you can just imagine the hell beast from *Pet Sematary* lurching out of the brush to chase your car. Then there's tourist Maine. Boutiques selling lavender sachets. Restaurants where you wait an hour to eat a forty-dollar lobster roll. Neither shows you what Maine was like in 1812, when Henry Varnum Poor was born there, in the town of Andover.

Then, it was frontier.

Some folks romanticize the frontier. I am an effete New Yorker. I send T-shirts to the dry cleaner. To me, frontier life sounds brutally hard.

Henry Varnum Poor was the son of the town doctor. He was the first person from Andover, Maine, to go to college. But even someone like Henry—son of a doctor, college bound—still had to tend the sheep. Shear them in springtime. Spin wool into thread. Weave that thread into clothes. His *own* clothes. Tend the cows. Sow, plow, and reap his own food. A subsistence-level life.

Henry Varnum Poor later developed a pet theory about this. His theory was that the isolation of American villages and hamlets was caused by a lack of market towns. "Take England, for example," he wrote. "Every farmer lives in sight of a market." In England, as an older culture, there were plenty of cities. Those cities were widely distributed. They were market towns. Trading hubs. So, if you were a sheep farmer, you could bring wool to the market and trade it for vegetables. You could specialize, make a profit, break out of subsistence farming. The

American farmer, Poor observed, "has no home demand for the wheat he raises, as the surplus of all his neighbors is the same in *kind*." In other words, if Andover was great for sheep farming, then everyone in Andover—and then the next town over, too—would raise sheep. And there would be nobody to trade with. No specialization. No profit.

Which was why Henry Varnum Poor became obsessed with railroads.

Railroads were the great connectors of the 1800s. They linked all those isolated American villages. With a railroad, the sheep farmers in Andover could trade with the weavers in Rumford, who could trade with the vegetable growers in Livermore Falls. Everyone could trade, specialize, and profit. Railroads were the key to breaking out of a subsistence cycle. Railroads were, for Poor, a catalyst for "progress . . . in intelligence, in wealth, and in social comfort."

Henry's brother Johann went into the railroad business. Johann was the charming one, the one you wanted to schmooze the bankers in their boardrooms or the legislators in the state house.

But Henry was not a railroad tycoon in-the-making. He was a railroad nerd.

Henry was a lawyer by training. Fastidious. For fun, Henry drew fifteen-foot maps of the western territory so he and his pals in the American Geographical and Statistical Society could speculate on the best route for a western railroad. When you see him in a rare photograph, Henry Varnum Poor wears a dark suit. His brow juts out like it needs extra room for all those brains. He glares at the camera like that one smudgy, precocious kid at the birthday party. The one who stares at you a little too long, whose laser vision cuts through the fact that you're a grown-up and cuts right down to that patchwork of flaws you call a self.

So Henry Varnum Poor quit working with his brother. He did what a lot of American nerds do when they come from outlying states and they're a little too book smart for their own good.

He moved to New York City and got a job in publishing.

• • •

IN THE LINGO of magazine publishing, there are B2C magazines—or "business to consumer," which is like *People* or *Vanity Fair*—the periodicals focused on a wide audience of readers. And then there is B2B, or business-to-business publishing. B2B focuses on a narrowly defined professional audience. Sometimes called "the trades."

I have worked in trade magazines. It's not very glamorous. I always found them slightly depressing. It's like, if you could really write, if you were a real editor or journalist, you'd be vamping in DC or Silicon Valley or Hollywood for *Vanity Fair* or the *New York Times* or maybe glammed-up business periodicals like *Wired*. But trades? *Progressive Grocer*? (An actual magazine, which you will hear more about in a later chapter.) *Hospitality Design*? (Yes, there is a magazine for choosing the carpets and lamps that go into hotels.) Really? You're going to expend your business genius writing about somebody else's business genius? The deal of the week by the dealmaker of the month—who wasn't you?

Henry Varnum Poor went to work in B2B.

Railroad trade magazines. Of course. He became the editor of the *American Railroad Journal*.

His competition was the *Railway Times*, the *Railroad Record*, the *Railroad Gazette*. His idea of fun was to travel to England and meet the prominent railroad engineers of his day. He met the *inventor of the railroad switch*! He wrote passionate editorials about financial reform.

Every day he went to an office on Spruce Street, in the financial district.

New York City at the time was packed with financiers raising capital for the big railroads. Moguls. They were probably as interested as anyone in positive press. But they did not invite Henry Varnum Poor to their parties on Fifth Avenue. No one wanted the weirdo with the staring eyes at their party, piercing their pretensions.

The whole *point* of a Fifth Avenue party is pretentions. That's the uptown life.

Henry lived downtown, on Saint Mark's place, where later generations of bohemians and literary types would live.

Poor sold subscriptions. Poor reported. Poor published.

He kept his editorial distance. And he was never cool.

WHAT HE DID do was study the railroad business. Yes, he believed railroads were a source of American greatness. He also saw that it was a patchwork of flaws.

The first and biggest problem was raising money.

Building a railroad was a multimillion-dollar project. A company like the Pennsylvania Railroad Company owned and leased more than two thousand miles of track. It raised $120 million in equity and debt. The equivalent of $3.6 billion today. The debt would be raised in two forms: Municipal bonds, when the state or local government financed the railroad, or private loans, where firms and banks supplied the capital.

How did the bankers know whom to trust?

They were just finance people, sitting behind desks, mostly in Boston, Philadelphia, and New York. They didn't know the railroad business.

To know the railroad business, you had to know the local terrain. Bald Eagle Valley and Belvidere. Gettysburg and Girard Point. Long Beach and Louisville. Shamokin and the Shenandoah Valley. You had to know the grade of the land. Where the swamps and mountains were. You had to know the dozens of villages on the route, all the little Andover, Maines, each one petitioning you to make their town the one with the railroad stop. So *they* could be the market town.

And not just locally. This was the era of the western rail. Those wide spaces, stretching to Colorado and Wyoming and even California, where Providence and rattlesnakes and deadly desert heat awaited. Try finding a local surveyor *out there*.

Then came the construction. Locomotives had to be built in H-form manufacturing machine shops, with foundries and smithies and carpenter shops. Rails had to be procured, either four feet eight and a half inches, which was standard gauge, or four feet three inches for the Delaware and Hudson gauge, or four feet ten inches for Ohio gauge. Manufacturing had to be set up locally. Sheds and workshops covered *acres* of land. The hammering, sawing, and smithing would go on for years. You had to buy the real estate for your depot, your terminal, your stations, warehouses, grain elevators, shops. You had to hire crews to build, to maintain. You needed skilled workers and experienced managers. You needed to keep your workers safe from inhaling enamel dust or drinking on the job and losing a limb.

Then you had to know the railroad business. The rates charged for passengers, for freight. Financial management. Death and disablement benefit liabilities for the workers. Rental and interest earned. Interest paid. Cash balances.

And to build the physical railroad, in a sense, was the simple part.

Because what was complicated was to manage the web of conflicting incentives that would cause players in this great scheme to lie.

Citizens wanted railroads and had an incentive to overstate the attractiveness of their region for a new line.

Railroad owners wanted financing and had an incentive to overstate their prospects to their lenders.

Stockholders relied on a board of directors to represent their interests, but management had an incentive to hide bad news from the board.

Everybody could have lied. (And often, they probably did.) Because, at that time, there was no regulation. The state governments, and certainly the federal government, did not require any kind of disclosure. It was all voluntary.

So Henry Varnum Poor, with his receding hairline and his prominent forehead—he looks a little like the actor Kurtwood Smith who plays the dad in *That Seventies Show*—sat in his Spruce Street office and agonized. Because he perceived a paradox.

Railroads were the single most important driver of American connectedness and prosperity.

Yet at its center loomed a colossal information problem.

A problem of expertise and incentives.

And motivation for lying galore.

AND THIS IS where fate intervened. Poor retired from the *American Railroad Journal.* He lost his retirement money in a stock market crash. Like Carlene Balderrama, he almost lost his home. He was middle aged. Worried. And that was when Poor's son, a grown man at this point, made a suggestion:

"Dad, you've been obsessed with railroad metrics for decades. Just . . . publish those."

And with that boost of love and support, Henry Varnum Poor had a late-career inspiration.

He had had this idea, back in the 1850s, of sending a questionnaire to every railroad company and asking them to self-report the details of their operation. Well, he would try again. Henry Varnum Poor still had clout. People remembered him. Poor would get the responses back from the railroad companies and publish—as almost a book, a directory—a summary of all their responses. It would contain all the critical information needed by the major stakeholders in a railroad company—the bankers and the citizens and the managers. It was a simple vision.

Poor mailed out 352 questionnaires. He received 330 replies.

He pounded the railroad tycoons with requests. He wanted their title. Their charter. Their costs. The gradient of their roads. The pattern and weight of their rails. They couldn't hide. Henry Varnum Poor knew their business cold. Henry Varnum Poor wasn't just *a* railroad nerd. He was *the* railroad nerd.

The data came in. Each statistic was painstakingly checked. Then, at last, published. *Poor's Manual of Railroads* was born. It was a masterpiece of metrics.

Line of road (miles). Sidings (miles). Rolling stock, in numbers of cars: By passenger, freight, with freight subdivided into box, platform, baggage, stock, coal, dump, fruit, and caboose. Mileage, by passenger and freight. Passengers in number. Freight in tons. Then the financials. Revenue, expense, stock, debt. Rates per passenger, per freight ton.

Each company's entry was placed in a standard form. So you could find the info on everybody.

And he named names. He named each director, of each board, of each railroad.

Vernon D. Price of Louisville, Kentucky.

Walden Eddy of Greenwich, New York.

Elisha P. Wilbur of Bethlehem, Pennsylvania.

"Daylight should be let into every department of service," Poor pronounced. "Concealment is certain to breed disease."

WHAT IS NEARLY as miraculous as the metrics in *Poor's Manual of Railroads*—or at least to the modern reader holding a leather bound copy in your hand and smelling the old paper and glue—is the advertising. I like to imagine an overly chipper clerk with a newsreel middle-Atlantic accent reading the ads out loud . . .

"Rumsey and Company, Fire and Engine Works!"

"Iron Clad Paint!"

"Fisher Rail Works! Fully Warranted against breakage of any part!" (With a helpfully labeled "side view" of rail joints . . . basically a cross-section view, of a log.)

You get the impression of a crowded bazaar, a whole industry converging on the page. A book, like some Harry Potter magical object, where the sounds and smells of iron works and sooty laborers and western dust rise off the page, so real you have to wipe your face with a handkerchief after reading.

In later years, the successor organization that we know, Standard & Poor's, in one important way, improved on its forebear. It crystallized all that complexity, all that richness, into one sharp little number that anyone can understand.

How risky is the loan of a giant complex company like the Pennsylvania Railroad?

They get a grade, just like in school.

If you are a AAA rating, you are not risky at all. You are "investment grade." You are a boring and safe country to loan money to, like Canada. You are a company like Johnson & Johnson that sells Band-Aids and Tylenol.

You can be AA, A, BBB, and so forth. If you are a C, you are "highly vulnerable to non-payment." If you are a D, you are basically bankrupt. (Why is there no F? Grade school stigma, I guess. Or, simply, too late.)

It took Henry Varnum Poor 238 pages to bring his *Manual of Railroads* to life. A hundred years later, the S&P could conjure up whole companies, whole industries, even whole countries, in a few letters. They advanced Poor's vision of crystallizing information to a new apex of brevity and power.

AAA?

Everybody can understand that.

What this shows us is the power of data to crystallize incredible complexity. And not just, like, adding up and averaging a set of numbers in a column. Real complexity. The complexity of economic life.

Yes, *Poor's Manual,* and the successor S&P ratings, summarized the sprawl of a company like the Pennsylvania Railroad or a Johnson & Johnson. But those metrics also—at their best—resolved conflicting incentives. The incentive of the lender to lie to the borrower. Or the manager's incentive to hide bad news. And it was more than that. In the 1800s, remember, railroads were new. No one in history had ever before built, managed, and financed a *two-thousand-mile railroad.* Especially not one stretching out into unmapped land.

Numbers, distances, human nature—all could be harnessed by a letter grade.

MAYBE POOR WASN'T cool enough to be invited to moguls' parties. But down in his little office on Spruce Street, Poor, in a sense, *was the one judging them.* He literally evaluated the moguls. Once a year, he published a 238-page picture of *who they truly were.*

That was what Kathleen Corbet and the S&P of the '00s had lost. Her S&P took the money. They went directly to the bankers, held out their hands, and got paid. Far from eliminating concealment and, with it, the ability for the various players to lie, they lied themselves. They published false ratings. The result was death and disaster.

Carlene Balderrama picked up a rifle on that dark day in Weir Village, Massachusetts, because she did not have Henry Varnum Poor—obsessive, detail-oriented Henry Varnum Poor—to look out for her. Because of his distance, his impartiality—because he lived on Saint Mark's Place and not Fifth Avenue—Henry Varnum Poor brought the daylight.

Carlene Balderrama, and so many others at that time, could have used it.

KEY POINTS IN CHAPTER 11

- Data helps people make decisions. In the context of the S&P ratings, it is usually: Should I lend money to this organization, and what is a fair rate for my risk?

- Doing so requires considering an impossible amount of detail. How much money does the company make? How solid is its management? Its processes? Its customers and all their businesses? It's a sprawling spiderweb of questions that ultimately must be reduced to something manageable.

- There is an ethical component too: By crystallizing information, data people take responsibility for what happens with their information. So it must be as accurate as they can make it, to shed "daylight"—not the opposite.

THOUGHT STARTERS FOR YOU

- Henry Varnum Poor did not leap straight to a AAA bond rating. First he crafted a question. How valuable or trustworthy are the railroad companies?

- Then he found data on different areas of the railroad business and rolled it up: Revenue, operations, assets.

- Try thinking about your crystallization challenge by breaking it into a hierarchy. Group many metrics into families of metrics. Then roll up those families so you can see the whole.

WHERE DO WE GO NEXT?

Data confers superpowers on humanity: Omniscience, directing resources to where they are needed most, shedding light on "dark rooms," crystallizing complex information. But what about more specific uses of data? What follows next are some of the common themes, or principles, I have seen in data in my career. It's used for counting, tracking, anomaly detection, identity, matching, certifying, scoring, and performance measurement. Naturally, this is just the beginning. And none of these uses stands alone. They are connected.. But if you understand these uses, even most of them, you will be a data person.

PART FOUR

How We Use Data

I have bedimmed
The noontide sun, called forth the mutinous winds,
And 'twixt the green sea and the azured vault
Set roaring war; to the dread rattling thunder
Have I given fire, and rifted Jove's stout oak
With his own bolt; the strong-based promontory
Have I made shake, and by the spurs plucked up
The pine and cedar; graves at my command
Have waked their sleepers, oped, and let 'em forth
By my so potent art.

—SHAKESPEARE, *The Tempest*

CHAPTER 12

Counting

The Idea of Three

The funny thing about Susan Whiting is she really is the nicest person you've ever met. She's basketball-forward tall, has lemon-blond hair, glasses. When folks say someone "moves like a natural athlete," if you can imagine the opposite of that, that's Susan Whiting: She moves like a natural reader, someone built to sit in a library carrel. When you ask her her greatest accomplishment, her reaction is, "Oh gosh."

None of this would be surprising if she were, like, a molecular biologist or a scholar of ancient Assyria. But Susan Whiting was a CEO of a company doing business in a hundred countries with thousands of employees, the first female CEO in her company's history. Soon after achieving that position, she showed up for a speech in her hometown of Chicago facing protestors with hand-painted placards that read, "You're Fired" and "African Americans for Accuracy." The protestors marched. They yelled through megaphones, denouncing Susan Whiting and Susan Whiting's company like it was a political protest, a labor rally, implying she was racist, that her company was racist, that they had had enough, the sounds of shame and denunciation echoing through the square. And it all had to do with counting.

Susan Whiting was CEO of Nielsen Media Research, the company that tells TV networks how many people watch their shows. TV ratings matter to a lot of people. They matter to normal folks because we like to know what shows are popular, the way we like to know which sports teams are ahead in their league or what songs are number one hits. The ratings matter even more to TV networks. Because the higher a TV show's ratings, the bigger the audience; and the bigger the audience, the more the network can charge for a TV ad and the more money they make. Like the Super Bowl, where the game can reach a hundred million people and every thirty-second ad spot costs millions.

But of course not every show is a Super Bowl, and the ratings don't always go up. If you have a show that reaches five million people but then one day Nielsen Media Research tells you it only reached four million people, well, you, as the TV network, have just lost a butt load of money. You've lost 20 percent of your advertising revenue. And if you arc that TV network, having just lost all that money, you will be furious. You might turn around and wring the neck of your showrunner for making bad choices. You might also try and wring the neck of Nielsen for counting the audience unfairly or inaccurately—the same way a team is inclined to blame a loss in a close game on the ref.

In Nielsen's case, in 2004, you wouldn't have been wrong to do so. At that time, it's hard to believe, but Nielsen would mail paper diaries—little blue books, like those exam booklets college students take exams in—to every so-called Nielsen Family. And the Nielsen Family would be expected to write down everything they watched, in pencil.

Or everything they *remembered* they had watched.

Now 2004 doesn't seem that long ago, at least to me. It wasn't like people were still listening to gramophones and riding horse and buggies. But the internet was new (just over ten years old), and companies were still adjusting, and Susan Whiting—being a responsible executive trying to keep her company with the times—decided to replace the diary approach to ratings with a technology. Specifically, a lightweight tech called a Local People Meter that plugged into your TV and captured what you watched without you having to do anything—like write it all down in a blue book.

Which all sounds very sensible.

Except for the fact that it *changed* the TV ratings.

You would think the Local People Meter technology would capture the same data as the diaries, only with a little more accuracy and without all the fuss and mess.

The problem was that those little blue exam booklets had already introduced bias to the data. People *remembered* they had watched a show when that show was really popular, and everyone was talking about it. But if they had watched some obscure documentary on cable about, say, Brazilian dolphins, they would probably forget the name as soon as they turned off the TV. And when it came time to scribble down the names of the shows they had watched that week, the dolphin doc was long gone, erased by paying bills and doctor visits and all the daily ridiculousness of life. So the data gathered was biased toward shows that were already famous and biased against shows that were hard to remember, or maybe embarrassing to write down. (Once when my kids were little and I was on an airplane traveling for business, I poked the button on the airplane entertainment system to watch *SpongeBob*. And it wasn't like nostalgia watching, like oh, I miss my kids, I'm going to watch *SpongeBob SquarePants*. No, I had been watching a lot of *SpongeBob* with them, and now, on my own, I wanted to watch *SpongeBob*. But of course I was having problems with the system, so I had to call over a member of the crew. And of course she was young and attractive and while fixing the system, she couldn't help herself and her tone grew as dry as a gin martini as she asked me, "*SpongeBob*?" In that moment, I remembered that grown men are not supposed to watch silly kids' cartoons when they are alone. And had I been a Nielsen Family, alone with my blue book, my pencil would have hesitated over the page, as I balked at committing my weirdness to paper. That's bias in your sample.)

The bias did benefit one group, however: The major networks like NBC and FOX. Those networks had a lot of marketing muscle to promote their shows, so people talked about those shows, they remembered those shows, and they remembered those shows when it came time to scribble in their TV diary. The diaries weren't so great for all the little cable networks showing dolphin documentaries.

So when Susan Whiting introduced the Local People Meters in June 2004, that was a big change. Suddenly, the TV ratings didn't rely on human memory and weren't filtered by self-consciousness. They just relied on data. People didn't have to remember the name of the show on cable. The meter did it for them.

And FOX's ratings plunged. Their advertising sales plunged. FOX was furious. Other big networks were furious. And along the way someone noticed that the shows whose ratings plunged were, among others, shows about Black and Hispanic people. And suddenly the metering technology appeared, somehow, to be racist. Or maybe it was the sample—the ways the Nielsen Families were chosen—that was racist, or at least not race-aware enough. A coalition was formed: Don't Count Us Out / Queremos Ser Contados. Black and brown people felt they were excluded from the TV ratings, from the sample. Univision, the Spanish-language network group, sued Nielsen. And Susan Whiting—I mean her name was *whiting* for goodness' sake—goes to an event in Chicago and, instead of dealing with all the arcane nerdery of TV ratings, faces accusations of racism.

Yes, later, it turned out that Don't Count Us Out was funded by FOX. Counting, in the TV business, had become the way tens of billions of dollars traded hands. And whether the cause was cynical TV networks like FOX losing money or Black people tired of not having shows about them reflected in the culture, the fact remained that counting, and getting it wrong—or even changing how the ratings were counted—meant facing somebody's wrath.

• • •

COUNTING IS MAYBE the most elemental idea in data. It is so elemental, you have to go back to the beginning of human society to understand it.

There's the baboon fibula, fifteen centimeters long and twenty thousand years old, known as the Ishango Bone, found in the Congo, with mysterious notching systems etched into it suggesting a counting method based on the number twelve.

There's the eight-thousand-year-old Mesopotamian trading system—not too dissimilar to the Nielsen Ratings—where two parties traded based on pebbles. A buyer and a seller would strike a deal—let's say they were going to exchange three sheep—and so three pebbles or other tokens would be embedded in clay. To seal the deal, the clay would be baked with the correct number of tokens inside. If they ever needed to reference the deal terms, they'd smash open the baked clay balls, witness the three tokens inside, and resolve any dispute they had about how many sheep they had agreed to buy and sell.

But when you slow down and think about the step that preceded this, there are more than pebbles embedded in that clay ball. It's kind of a miracle.

Because some human had to look at three sheep . . .

Then look at three trees . . .

Then look at their three children . . .

Then the three people standing up there on the ridge, outside the village, at sunset, swathed in all that luscious pink light: Their neighbors Brown, Jones, and Robinson . . .

. . . hold in their hands the three pieces of fruit they're about to eat for lunch.

And say, "Wait a minute."

Someone in our species had to reflect that there is a level of abstraction beyond those *instances* of three things. That there is, in fact, an *idea* of three things. And that idea, that abstraction, can be applied to any instance of three things in the observable world. Bertrand Russell, in his *Introduction to Mathematical Philosophy*, speaks about it as if it were the birth of the number:

> A particular number is not identical with any collection of terms having that number: The number is not identical with the trio consisting of Brown, Jones, and Robinson. The number is something which all trios have in common, and which distinguishes them from other collections.

The ability to abstract the idea of three represents a massive leap, and not just for mathematics, but also for data. It reinforces an idea from earlier chapters: That data is a representation of reality. Three, applied to sheep, is data (three) about reality (sheep). It's linking an aspect of the wild world to a descriptor of that world.

But we're not there yet—the idea of three is not yet data.

First, the idea of three must somehow be *recorded*. The idea of three must be communicated . . . communicable. That first observer of trios must be able to share their observation with someone else and have that other person get it. Oral communication about counting might have been enough for a period in human civilization. But then emerged the need for records, which gave us clay balls with tokens baked inside. And finally something else happened, in the telling of the cognitive linguist Caleb Everett—a fiftyish, bearded professor and an associate dean at the University of Miami—"The system gradually transitioned from a three-dimensional one, to a two-dimensional one. That is, rather than encoding the quantities of trade items with actual tokens inside clay containers, the quantities were simply depicted on small clay tablets."

Cuneiform writing was born! The number three was written down! And with it was born the kind of data we know today. Because now, data has a few essential ingredients:

The observable reality. (Sheep.)

The abstract-able characteristics of that reality. (There are three of them.)

The connection of that snatch of reality to its characteristics. (Someone observes it.)

A way to communicate that record to anyone. (Someone writes it down.)

Without these foundational steps, all the other concepts about data in this book cannot exist. I sit in wonder at the Big Bang quality of this moment for our civilization.

I also wonder, in a smaller way, at the persistence of the human impulse surrounding counting. Susan Whiting and Nielsen had gone into the clay ball business. And—right or wrong—FOX thought Nielsen had got it wrong. And they were pissed. As pissed as our friend in Mesopotamia might have been when their trading partner showed up with two sheep, not three, at the trade—when the clay ball in his pocket contained three pebbles.

Susan Whiting has one more lesson for us.

You'll note that FOX was angry at Nielsen during this transaction.

But wait a minute: Nielsen was not selling sheep. Sorry—I'm getting too into this early civilization theme—Nielsen was not buying or selling advertising. Nielsen didn't refuse to pay for an ad campaign or renege on a contract for a Super Bowl ad. So why was FOX pissed at Nielsen?

Because FOX was paying Nielsen to do the counting—for the TV ratings.

And why is that important?

Because suddenly the scribbles on the clay tablet had become *an asset*. The observation about the number of sheep—the clay ball—was not just useful. Clay balls had value, like the sheep themselves. Maybe not the same value. But enough to be worth money. When I worked in corporate strategy at Nielsen we usually assumed we could make 1–2 percent in data fees from the value of the original marketplace. In other words, if $100 billion traded hands in the TV advertising business every year, we reckoned we could make $1 billion or more. And we did. If you walked into the secret halls of Google or Facebook or Amazon today—or, for that matter, simply read their financial statements—you would see how crucial data is to these insanely successful businesses. It fuels their ads business; it fuels their cloud storage businesses. And it goes without saying—but I already did in earlier chapters—how crucial data is to the development of large language models, or LLMs, which were the explosive factor driving AI.

With those clay tablets, data went from being merely a recorded observation to an observation that itself had value.

Data became a thing. Not just a thing *about* a thing.

THE UNIVERSITY OF MIAMI professor Caleb Everett, whom I mentioned above, has a unique perspective on counting. As a boy, he lived in the Amazon region with his missionary parents—who also happened to be linguists—with a tribe called the Piraha. There are only a few hundred Piraha people. You need a sea plane to reach their network of villages. According to Everett, and other sources, the Piraha are hunter-gatherers who have lived in the region for more than ten thousand years and who have resisted integration with twenty-first-century culture. Everett's family lived with the Piraha for years, and got to know them as well as any outsider could. And there was one thing outsiders noticed:

The Piraha did not use numbers.

They had three numeric words.

The word for the number one is *hoi*.

The word for the number two is *hoi* (with the emphasis changed to the last syllable).

And then there is a word for "many": *Aibaggi*.

And that is pretty much it for the numbers. No three, no four. Forget about getting to, like, eleven. Just one, two, and many.

So, in effect, the Piraha do not count. They don't have calculators. Rulers. They don't make complicated buildings—at least, not in an engineering sense—so there are no architectural drawings or schematics lying around. They don't do accounting. They don't calculate the value of a share of common stock or use the Black-Scholes model to value a call option. They simply don't learn or use math.

In fact, not only do the Piraha not count, but they seem to have sidestepped Bertrand Russell's leap into abstraction altogether. They don't have words for colors, for instance. In a *New Yorker* profile of Everett's father, he is quoted as saying: "If you show them a red cup, they're likely to say, 'This looks like blood.' Or they could say, 'This is like vrvcum'—a local berry that they use to extract a red dye." In the Piraha universe, not only is there no concept of the value of "three" abstracted from some collection of observable trios, but there is also no concept of "red" abstracted across blood or berries. The Piraha live in open huts with no walls or furniture. They don't stockpile possessions. They don't even store or preserve food—no smoking, no pickling, no jams, no salting. They live off fish and game they catch. They don't grow food. No agriculture.

Because this quality of Piraha language and culture is so striking, it has been the subject of academic papers. Even academic squabbles. Most of the hubbub focused on (to my ear) obscure arguments about linguistics—whether a human language without numbers proves Noam Chomsky wrong about whether all language is hard coded with the same general tool kit. I couldn't care less. For me it seems that the Piraha are a natural experiment that we should treasure. *What happens when you don't count?* When you don't let in the outside world? When you don't set time in motion?

• • •

AS A YOUNG and impressionable professional working at Nielsen while the Don't Count Us Out controversy was underway, it felt like an education.

Today, steeped as we are in the concept of systemic racism, we would be inclined to take the claims, and the anger, of the coalition at face value.

But it appears the Don't Count Us Out coalition was created—from whole cloth—by the Murdochs, especially Lachlan Murdoch, who at the time was just emerging as a key player in the family. "Liberal politicos," wrote *Variety* at the time, "characterizing the ruckus as a question of racial equality have been snookered—and by a studio well-known for backing conservative causes, no less." In other words, to pressure Nielsen to change its methodology to preserve FOX ad revenue, FOX had found enough support for the racism charge to make Susan Whiting's life hell, at least for a time. The lesson for me, hearing these insinuations, was a wide-eyed understanding that, yes, appearances could be manipulated. That cynicism, where money was at stake, knew no bottom. If it meant saving a few bucks, why not publicly denounce someone as racist?

Then there was the take within Nielsen that Susan Whiting had successfully played the rope-a-dope with her adversaries. She let them take their shots. She waited out public interest in the topic—which, given that is was about statistical samples and methodology, wasn't very deep to begin with. And she diffused the entire affair and protected hundreds of millions in Nielsen revenue from FOX and the other broadcasters with the announcement of a $2.5 million research fund into the topic and an eight-page letter detailing how Nielsen would respond methodologically. A hero: Successful because she expressly did not look or act heroic. The lesson for me was in shrewdness.

But as I sought out Susan Whiting to interview for this book, and our meeting kept being rescheduled, I eventually was told the reason: Now in her late sixties, *Susan was ill, and receiving treatment, and getting better, but yes, difficult to schedule, she would be in touch soon.* I had no reason to think the illness was life threatening. Yet I found myself growing emotional. I went for a run. I played the same song on repeat, as I sometimes do. I ran up a long hill, in a heat wave, and sweat drenched my shirt, hair, then forehead, eyebrows, and then eyes. And then tears came. Why? I had known Susan Whiting a little at Nielsen. I thought of her with some affection: Kind people in power are rare. But there was something else here. Susan Whiting was a parental figure. Protective, tall, reassuring. And could she really die? Was I having some sort of substitute mourning for my relationship with my own mother (another tall, bookish blond), which had grown frayed and mistrustful?

Yes. And there was still more to it. It is ridiculous and corny to say so, but I felt, as I grew red eyed and weepy on my run, that I was crying for everyone. That one person who had seen the three sheep, or the trio of Brown and Jones and Robinson, and abstracted a number out of the experience? They advanced our civilization. They leaped us forward. They gave us the power to count our minutes. Advance time. And in doing so, I felt, they had allowed billionaires to gin up scandal, allowed protestors to be angry, businesspeople to bicker, and allowed all the ragged conflicts of the world to happen. They allowed Susan Whiting—not today, maybe, but sometime—to die; the tall, bookish, lemon-haired warrior of the rope-a-dope. And the Piraha, by avoiding abstraction—by not counting the minutes or abstracting anything—maybe had cheated time, cheated greed and disease and death.

I ran up the hill, gasping, determined not to stop, eyes squeezing tears for Susan Whiting, for my naive professional youth, for my lack of a loving relationship with my mother, and for all of us. Because we live in a world of magic and wonder and powers; but a world where troubles come from those powers, too, from permanently separating ourselves from merely seeing sheep to counting them. "But of the tree of the knowledge of good and evil, thou shalt not eat of it: For in the day that thou eatest thereof," God warned Adam and Eve, "thou shalt surely die." The idea of three allowed us to count, trade, do business. And as soon as we had it, the Garden of Eden was gone.

KEY POINTS IN CHAPTER 12

- Counting is the most fundamental way we work with data. But it's more subtle than we think.

- It involves connecting a reality (sheep), to an abstraction (the idea of three), to make an observation you care about (three sheep), to making a record of that observation (writing it down).

- Counting is the heart of commerce, dealmaking, recordkeeping, all of which define our society. The absence of counting exists in some cultures, like the Piraha tribe in Amazonia, an intriguing comparison to our own.

THOUGHT STARTERS FOR YOU

- Where are there gaps in quantification in your domain? Do you count the number of visitors to your organization? The number of users who share a password? The number of the various types of products you sell?

- What kind of power would you take on if you knew this information? Could you make a case for more funding? Could you kill products that don't sell and use those resources to nurture products that do?

- What about counting as an asset in itself? Are there transactions, events, or objects that only your organization can see? What stakeholders would benefit from having this knowledge?

WHERE DO WE GO NEXT?

Now that we have grasped the value of counting, let's add the dimension of time. If you count the same thing, over time, you are in the business of tracking, which has a value all its own.

CHAPTER 13

Tracking

The Power of One Number

I n summers, Missy Pollock would sit at the kitchen table eating a sandwich her mom made her. Tuna fish maybe. Or turkey and cheese. And while she was sitting at the table, feet dangling, the radio would sound this jingle, like a cheerful robot, for its noon broadcast. *Do do do-DEE do do dee . . . DOOOO!* and a man's voice would come on the radio, WKTN, kind of driving and intense. "*This* is the Ohio Ag Net!" And it would be the Ohio State Department of Agriculture Commodities Report. "Corn prices are trading lower. Soybean futures rose eleven cents per bushel . . ." Missy's grandparents were soybean farmers. Her mother was a nurse.

"This is pre-internet," she remembers now. "Not a lot of exposure to what the world was like. But I always knew that there was something more out there for me. It was like, I'm gonna get out. I'm gonna go do something." She got a graduate degree in economics. She moved to New York City. She became an economist. And as if growing up in a little railroad town like Kenton, Ohio, with its radio commodities reports—with its rattling trains carting tons of corn and seed and soybean—had drummed some kind of rhythm into her, like an analytic tempo for commodities, Missy, now Melissa, set aside a successful corporate career at American Express and went to work for the government, tracking inflation. Tracking prices, in fact, helping to create, once a month, without fail, the United States of America's mighty Consumer Price Index.

What makes the Consumer Price Index, or CPI, mighty? It doesn't sound mighty. It sounds on one level like a screaming bore. First, it's an acronym. Second, it's created by the federal government. Third, it's created—within the federal government—by the Bureau of Labor Statistics, which (in the parlance of the Gen X women I know reared in the age of *Sex and the City*) is not exactly a panty dropper. And fourth, it is crafted with painstaking care, with layer upon layer of meticulous data gathering and statistical calculation.

Yet the CPI affects almost every dollar of wealth in the United States. Maybe the world. And it does so every thirty days.

The Consumer Price Index is, essentially, a measure of inflation. The Bureau of Labor Statistics defines a basket of goods. Then they track how prices change for those goods over time. That's inflation.

Down on Wall Street and in Midtown Manhattan, in all the offices of Morgan Stanley and Goldman Sachs, all the boys in dress shirts and ties and the girls in blouses and pencil skirts, all the twenty-something analysts are, figuratively speaking, poised over their laptops ready to type numbers into their financial models when the inflation numbers come out.

Because—in case you missed this in finance class or neglected to sign up for finance class or never dreamed that taking a finance class was a good idea in the first place—stock prices are the *net present value of all future cash flows*.

In English? It means a company's stock, today, is worth a total of all the money it will make in the future.

Weird, but makes sense.

That's the "all future cash flows" part of the definition.

The "net present" part is where the definition of a stock price gets interesting.

Because money you get paid in the future is not as valuable as money you get paid today. You can prove this for yourself with a simple thought experiment. If I offer you $100 today or offer you that same $100 exactly a year from now, you'll say, "I'll take $100 today." You just know intuitively that the gap between today and this date a year from now will create risk. I could forget about my promise, or I could go broke and not be able to afford $100 anymore. Or a million other things that might intervene that we couldn't dream up. And one of those million things is inflation. Because as the world knows, having gone through the postpandemic rise in inflation, inflation makes money worth less. If three years ago a gallon of milk was worth three dollars, and inflation has been skyrocketing, and the milk now costs five dollars, then your three dollars that used to be worth a gallon of milk is now only worth three-fifths of a gallon of milk.

So the higher inflation is, the less milk you can buy. Because inflation reduces the value of your money.

The same is true for stock valuation. The higher inflation is, the less all those *future cash flows* will be worth.

In other words, if a company was going to pay you $100 a year for ten years, that would be worth $1,000.

But with inflation, that same promise for $100 per year for ten years might be worth $600.

Which is why all the young analysts in their ties and skirts are poised over their laptops ready to tap the inflation rate into their financial calculations. So they know how much to discount the future cash flows of every publicly traded company in the United States.

So inflation affects the value of *every publicly traded company's stock*. From Walmart to Build-A-Bear.

Which is *fifty trillion dollars'* worth.

But it doesn't stop there. Inflation is used to calculate cost-of-living increases at your employer, which affects how much of a raise you get in January. It's used to calculate interest rates, which affects how much you pay for a mortgage or a small-business loan.

And so on and so on.

And then, in a two-day stretch in the summer of 2022—August 15 and 16, to be specific—the Consumer Price Index took on even more special significance. On the fifteenth, the CPI updated its August numbers. Another monthly uptick in a hot run of inflation that had global investors—and citizens—scared that the gloom of the pandemic would extend into the misery of a recession. Then, on the sixteenth, the Inflation Reduction Act passed.

The Inflation Reduction Act. The most ambitious, sprawling climate legislation in American history.

Wait . . . climate?

Almost $400 billion in loans, grants, and incentives for heat pumps, domestically produced batteries, zero-carbon electricity, nuclear energy, clean transportation, and upgrades to the grid.

So why was it called the Inflation Reduction Act and not, say, the Climate Change Reduction Act?

The short answer: Because inflation is tracked.

And climate is not.

TRACKING IS WHAT you do when you care so much about a phenomenon that you invest time, effort, and resources to monitor it.

That's fine as a definition. But it's a little circular. I'm just substituting the word *monitor* for *tracking*.

We might understand the power of tracking best by its absence.

Lack of tracking. Now there's a feeling.

It's itchy. Uncomfortable. Anxious. Something is going to come at you and mess you up—but you're not sure when, or from where.

Let's use a scenario.

You're a small-business owner.

A new competitor, call them Competitor X, is winning business from you. It's serious, but you're not sure how far things have gone. You wished you had tracked their inroads with your customers. You wish you had started doing so months or years ago and seen the warning signs. Now you're losing money. No wonder you're anxious.

That lack-of-tracking feeling is not only anxious but also itchy and uncomfortable because of the number and complexity of the unknowns. You might have heard about Competitor X from one of your salespeople here or there. You might have seen their booth at the expo. You might have seen their ads in the trades. But did that mean they were a serious threat? How would you know? Again, you need customer sales data. You need to know your market share—and Competitor X's market share. But it's hard to gather that information. You'd have to survey all your potential customers to find out how many of them use Competitor X and how many use you.

Okay, let's say you did that. You did the survey. And you got the survey back and it turns out 20 percent of all the customers in the market love your product. But 5 percent love Competitor X.

Five percent. That seems like a decent amount but not overwhelming. The nuances now become essential.

Is it 5 percent, up from zero in just six months? That would be a major threat.

Is it 5 percent, up from 4 percent in one year? That would seem more stable and manageable.

But to get that information, you would have to track your market share *over time*.

So let's say you did that too. Or tried. But you're not trained at doing customer surveys. So maybe you kind of screw it up. And while your first survey had a hundred customers responding, your second survey had only twenty customers responding. And suddenly the survey says Competitor X has 10 percent market share. Terrifying! But what if your survey went out on a holiday, so you got a weird, biased mix of people responding. And you're not sure if you believe the 10 percent number.

To really get an accurate picture, you would have to do the tracking *over time* with a *consistent methodology*.

Which means someone has to focus on it. And it takes money to hire that person. And they'd have to have the right skills in survey research. And you'd have to pay attention to it.

And you're so busy. And numbers and surveys are not your thing anyway. And going to all this effort just to see Competitor X slowly kicking your ass is kind of depressing. So, to be honest, you were a little avoidant. And you didn't bother.

Only here you are, a few years later, and your biggest customer just fired you to go to Competitor X, and suddenly you look at your books and you realize with horror that if things keep going like this, you could go bankrupt.

Those dynamics: The inconvenience, the avoidance, the neglect?

That's pretty much where we are with tracking climate change.

IN 2015, A United Nations subgroup dedicated to climate change called the Conference of Parties (COP) gathered in Paris. It was the twenty-first time they had gathered, so they called this meeting COP21. They gathered with the goal of getting everyone in the world to limit "the temperature increase to 1.5 degrees Celsius above pre-industrial levels." They signed a paper to this effect, which became known as the Paris Climate Accords. One hundred ninety-six parties signed. It was legally binding. They agreed to come back together and share information on progress. They agreed on metrics. They documented everything.

The UN group, in other words, had done something incredibly meaningful. They had identified a problem. They got leaders from all over the world to agree on that problem. They understood that data was key. They understood that there were consequences to failure. And they knew the consequences of failure would be irreversible. They got to work. And they started tracking their progress.

Kind of.

Actually . . .

Not really.

The UN Framework Convention on Climate Change (UNFCCC)—the group that gathered everyone together in the first place—is a case study in being a near miss, in tracking.

The main problem is that "to limit the temperature increase to 1.5°C above preindustrial levels" is not a tracking idea. It's a target. It's a goal. Tracking, as we observed above, is about setting a metric and measuring it over time with a consistent methodology.

Tracking is less in the spirit of goal setting and more in the spirit of, well, just tracking for its own sake. Yes, when you track, you should know what's good and what's bad. (Usually up is good—more market share! But not necessarily. Down could be good if you're tracking, say, manufacturing errors.) When you track, you monitor your metric obsessively.

Have you ever seen, at payout time, a sales force that's compensated based on a certain metric? Oh Lordy, you've never seen so many C students become expert mathematicians overnight. "That baseline number was incorrect!" "You're not taking seasonality into account!" "Last year November was a five-week month!" To them, the metric means hard cash. And that's what they're trained to fight for. To them, the metric is life or death.

And in the case of climate change—it is.

Yet the UNFCCC went hard at the target and soft on the tracking.

The first and most obvious problem is that they set a target in terms of temperature change versus preindustrial levels and then, oddly, didn't seem to have an approach to tracking that metric. We *should* hear the UNFCCC once a year at COP22 and COP23 and COP24 saying, "Well, last year global average temperatures versus preindustrial levels was 0.6 degrees Centigrade higher, and this year it's 0.9 degrees higher. That's a huge increase. We need to do something fast, or we're doomed."

For some reason, UNFCCC does not do this. There are challenges, for sure. Creating a consistent methodology is tough. If you're comparing to "preindustrial levels," well, there could be debate and squishiness about what "preindustrial levels" really means. Is it temperatures in the year 1850? Or the year 1900? Or the average between 1850 and 1900? Or maybe it's hard to gather and you agree on the concept of a "global average temperature." Is that land surface temperature? What about the temperature over the oceans? The UN does have a "Global Stocktake"— their way of holding the 196 signers of COP21 accountable. But the documents cover seven *types* of data and eight *sources* of data. That's a lot.

Still, I don't believe complexity is the problem. As discussed in other chapters, reality is infinitely complex. Having seven types of data and eight sources of data, to measure a whole planet, doesn't seem so terrible as a *starting* point.

The problem is letting the data *remain* complex.

Because when the data remains complex, human psychology takes over.

Or rather, it does the opposite: The human brain shies away from complexity. It becomes anxious and itchy and uncomfortable.

And no one pays attention.

LET'S GO BACK to the analysts in the midtown offices of Morgan Stanley at seven on a Tuesday morning waiting for the release of the Consumer Price Index.

First observation: They care. Look at them, sitting there waiting. Maybe they have doughnuts and special coffee for the occasion. They're as focused on their metric as an argumentative sales force on payday.

Second observation: Part of why they are poised and focused is that the inflation number is one number. *One number*. It's a percentage increase in CPI over the same period a year ago. They know what it means. They don't have to wonder. They don't have to interpret—or very little, anyway.

Third observation: It's not just Wall Street analysts who anticipate the inflation metric. Inflation is published on the front page of the newspaper—or at least, the business section—every month. If you're American and you've ever had a salaried job with an annual increase, you pretty much understand "inflation, because you want your annual pay increase to be above zero and at least as much as inflation." You get that 1 percent is low inflation and 3 percent is high-ish inflation and anything above 3 percent could mean tough times. Newspapers and cable networks think inflation is interesting enough to publish about because it affects everybody. Everybody gets it; and everybody gets it because—again—it's just one number.

But that doesn't mean inflation is simple.

"HOW DO WE know what we *want* to price?" Melissa Pollock asks. For the inflation calculation—remember it's really the Consumer Price Index—"we need to price the things that people are buying, not the things that people aren't buying." So Melissa and other members of the Consumer Expenditures and Income team recruit people to fill out surveys. Keep diaries of what they buy. "What we call in economics, the market basket of goods." They do this to avoid what Melissa calls "substitution bias." In other words, they don't want to anchor our national inflation rate to the price of Peloton bikes if the Peloton bike craze has faded.

Then, "once we know what they're buying"—what US consumers are actually buying, based on their diaries—"we can price them over time."

The pricing part is where is gets kind of crazy.

The Bureau of Labor Statistics breaks down America into geographies. There's the four geographic regions (West, Midwest, Northeast, South). Census regions (such as West North Central, East North

Central). Then twenty-three metropolitan areas (from Miami–Fort Lauderdale–West Palm Beach—yes, that's just one metro area—to San Diego–Carlsbad). To represent reality properly, the CPI team must gather up-to-date prices on all the goods Melissa and her colleagues have identified in the consumer diaries—the goods people are buying.

CPI workers go to stores. They go to websites. They gather data on ninety-four thousand products and services per month. Ninety-four thousand! The goods they track are in eight major categories. There are the basics of food, clothing, and shelter—in Bureau of Labor Statistics parlance, food and beverage, apparel, and housing—then the other stuff like transportation, medical care, education, recreation, and, of course, other. Underneath these, there are two hundred subcategories. When you read them, it's like this absurdist, arrhythmic, clinical song of our consumer selves.

- Infants' Play/Dress/Sleep Wear

- Men's underwear, nightwear, or swimwear

- Girls' footwear

- Women's footwear

- Powdered drinks, cocktail mixes, or ice

- Window coverings such as curtains, drapes, or blinds

- Mass transit

- Airline fares

- Butter or margarine

- Candy or chewing gum

- High school books

- College tuition

- Luggage

- Jewelry

- Watches

- Tires

- Pork chops

- Lunch meats

- Uncooked other beef and veal

And on and on, until the inevitable:

- Tax return preparation

and

- Funeral services

It's an extraordinary feat to pull off every thirty days. All those geographies, all those categories, all those products. It's painstaking; it's methodical. "Sometimes the data itself is dramatic," Melissa says. But not the process. "You don't want drama," she says, "for official government statistics."

And its greatest triumph may be in its simplicity. The BLS does all the methodology, all the weighting and the substitutions and the statistical calculations, so that by the time they're ready to publish it's just . . .

One number. On August 15, 2022, it was 8.3 percent.

Markets moved, salaries changed, houses were bought and sold. Everybody cared.

•   •   •

THE TRAGEDY OF climate change tracking is not in its lack of data. Climate change data exists in quantities and complexities that rival the CPI, and then some. The International Monetary Fund tracks emissions in CO_2 parts per million. The Greenhouse Gas Protocol adds three levels to this: Scope 1, Scope 2, and Scope 3. The UN Food and Agriculture Organization tracks land cover change in hectares. The Laboratory for Satellite Altimetry tracks change in sea levels in millimeters and sea ice thickness in centimeters. There are metrics for ocean heat, ocean pH, sea surface temperatures, atmospheric temperatures, and, of course, natural disasters. The disasters have their own taxonomy: Drought, extreme temperature, flood, landslide, storm, and wildfire.

We have Melissa Pollock and the thousands of employees of the Bureau of Labor Statistics to help us simplify pricing into twenty-three metropolitan regions and two hundred goods and services subtypes. What hero has stepped forward to simplify climate metrics? To make climate change tracking simple, ongoing, and consistent?

Perhaps whoever that hero is could take a cue from the BLS and create a taxonomy of climate metrics that they could roll up into simple groupings. Not food, clothing, and shelter but land, sea, and air.

How about:

Land (land cover, drought, wildfires/floods)

Sea (sea ice, ocean pH, ocean temperature)

Air (CO_2 emissions, surface temperature)

And then, of course, that hero would need to roll it all up into—say it with me—one number.

So far, no one I know of has embarked on this quest. The scope remains overwhelming. Or I should say, it *appears* overwhelming. But it is doable. I promise. We, collectively, have the data and the expertise in abundance.

Perhaps you or I will set this chapter down and, like the hero in a fairy tale, set out to seek our metrical fortune. Maybe, like Melissa Pollock, we believe *there is something more out there for us. That we're gonna do something.* And maybe, sure, maybe there is no fairy-tale ending. Maybe once we have imposed order on the overwhelming complexity of a planet's worth of data, the facts we reveal *won't* uplift us or inspire us. Maybe the data will make us cry.

But then, at least, we'll know.

KEY POINTS IN CHAPTER 13

- Tracking requires a consistent effort and methodology to monitor a number over time.

- The number is important (or you wouldn't be tracking it) mainly because it allows you to act. You adjust your actions based on whether the number is too high or too low.

- Complexity is the enemy when it comes to tracking. Any metric that's too complex boggles the brain, and you lose people's attention and focus.

- Tracking is incredibly powerful, with a positive example in inflation / Consumer Prices Indices, which is one number and changes the wealth of everyone in the world, versus climate change, which is not tracked as one number and feels like it's out of control.

THOUGHT STARTERS FOR YOU

- What are two or three metrics in your domain that, if tracked, might give you more control? Number of customers? Average revenue per customer?

- What if the data for these metrics is not readily at hand? And what if gathering the required data is complex? How can you mimic the Bureau of Labor Statistics (in your own smaller way, hopefully) and craft a structure for pulling together what you need?

WHERE DO WE GO NEXT?

Tracking is picking a number and watching it go up or down, in a trend, over time. The reverse of that is watching a number and waiting for it to plunge or soar in a terrifying way, watching for an abnormality that serves as a warning.

CHAPTER 14

Anomalies

Hunter of Earthquakes

I t is 5:04 on a balmy October evening in San Francisco. In thirty-one minutes, the Oakland A's are about to play game 3 of the World Series against the San Francisco Giants. As the players prepare to take the field, they feel a ripple under their feet. Sportscasters freak out. Then the TV broadcast cuts. During that news blackout, sixty thousand fans in Candlestick Park feel the steel and concrete stadium sway. An earthquake shakes the city. Buildings collapse. A fifty-foot chunk of the Bay Bridge upper level falls onto the lower level. The one-mile-long Cypress Street Viaduct section of Interstate 880 completely collapses. Fifty-seven children, teens, and adults are killed. One is Scotty Dickinson, an infant. His mother, Carol, was carrying Scotty to the changing table in their first-floor apartment on Cervantes Boulevard when the quake hit. The building collapsed on them. They were buried in rubble. Firefighters rescued Carol. But her baby's lungs couldn't filter out the concrete dust. Scotty died in her arms.

At that same moment, on that October afternoon, Tom Bleier, an electrical engineer, had just stood up and welcomed a group of scientists to the Stanford Research Institute.

At the first vibration, Tom joked about it. "We arranged to have an earthquake on your visit to San Francisco, so you'd have a little bit of fun."

Heh heh.

Seconds later, no one was laughing. Afraid that the glass conference room windows would shatter and slice them to bloody ribbons, Tom dove under the boardroom table. As the earthquake shook the building, an urn of scalding hot coffee vibrated its way across the table to where Tom sheltered. The quake stopped just before the urn reached Tom. It never spilled.

Tom Bleier emerged from under that conference table a different man. He was an electrical engineer by training—trusted by the US government, think tanks, and major corporations with classified research related to satellites.

He also had a passion for earthquakes, which, on that October day, he would make his obsession.

It all had to do with his first house.

TOM IS IN his seventies now. I'm talking to him via Zoom. In the background I can peer into his multilevel house with its wood beams and art and an air of rambling comfort.

I have this flash of thinking: *Tom Bleier would make a cool father-in-law.* Easygoing, smart, still fit. He has that crackly, old-world kind of voice—at least one part Jimmy Stewart—that, combined with his youthful enthusiasm for earthquake hunting (he calls the company he founded Quakefinder), makes you see him as a grown-up version of a kid from some '40s and '50s boys' adventure tale. Crew cuts and Swiss Army knives and muddy science projects piled in the back of a red Radio Flyer.

"I moved to California with Kodak, in 1969," he tells me, "from Rochester, New York. Kodak was having trouble staffing their engineering group out here. So they were offering young guys out of engineering school to come out, and they would pay your housing. I came out. And I met my wife in a singles-only apartment complex. Two thousand people, all singles." I note that this sounds very 1969. Tom adds, a little wistfully: "Those didn't exist back in Rochester."

So Tom and his bride bought a property. And Tom, being an engineer, and being a grown-up now, with grown-up-sized Swiss-Army-knife projects, decided to build the house himself. It's not clear to me at what point in Tom's journey to buy the property and build the house he found out the following information. But it must be true because the house I see in the Zoom background is the very home itself.

"It's a thousand feet from the San Andreas fault line," he tells me. "The actual line you see on a map." The San Andreas fault was the source of the great 1906 earthquake in San Francisco.

Out of necessity, then—or as a defensive strategy—Tom Bleier began educating himself about earthquakes.

What he found was that—not surprisingly—earthquakes are a major problem. Not just in San Francisco but globally. Just since the millennium, more than five hundred major earthquakes have killed more than four hundred thousand people. Maybe more surprisingly, he found that people considered detecting them—ahead of time—basically impossible.

"The USGS [United States Geological Survey] does a wonderful job keeping track of earthquakes and making statistical projections," he says. For instance, the USGS might predict that in a thirty-year period, "There is a 70 percent chance of an earthquake occurring in the Bay Area." That might be a hell of a precise prediction in the context of the yawning eons of geological time. But to—say—sixty thousand fans sitting in Candlestick Park, or motorists crossing the Bay Bridge, to Carol and Scotty Dickinson, that level of precision is not useful.

Then there's the computer-linked seismometer networks set up by UC Berkeley and the USGS. "When two or three seismometers pick up the quake, it will message the network. As you go away from the quake, it will tell you how many seconds it will be before it hits. Unfortunately, if you happen to be in the epicenter, you get zero warning. And that's typically where the most damage and greatest loss of life occur."

In other words, we, as dwellers on the earth's surface, have gotten good at predicting earthquakes decades into the future, and seconds into the future, but we are helpless at predicting them in that sweet spot of hours or days ahead, where you have time to evacuate buildings.

Tom, the electrical engineer, in his research, was struck by stories of "earthquake lights." This sounds like science fiction, but it is documented reality: Earthquakes send up these lightning-like flashes before or during the quake. (When you see them on YouTube, they look like lightning during a summer storm.) The flashes come from great pulses of electromagnetic energy shot out by the tectonic plates rubbing together during a quake.

Based on this simple and irrefutable fact—that the earth itself shoots up its own massive flares *that announce the presence of an earthquake*—Tom made a few assumptions.

First, there is a normal level of electromagnetic energy when the fault lines are not crunching against each other.

Second, there is an abnormal amount of electromagnetic energy stirred up when there are quake conditions.

Third, it's likely that this energy builds in the lead-up to an earthquake.

And fourth, that you can measure this energy buildup, and hence, the earthquake can be detected. Not a decade in advance. A few days in advance. That missing sweet spot of warning between thirty years and three seconds.

Tom Bleier was sure that, using his training, and his unique fate as the guy who built his house on top of an earthquake zone, he could be the scientist to spot that anomaly—that deviation from the norm—in the earth's electromagnetic energy and save thousands of lives.

I AM IN Las Vegas. I hate Las Vegas.

I hate the strip clubs and the creepy magician shows. I hate the rooms that don't have minibars so you're forced out into the casino. I hate the shady shops along the Strip blowing ventilated air that somehow smells like lube. I hate the cab lines, the expensive food, the tinted hotel windows, the nine-dollar surcharge for withdrawing cash. Visiting the city for business feels like someone laying you down on a conveyor belt so a thousand merchants can paw you and take your wallet, watch, jewelry . . . and cop a feel while they're at it.

So, of course—of *course*—it's in Las Vegas that someone steals my credit card number.

I'm here for the Consumer Electronics Show. I'm up in the Samsung suite, a twenty-first-floor oasis looking down on the chaos. The phone call comes in the middle of our welcome party. My card is showing unusual activity. The bank fraud representative recites charges that are real. (Yes, I managed to find someone selling apples and yogurt in Vegas.) And some that were not me. I wasn't buying gas in Pennsylvania while I'm here in Vegas, no.

In all, $356 of not-me. They freeze the card. How was the card stolen when it's still here in my wallet? The nice kid in the fraud department couldn't say. I hang up feeling paranoid. And oddly in sync with my surroundings. Getting ripped off in Vegas . . . maybe I should buy tickets to a creepy magician.

How did my bank know that the e-commerce charges had been fraudulent?

Anomalies.

I didn't quite understand how much work went into this until I called my friend Brendan Goode, formerly of Homeland Security, now the chief security officer at Commonwealth Bank in Sydney, Australia.

"The old rules-based approach would say: If Justin is buying something in Brooklyn at 3:00 p.m., there's no way he's buying something in Thailand at 4:00 p.m.," he tells me. Now there are more sophisticated ways to detect fraud, through statistical models. "The model is based on features about you. Spending patterns. What time of day you spend. How much you spend." The models identify those patterns. Then the model, in essence, draws a boundary around what it considers normal behavior. "When a purchase pops out of the boundary, we'll send you an alert."

A group of researchers at eBay put it slightly differently in a 2019 paper on credit card fraud detection. "We hypothesize that good behavior does not change with time," they wrote. "Data points representing good behavior have a consistent signature." As a result they created a "consistency score" and developed a technique to score every purchase based on its consistency with past behavior.

I like this idea of a Consistent Self. Like there's this solid citizen version of me living in my bank statements: Dr. Jekyll. He is a good person. Or, at least, uses his credit card like a good person. He buys apples and yogurt. The laws of statistics imply that his goodness is persistent.

So when Mr. Hyde steals his credit card, Dr. Jekyll's consistency scores flip negative. And people like Brendan Goode, and the analytics folks at eBay, can watch the purchase pattern change. "Those purchases sitting outside the boundary of your established pattern are going to be anomalies," Brendan tells me.

WITH BANKS AND credit cards, finding the anomalies is relatively simple. They already have the data. The problem with earthquakes was: How do you gather the data?

Tom Bleier was burned out working on secret satellite projects, and to keep himself happy, kept up his tinkering with earthquake detection. He went to work for a small aerospace engineering company called

Stellar Solutions, which had the vision to "satisfy customers' critical needs while realizing employees' dream jobs."

"So I said, 'I have a dream'!" He laughs.

That was when Tom Bleier—the man who built his own house—picked up his Swiss Army knife again. Only this time, with Stellar Solutions funding.

They created earthquake detectors that look like a cross between Wall-E and a space-age lawn chair. Also, three-foot magnetometers buried in the ground. And white plastic ion sensors to detect shifts in the electromagnetic energy in the air. Geophones to detect ground movement, to filter out noise from their measurements. And a shiny silver solar panel to power mobile modems sending thirty-two samples per second.

That was when they created their own version of the consistency score, the baseline against which they can measure anomalies. "We would see an average of about ten pulses per day," Tom said. "We noticed there'd be little periods of activity, maybe a couple hours, even a day long, but they would go away. The fault was moving. It was cracking. It was creating these little bursts of current." But it wasn't sustained.

Until the Alum Rock earthquake, magnitude 5.4, the biggest in California since the Loma Prieta quake rocked the World Series. "We saw clustering," he said. The readings spiked. They came regularly. The pulse count boosted for two weeks. The quake hit, fifteen miles east of Milpitas in the Calaveras fault area. And then . . . they went away.

Jekyll. Hyde. Jekyll again.

Tom Bleier had found his anomaly.

Stellar Solutions built sensors and deployed them to 125 sites, across the San Andreas fault, the Santa Cruz Mountains (the origin of Loma Prieta), the Heyward fault, the Calaveras fault, San Jacinto, the Sierras. They persuaded seven high schools, which happen to be built along the Heyward fault, to join the earthquake hunting, deploying and maintaining ion sensors. To independently verify the research, they partnered with Google. They published their findings.

"We observed a modest association between the magnetometer measurements and earthquake occurrence 2–3 days later. The signal is not strong enough to provide useful predictions, but it does suggest a relationship that could be explored." Further study, in other words, is required.

THE WEEK I am writing this chapter, two things happen. In Wajima, Japan, a 7.6 magnitude quake hits, toppling buildings right over on their sides. Forty-eight people die, including nineteen at the epicenter. Tsunami warnings are issued. People post videos of department stores shaking, merchandise spilling off shelves, terrified Japanese shoppers running for safety. Clearly, neither Tom Bleier's, nor any other technique, has completely solved the mystery. In that same week, in the *MIT Technology Review*, a seismologist PhD named Allie Hutchison published a summary of all the new science, and data science, being deployed to predict earthquakes. Neural networks, machine learning, GPS, paleoseismology, even the observations of earthquake-sensitive catfish. "It may be decades before we can look back on this period in earthquake research with certainty and understand its role in advancing the field," she writes. "But some are hopeful."

KEY POINTS IN CHAPTER 14

- Watching for anomalies is probably boring most of the time, because you're fixated on a baseline you've established, and you're watching it like a hawk, hoping it won't move.

- In earthquake hunting, this is watching a normal or consistent level of electromagnetic energy. In credit card fraud, it's monitoring purchase patterns for consistency.

- Only painstaking data gathering can identify these normal levels. What is a ho-hum day like? Thousands of ho-hum days?

- But when the deviations happen, the stakes can be incredibly high: Lost funds, earthquakes.

THOUGHT STARTERS FOR YOU

- Where do anomalies play a part in your world? In my team at Samsung, it's a narrow but important use case: When does the data load wrong? When it does, and it's undetected, everything downstream from that is screwy and has to be reworked.

- If anomaly monitoring is boring, how can you automate it?

WHERE DO WE GO NEXT?

Now we pivot a little bit and move away from counting, counting over time, and tracking deviations. Now we're going to focus on something permanent: Identity. Think of identity as a locus, a point on a graph. Identity is the name we give to the thing we're counting or describing. Not just the trio concept Brown, Jones, and Robinson. But actually Brown, Jones, and Robinson. And why do we care about permanent names for them? So that in the sea of data, we can find them again, whenever we want.

CHAPTER 15

Identity

"The Greatest Business Day of My Life"

You know on your mattress where there's this tag that reads, DO NOT REMOVE THIS TAG UNDER PENALTY OF LAW? And there's this childish part of you that's terrified of what would happen if you accidentally did remove the tag—and then lose it? That's pretty much what happened to Rhona Hoffman, who runs a well-known art gallery in Chicago. Rhona Hoffman really did lose the tag. Not to a mattress. To a million-dollar work of art.

Sol LeWitt was a modern artist famous for wall drawings and wall paintings that are "site specific" (to use art world lingo). This means his art is often created just for that one exhibition space. If you drive a few hours north of New York City, there are Sol LeWitt drawings in a museum called Dia Beacon in the Hudson Valley. They're wonderful. They're pencil drawings, mainly of lines and patterns at a large scale, as wide as your spread arms. The little graphite lines come at you as plentiful and rich and varied as a snowstorm, and as you stare at them you kind of can't believe that it's as simple as that, to have just a bunch of lines on a wall that make you feel like you can close your eyes and feel snowflakes on your eyelashes. It's also the kind of modern art that, when you bring along your six-foot-three cousin whose idea of fun is blasting shotguns at a range, he will be boorish, and snort, "I could make that."

And, oddly, you're both right. Because Sol LeWitt came up in the art world not as a fine artist but as an employee in an architecture firm. His perspective was: An architect isn't laying the bricks, but that doesn't mean the building is not the architect's creation. Sol LeWitt wouldn't necessarily *make* his art. He would create *instructions* for his works like an architect creates instructions for a building. Then he would let other people, you know, lay the bricks. Or, in his case, do the actual drawing.

"On a wall surface, any continuous stretch of wall, using a hard pencil, place fifty points at random.

"The points should be evenly distributed over the area of the wall.

"All of the points should be connected by straight lines."

Those are LeWitt's instructions for Wall Drawing 118. But LeWitt didn't do the drawing for Wall Drawing 118. Other people did. Just whoever. People hired for an hourly wage. Or students.

So, as an art collector, when you buy a Sol LeWitt—say, Wall Drawing 448—sometimes you'll get a work of art. But sometimes you won't. Sometimes you'll just get a sketch of what the drawing is supposed to look like when it's done, along with a little certificate of authenticity. And then you're free to make the art yourself. I mean it is a little odd, when you think about it. To "put up" a Sol LeWitt wall drawing you would need to create a little art exhibit space in your home or office, hire a crew of pencil drawers, and supervise the project, which is a lot of trouble. So, instead, while you wait for all that to come together, you might ask a gallery owner like Rhona Hoffman, for a fee, to store the sketch of Wall Drawing 448 and the instructions and, of course, the certificate of authenticity for you.

But what happens if Hoffman loses the certificate? Then what you have, as we say down South, is *a whole lotta nothin'*. And if the drawing is worth $1.4 million, then you might sue Hoffman. Which is exactly what happened to a collector named Roderic Steinkamp. And you feel his agony. I mean, he had the sketch and the instructions. He could make as many as he wanted. He could make a hundred Wall Drawing 448s. But they wouldn't be anchored, pinned down, to a proper identity.

And, as such, they wouldn't be real.

WE'LL COME BACK to Roderic Steinkamp and his unmoored wall drawing. But first let's talk about the alligators.

AT THE BEGINNING of this book I told the story of how private equity firms took over the data and research company I worked for, the famous Nielsen Company, home of the Nielsen TV ratings. And how all the executives were terrified they would lose their jobs.

All that happened.

The private equity firms bought Nielsen. They installed a new CEO. The man they picked had run the aircraft division of Jack Welch's General Electric, a man named David Calhoun, who later went on to become the disgraced chairman and CEO of Boeing while Boeing was smashing 737s full of people into the dirt in the name of cost savings. At Nielsen, Calhoun came in, fired a bunch of senior leaders to send a message that there was a new sheriff in town, and when the dust settled, he invited the remaining leadership group to Florida—where the famous TV ratings operation was based—for a rah-rah corporate get-together. It was meant to be kind of a kickoff of the rest of our lives as members of the new, improved crew.

Only, as you might have guessed, everyone showed up kind of rattled. I mean, sure, some of the old guard who had been fired were swaggering, complacent bullies. (See the earlier chapter.) But they were kind of bush-league bullies, guys who were dumber than they should have been and more arrogant than they deserved to be. When David

Calhoun brought in a cohort of his own guys—former GE types and others of that stripe—it was sort of like when Voldemort's Death Eaters took over Hogwarts. They weren't even data people. They didn't love what we did. We could have been a carpet company. Their mission was to rip out costs, mostly by firing people, to make us more profitable so they could resell Nielsen for a monstrous profit. For everyone at that Florida meeting, it was like, *Oh wow, this is serious. This is real.*

The first day of the conference, I went for a run on the hotel grounds to clear my head. You had to get up early because the heat and humidity would kick in by nine. And there were these concrete gullies full of still water alongside the running paths. I gave them a wide berth because it seemed perfectly possible that an alligator would leap out of the slime and bite my leg off at the femur.

That was the vibe of the conference.

As if to confirm it, Calhoun—a handsome, slim, midheight, midlife CEO who by looks might have been Bob Iger's little brother, who did possess a certain straight-talking charisma, and who was known among his new sycophants to be a "scratch golfer," whatever that is—got up in front of this crowd of his new team and, instead of giving a barnstorming speech titled "Data Is the Future, and You Are Part of That Future," gave this weirdly shrill, hectoring sort of speech about how if people cheated on their expenses he would fire them. And it was like, *Do we clap?*

And then Scott Taylor took the stage.

Scott who?

Every company is like a high school. There are cliques. At Nielsen there were the swaggering data guys who focused on the grocery business—the jocks. And there were the elite and aloof profit-driving TV ratings clique—the beautiful people. There were even a few data entrepreneurs worth millions because Nielsen had bought their companies from them—the tech club.

But nobody had heard of Scott Taylor. He ran this obscure business unit called TDLinx that, also, no one had heard of. Scott has a

pile of dark curly hair, wire-rim glasses, and the braying baritone of an
aggro comedian. Scott Taylor was class clown. Or would have been if
this had truly been high school. But it wasn't. This was a ballroom in a
Florida luxury hotel, with the windows steaming from the growing heat
outside, while inside, 150 executives gazed up at the stage, aching for
someone to tell them that there was meaning to their professional lives
beyond clinging to a paycheck and flinching before the corporate ax.

And this is exactly what Scott Taylor did.

SCOTT TAYLOR'S STORY was a perfect data story. Part of what made it
perfect is that, like Scott himself, there was nothing pretentious about
it. Like Henry Varnum Poor, Scott got his start in a business-to-business
trade magazine. In this case, one that was even less sexy than *American
Railroad Journal*. Perhaps the least sexy magazine title on the planet:

Progressive Grocer.

Progressive Grocer started in 1922. Its first issue makes references to
the retail market following "the war"—you know, WWI. *Progressive
Grocer*'s website today has explainers about Amazon, retail technology,
and product showcases for Jim Beam Kentucky Coolers, Manischewitz
Frozen Knishes, and Funfetti Ice Cream Cake. (Which actually sounds
like a decent party.) Nothing really screams data—yet.

But Scott pointed out that, in 1969, "There were two magazines
on earth that had computerized subscriber lists: *Time* magazine and
Progressive Grocer. This was a huge deal at this time." And by the time
he arrived, in the '90s, "Somebody realized we are sending a magazine
to every store manager in the country.

"And the database was born."

The data had value. The little code on the magazine circulation
label, part of that text-y jumble, was, in fact, a unique identifier for
every grocery store in the United States.

"We defined what supermarkets were. In other words, if the store
wasn't in the *Progressive Grocer* list, it wasn't a store."

The problem was, *Progressive Grocer* didn't know what it had.

"I go in and the first day the sales manager comes in and said, 'We're going to take you through the pitch.' He flipped through this book. It was inches thick and impossible to understand. I remember thinking, *I'm getting paid to sit through this. I can't imagine anybody else is gonna sit through this. What the hell does this mean?* They have all these internal IT names. Nothing was marketable."

So Scott changed the labels on the data to make it intuitive. Data about a market would be called a market file. Data about stores would be called a store file. And so on.

But still, Scott was the low man on the totem pole, and management wouldn't let him go near the fancy accounts—the Procter & Gambles, the General Mills, the Campbell's Soups. So Scott is given the assignment to sell the data to in-store media and promotion companies, which nowadays is a huge business. But back then, it was the companies who set up card tables to offer samples and hand out coupons. Not fancy. But Scott makes decent headway.

And then one day Scott gets a call from "some, like, admin at Nabisco." And the admin tells Scott:

> Well, we've been trying to coordinate all our in-store promotions— all the vendors we use for setting up card tables to pass out samples and coupons.
>
> We want to know where they're doing work for us. But each retail company has a different way of identifying stores.
>
> There's Albertsons and Publix and Piggly Wiggly and Kroger and Walmart and Safeway and Food Lion and Whole Foods and Hy-Vee and Stew Leonard's and Aldi.
>
> And the only solution we can find, to keeping all these stores straight, is the *Progressive Grocer* ID. [The little code at the corner of the subscription label!] So . . . could you sell us a license to the ID?

And Scott is thinking: Nabisco! The National Biscuit Company! A pedigree going back to the 1800s! National brands! Oreos and Chips Ahoy and Nutter Butters and Fig Newtons and Saltines and Wheat Thins and, my god—Lorna Doone shortbread! Nabisco is legit. So, even if no one was seeing the data the way Scott was, if Nabisco wanted it, it must be real.

But more importantly, because Scott Taylor is a data person, he is focused on what the admin from Nabisco is telling him. About how they are using the data.

They are telling him that their life is chaos.

That, to them, the United States grocery market is a mess. It's just this tangle of stores that you can categorize in all these different ways. By street address or by format (grocery, big box, wholesale, discount, drug and pharma, convenience, gas station) or by latitude-longitude or by size, region, or ownership chain.

And all the Nabisco salespeople who are out there trying to sell to all those buyers, in all those stores, and all those operations teams trying to ship cookies and ensure those cookies are received and logged and accounted for—it's all happening based on what? Best case, a spreadsheet. Worst case, some, like, leaf of typing paper, Scotch-taped to the ops manager's wall, with little scribbled store names written in ballpoint pen, scratched out, and corrected in pencil.

No one, in other words, really knows what stores they're selling to. Or how many stores there are in that chain. Are they selling to *all* the stores? Or are they missing some—and thereby missing sales? Are they shipping the pallet of Nutter Butters to the right Piggly Wiggly in Kinston, North Carolina—the one on Route 11—or the wrong one, down the way on New Bern Road? Problems like this, multiplied by the eight hundred thousand stores in the US? Chaos!

But if Nabisco (which is now part of the food giant Mondelez) *did* employ *Progressive Grocer*'s little IDs from the magazine label, then every single store in the United States, every grocery and convenience and drugstore anyway, would have a unique code. And each code, in the database, would be linked to the store chain it belonged to. So no delivery truck would ever get lost. And no Nabisco salesperson would ever fly blind.

The data was, in a strange way, existential. The unique ID anchored the store to the map of the grocery world.

Does this thing—this store—exist or not?

And Scott Taylor, in that moment, realizes he is the one person in the world who gets it, who can help Nabisco untangle their entire sales and distribution operation. And maybe it could be more than Nabisco. Maybe *all* the manufacturers—of food, beverage, tobacco, alcohol, health and beauty. Maybe the entire grocery industry—which at that time was an industry generating more than $350 billion (today it's approaching a trillion)—needed to be untangled. And Scott could do it. He could do it with nothing more that the little ID number on the subscription label from everybody's copy of *Progressive Grocer* they got in the mail so they can see the product feature spread about Manischewitz Frozen Knishes and Funfetti Ice Cream Cake. As long as everyone used the same code—the sellers (Nabisco) and the buyers (the grocery stores)—then everyone could buy and sell in an operationally efficient market. As long as everyone bought the data from Scott.

And this, of course, is exactly what Scott persuaded them to do.

Progressive Grocer spun out its data business into a team they called Trade Dimensions, and Scott pulled the little ID from the corner of the subscription label and made it its own business called TD (after Trade Dimensions). TD Linx.

Onstage in Florida, telling this story, or a version of it, Scott has the audience in the palm of his hand. Every joke is landing.

"I'm going long, Dave," Scott mugs after a big laugh, to Calhoun, the fearsome GE head whacker. "I'm telling you now."

Every jittery division president and junior vice president is sitting up in their chair, eyes shining. Because Scott Taylor is reminding them what a data person does. They don't fire people and mop up the profit to get rich. A data person solves problems. A data person roots around in the boring and unreadable inch-thick IT-jargon binders until they find that kernel of truth that solves somebody's problem, then they simplify it so the client can understand, and then—yes, because Scott is the consummate salesman, he reminds us—they sell it.

"Because you know what happens when nobody sells?" Scott prompts from the stage. He waits one masterful beat, then tells us:

"Nothin'."

The joke lands. The applause is uproarious.

Decades later, Scott and I have a little reunion. Does he remember the effect he had on people that day in Florida? When we all needed a lift so badly? He does.

"It was one of, if not *the,* greatest business day of my life," he says.

THE BUSINESS WORLD is full of these tangles.

There are items we can describe in a thousand different ways.

There are albums. By artists. With songs on them. There's the studio version or the live version or the remastered version or Taylor's version. There's the version on the original album. Then there's the same song but on the greatest hits album or on that movie soundtrack or on the '90s dance hits collection. That's why there is—there must be—such a thing as the International Standard Recording Code.

There are books. You can think of a book by its author, title, publisher, or release date. Or its editions: Hardcover, paperback, ebook, large print, audio, and braille. In books, your life is chaos without the International Standard Book Number (ISBN).

Or there's the International Statistical Classification of Diseases and Related Health Problems (ICD) I mentioned at the beginning of this book to identify my potential colon condition.

In all these cases, there is a complex set of stakeholders that need to agree on the identity of something.

Is it reassuring to think that somewhere out there, there are teams of data people trying to keep us from the chaos by applying systems of unique identifiers? Maybe, maybe not.

Identifiers, as Scott Taylor realized, anchor in reality things that are vague, or at least mutable—that is, things that may be seen from different angles. This is powerful. It helps us know where things are, no matter where they go. It makes markets possible: Grocery store distribution, books, and music.

Yet, like anything powerful, there is a dark side too. Just ask Winston Smith, the antihero of George Orwell's *1984*, who is known to Big Brother and the all-knowing state as *6079 Smith W.* Winston Smith is anchored in that identity. He cannot escape, or redefine himself, even inside his own mind, which, in the end, is possessed by Big Brother. This becomes the stuff of paranoia and conspiracy theories. Citizen ID cards. Government-issued vaccines that inject you with microscopic bar codes.

Does this thing exist, or not?

It is not for the labeled to say, but the labeler.

YET FOR RODERIC STEINKAMP, our hapless collector of Sol LeWitt drawings, we may safely say he wished his labeling system had worked better. Later, using nonfungible token technologies, the art world would cotton to labeling even easily recognizable works of genius— that no one could ever mistake, like a Georgia O'Keeffe—with unique identifiers. Had this technology arrived earlier, it would have saved Roderic Steinkamp $1.4 million and the unlucky gallerist Rhona Hoffman a lot of legal trouble and heartache. Instead, for Roderic, Rhona, and the world, Wall Drawing 448 was lost forever.

You have to wonder where it went. Or even how to think about it.

What happens to the drawings without authentication? To the books whose ISBNs are lost? The songs without codes? Do they cease to exist, once split from their identities? Or maybe they are more like Peter Pan separated from his shadow: Wandering, incomplete, yearning to be, in this one way at least, findable.

KEY POINTS IN CHAPTER 15

- Reality: Things are. Events happen. But they do so in unlabeled anonymity. This is good if you want to remain anonymous. It's bad if you need to keep track of a complex system or highly valued items.

- The company TD Linx gave every grocery store in the United States a unique identifier and, importantly, placed it in a hierarchy. This allowed buyers and sellers to track their operations and sales. Had they sold to all the stores in the chain? Had they delivered to store X or store Y?

- Each store, once assigned an ID, was then able to be described: Was it an Albertsons? A Piggly Wiggly? Was it a big-box or a convenience store?

- This became an opportunity for TD Linx to enhance their data asset. This is crucial. Once the store was anchored in a single identity, more information could be appended to it . . . really in an unlimited way.

THOUGHT STARTERS FOR YOU

- This is one area where a counter-example helps sharpen perspective. As does the idea of time. What aspect of your world gets chaotic over time if there's no permanent labeling?

- Maybe you're tracking biodiversity, but the taxonomy of plants is out of date, so you can't tell which species are coming or going. Maybe you're an art dealer or a museum and you don't know where your Picasso fits into all the other Picassos because no one's ever created an ID system. Maybe you have one of Picasso's only twenty woodcuts, which sounds valuable. But you wouldn't know, would you? No one went to the trouble of labeling them all and arranging them in a hierarchy.

WHERE DO WE GO NEXT?

The cancer professionals we meet in the next section would never have gotten anywhere if they did not have a powerful labeling system. In fact, an ID system is an essential precursor to our next data use case: Matching. Because you can't match if the data you are matching don't have consistent labeling. Fortunately for these professionals, and many cancer patients, the labeling system boils down to arrangement of four very consistent "characters": Adenine, guanine, cytosine, and thymine.

CHAPTER 16

Matching

The Coupon and the Cancer Genome

At last, Deborah Morosini was a doctor.

She had completed seven years of medical school. Five years of residency. During the last year of her residency, she had been chief resident of pathology. A thousand doctors and two thousand nurses at the Boston University School of Medicine relied on Deborah's team of pathologists to detect disease in thousands of tissue samples in the lab. Not to mention the autopsies. A high pressure role, at an elite medical institution.

There was one difference. Usually the chief resident was in their early thirties. Deborah was forty-four. After a divorce and two children, she had decided to become a doctor, following in the footsteps of her cardiologist father. She had studied English as an undergraduate. Learning advanced biology and organic chemistry had been like climbing Everest. But she did it. Sometimes her shift would end in the raw winter hour when dawn broke. She would drive home numb from squinting at slides under a microscope and supporting her team of anxious residents to pack lunch for her two boys, twelve and ten, who needed and missed her, who were cranky because she was not the apron-wearing stay-at-home mom they might have wanted. Yet Deborah was showing them something else: Determination.

It was Christmastime in Boston—the sun going down at 4:00 p.m., temperatures hitting the twenties—when Deborah got the call. Her mother, Helen Morosini, back home in Connecticut, had been diagnosed with ovarian cancer.

In February, Deborah's mother underwent surgery. Deborah's mother died during her postoperative recovery. It had been only two months since her diagnosis.

Then in July, while the family were still grieving their matriarch, came more bad news. Deborah's youngest sister, Dana, was diagnosed with lung cancer. Dana hadn't even smoked. But Dana had been a singer. She performed at clubs where the audience smoked. Deborah and Dana sang together. They sang at holidays; they sang at weddings. They harmonized; they improvised. They had been impossibly close—finishing each other's sentences, knowing what the other was thinking.

Six months later, the following January, Dana completed chemotherapy and radiation. Her tumor had shrunk. She was thinner, yes; she wore a wig; but she seemed ready to bounce back. She was full of optimism. An actress and singer, she was singing again—magnificently!—and publicly performed the Carole King song "Now and Forever." A comeback.

It didn't last. Less than three months later, on March 6, Dana also died. She left a son and two stepchildren behind. Dana was forty-four.

Deborah was devastated. To cope, she flung herself into the cause of curing lung cancer.

"What struck me was how invisible lung cancer was then," she said. "I was a single mom. In med school. So I may have missed a little bit [about what was going on]. Occasionally." Deborah has a way of breaking into a bright smile to show she's joking. "However, I'm a good physician. I'm a pathologist. I didn't know there was one cancer that killed more than breast, colon, prostate, pancreas, all together.

"It was wrapped up in the stigma of smoking," she went on. "Everyone focused on getting people to stop smoking. The focus was not on the cancer. How do I not know—and I'm a doctor!—that the survival rate for lung cancer had not changed in thirty years?"

It was then that Deborah Morosini, MD and pathologist, became a cancer warrior. Giving speeches. Testifying before Congress. Volunteering for the National Cancer Institute.

Yet it would be another fourteen years before she had her own breakthrough and helped to drive a revolution in cancer treatment, through data.

IN 2023, DIRECT mail marketers clogged up American mailboxes 59.4 billion times, with each household receiving 447 pieces of junk mail. Letters and postcards and flyers and catalogs. Previous generations thrilled at going to the mailbox. Maybe your best friend wrote you a letter. Maybe you'd been admitted to college. Maybe somebody sent you a check. Now the mailbox serves one purpose. It's a receptacle for direct mail. The new social compact is not that your girlfriend writes you a letter on perfumed paper. It's that Best Buy sends you a colorful blue flyer you hold in your hand only long enough to dump in the recycle bin. Goodness knows what the environmental impact is.

If it's so obnoxious, why do marketers still use it? Because—according to the people who sell such services—it works. Five percent of those mailed letters and catalogs prompt a response. That's a high multiple over, say, the click rate of digital banner ads. Maybe for this reason—ironically—big tech companies love old-school direct mail. Google, Uber, Amazon, and LinkedIn all use it lavishly. Direct mail is a $39 billion industry used by car dealerships, insurance companies, credit card companies, retail stores, and political campaigns.

But behind every single mailing is a simple idea.

The list.

The list is what every direct mail marketer starts with. Each list is compiled by a company called—intuitively—a list compiler. Lists contain the names and addresses of the people getting the mailer. The biggest compiled lists, such as those provided by the marketing data company Experian, contain every single postal address in the United States. Every state. Every county. Every neighborhood. Every street. Every block on every street. Every house, apartment, and business on that block. This information is gathered from the public record such as Department of Motor Vehicles information; birth, marriage, and death certificates; court records; and real estate transactions.

These lists make up a kind of map of American humanity. If you can overcome your distaste at how mercenary it all is, and how much annoyance all the mailings cause, the industry can also seem like a minor miracle of knowledge. One of those baby steps toward omniscience that data affords. Really? Every *single* house?

Yet for Google and Best Buy, and for the Random Hardware store in your neighborhood, the name and address is not the meaty part.

The name and address is simply a vehicle to get to the household's *attributes*.

If you're a marketer, you're looking for the people most likely to buy your product or service.

For instance, if you're the owner of a local hardware store—let's keep calling it Random Hardware—one group of people you really want to reach is people who have recently moved.

The industry calls these people new movers, and they are a popular list because people who have recently moved spend a fortune. They need internet and cable, paint and paintbrushes, sheets and towels.

If you're Random Hardware, these people are gold. If you're Random Hardware, you dream about that young couple standing in an echoing, dusty house full of cardboard boxes. You fantasize about that moment when they are putting away their dishes and glasses and silverware for the first time in their new kitchen, when they suddenly realize they need lining paper for their cabinet shelves.

It's a vulnerable moment. Everybody feels like a stranger in a strange land when they move. Random Hardware wants to be the one to make this young couple—let's give them a name: Dick and Barbara Shlep—feel welcome to the neighborhood. Dick and Barbara open their mailbox and they get that feeling that harks back to getting a letter from your best friend. Somebody knew I would be here! Somebody cares! And look—a 25 percent discount with this flyer!

So, to accomplish this, Random Hardware store calls Speedeon. Speedeon is a (real, not hypothetical) small data company based in Cleveland, Ohio. Speedeon specializes in new mover data. They build their database from multiple sources, including the US Postal Service's National Change of Address database, which is compiled from all those little cards people fill out in ballpoint pen when they're going to move. And Random Hardware is going to use Speedeon's data to tell them which people on their mailing list are new movers.

To understand this, we need to understand a concept in data: The match.

Random Hardware is a sophisticated operation, and they send out mailers all the time. So they already have a mailing list, comprising every name and address in their county.

But for this campaign, they want to send flyers *only* to new movers.

So Random Hardware matches their current mailing list to Speedeon's new mover data. (They have software that performs the match.)

How does the match work?

The software starts with this database:

RANDOM HARDWARE MAILING LIST
ATTRIBUTE: Potential customer.
TOTAL RECORDS: 12,219.
Record #10,987 is . . .

NAME: Dick and Barbara Shlep
ADDRESS: 12 Oak Street

Armed with that information, the software performs a match to the new mover list provided by Speedeon. The second database is:

SPEEDEON NEW MOVER LIST
ATTRIBUTE: New Mover
TOTAL RECORDS: 1,219
Record # 673 is . . .
NAME: Dick and Barbara Shlep
ADDRESS: 12 Oak Street

You probably see where this is going. It's very simple and not a trick. Random Hardware's software can match the first database (Random Hardware's mailing list) to the second database (Speedeon's New Mover list) because *both databases contain name and address.*

This is the final concept: The linking variable. Also known as the match key.

The name and address of the Shleps is what links the first database to the second database. It's a record that's common between one database and the next.

The match key enables, in effect, a little transitive property magic. If A = B and B = C, then A = C. If the Random Hardware customer database contains 12 Oak Street, and the new mover database contains 12 Oak Street, then Random Hardware knows the residents of 12 Oak Street are new movers . . . who really need to buy shelf liner at 25 percent off.

This is the concept of matching.

If you have a match key, you can walk over information from one database to another. Think about it as a bridge. You can walk over information from one data island to another. Without the bridge, the data is isolated; nothing to add. With the bridge, you can transport data ideas from one place to another. You can link new mover status to a name and address. It happens millions of times a year in the world of direct mail. It is a principle so basic companies can apply it to simple things like selling shelf liner.

Or to hard things.

Like curing cancer.

JOSH BILENKER WAS another English-major-turned-MD. He studied medicine at Johns Hopkins, specialized in oncology, went to work for the Food and Drug Administration (a useful background if you're going to work in pharma or biotech), then joined a venture capital firm. In 2013, Josh persuaded his partners to spend money on a failed pain medication called larotrectinib.

Medications fail all the time. After they fail, nobody wants them. If the treatment is already a proven loser, it has already cost someone a lot of money. The last thing any capitalist wants is to throw good money after bad. Failed treatments are the yard sale junk of biotech.

So why would the forty-one-year-old Josh, with his English degree and his first job in venture capital, stake his reputation on such a crazy bet? On a compound no one had heard of, larotrectinib?

Josh licensed the failed pain medication because he knew the medication inhibited a certain gene in the nervous system that helps regulate pain. The gene is called NTRK—neurotrophic tyrosine receptor kinase—which the pros pronounce as "Entrack." Why did larotrectinib, the pain drug, fail? Who cares? Josh was counting on the drug to do something else entirely. From his background in oncology—the study of cancer—Josh knew that that same gene, NTRK, played a role in certain cancers.

What happens is, sometimes the gene NTRK goes haywire. When it does, it links to, or "fuses" with, other genes. Kind of randomly. Not in a way that helps the body do anything useful. In fact, these fusions cause various cancers. Like lung cancer.

What if the unpronounceable larotrectinib, by inhibiting the NTRK gene, could also inhibit those cancers?

That was Josh's big gamble. And to convert his bet, he called Deborah Morosini—the single mom pathologist in Boston who had lost her mother to ovarian cancer and her sister to lung cancer.

SIX DAYS AFTER Deborah's mother, Helen Morosini, died of ovarian cancer on that icy February Friday in Connecticut, down in Bethesda, Maryland, the National Cancer Institute submitted a radical recommendation to its board: Spend $100 million and three years to launch a program on the genomics of cancer.

To most of us, cancer is this invisible monster that sneaks up on you and tries to kill you. Like a shark. We know, vaguely, that too much sun or smoking or living near a toxic waste dump can attract the monster. Blood in the seawater. Beyond that, we think of cancer as bad luck.

But by 2006 the National Cancer Institute knew that cancer arises when things go wrong in our genes.

DNA is the programming of our body—our cells' recipe for the proteins that make up every part of us. Cancer is what happens when those recipes get scrambled: Genetic "alterations" in the professional parlance. When "altered," our own DNA—due to an inherited mutation or the trauma we inflict on our bodies through smoking or sun exposure or living next to a toxic waste dump or just bad luck—can create cancer cells.

What the National Cancer Institute wanted to do with $100 million was to start mapping which cancers came from which gene alterations. For instance, to identify that breast cancer, the most common cancer in the United States, arises from alterations on the gene BRCA1 located on chromosome 17q21. They wanted to create a giant database of all the cancers linked to all the genes that create them.

On that February day, in other words, the National Cancer Institute came to terms with the fact that cancer was a data problem.

• • •

SINCE HER MOTHER and sister died of cancer, Deborah had become a triple threat when it came to recruiting patients for cancer trials. First, she spent four years as the head of patient engagement at a biotech firm. Haunted by her mother's and sister's failed cancer treatments, Deborah had become a full-time patient champion, finding the ones who needed treatment, directing how they were treated, focusing on those treatments' success. Second, she had joined the board of the National Comprehensive Cancer Center network, an organization dedicated to the highest standards of patient care. That meant Deborah had connections in thirty-two cancer hospitals, from Fred Hutch, fifty miles from the Canada border in Washington State, to the Moffitt Cancer Center in Tampa, Florida—and nineteen states in between. Third, and perhaps most importantly, Deborah is cool. She has platinum blond hair, twinkling blue eyes, the fashion sense of an off-duty rock star, and a laugh like somebody doing scales on a glockenspiel. People like her and want to be her friend.

In other words, Deborah was the person you called when you needed to recruit patients for a cancer drug trial. Which is exactly what Josh Bilenker, rising venture capitalist and new owner of a failed NTRK inhibitor drug, was looking for.

Yet even for Deborah, the challenge was enormous.

A genetics-first view of cancer was still nascent. And NTRK fusions are not a simple business.

The medical profession preferred to think about cancer simply, based on organs.

Organs are intuitive. Breast cancer. Lung cancer. Colorectal cancer. More than 260,000 cases of breast cancer are diagnosed every year, in women and men. That was a huge market for the drug companies—valued at $57 billion in 2021. As a result, most drug companies, and the genetic testing they asked for, focused on the big market opportunities. The organs.

But Deborah was hunting for patients with cancers caused by NTRK fusions.

This was not the language hospitals spoke. They spoke organs. They did not speak obscure genetic alterations.

NTRK fusions?

To make matters worse, cancers caused by NTRK fusions were esoteric even in oncology. They make up only a few thousand cases a year. Less than 1 percent of cancers. And even within that group, it's not simple. When NTRK fuses with other genes, all sorts of cancers result. When NTRK fuses with the gene LMNA, you get colorectal cancer. When it fuses with ETV6, you get breast cancer. When it fuses with TPM3, you get cervical cancer. And so on, for *twenty* types of cancer. There were a lot of people suffering and dying from those types of cancers. But they didn't conform to how the medical establishment categorized—much less treated—cancer.

"The drug companies were working on the big targets, because that was the largest market," Deborah remembered. "Nobody tested for anything else."

But in Deborah's travels she had learned the value of the patient advocate: A role in hospitals without a medical degree, whose sole job was to help patients navigate the complex world of the medical establishment. Deborah sniffed out the hospitals treating cancer cases who *also* performed tumor testing. She called the patient advocates. And she offered them a deal.

If they would introduce their patients with NTRK fusions to her, Deborah could put them into an experimental treatment program using Josh's unpronounceable drug.

"You would think the words 'experimental treatment' would send patients screaming," Deborah commented. "But these were people who had been given months to live. They had nothing to lose. They signed right up. No hesitation."

Deborah recruited ten patients. These included a forty-year-old mother. And an infant.

"We had to grind up the compound to administer it to the baby," she recalled.

Treating the alteration, not the organ, worked. The drug's success rate was more than 75 percent. Patients' response, Deborah said, was "Lazarus-like." Fifty-five patients participated in the trial, with different cancers, in different organs. Within two years, Josh's unpronounceable drug had received a fancy new name and approval from the FDA. Within five years, Josh's fledgling company had been acquired by Eli Lilly, the fifteenth largest drug company in the world.

DEBORAH AND JOSH and their team know something before everybody else, which the National Cancer Institute would later codify: "Cancers of different tissues can share the same alterations and be biologically more similar to each other than to other tumors of the same tissue of origin." In other words, cancers with the same genetic origin had more in common than cancers in the same organ. The industry had been approaching it upside down. The National Cancer Institute knew cancer was a gene problem. But the drug companies and hospitals had been treating it like an organ problem.

When Deborah called the hospitals, in an ideal world, they would have had a genetic database ready to go. That database should have been a simple bridge, a linking mechanism, just like in direct mail. Data point A links to data point B links to data point C.

In this case, you would have a forty-year-old mom with metastatic liposarcoma. (Data point A.)

Testing would tell you that a fusion of the gene NTRK caused this cancer. (Data point B.)

And the database would tell you that larotrectinib treats cancers caused by NTRK fusions with 75 percent effectiveness. (Data point C.)

If those databases had been as deep and wide as direct mail databases, then every cancer would be tested so it could be linked to its genetic alteration. The gene alterations would act like the name and address for the hardware store—the match key linking the cancer patient to the cancer *treatment*. The data would be bridged.

Cancer: Gene alteration: Treatment.

The day they made public his company's clinical trial results, Josh spoke on CNBC.

"One call to action I'd love people to hear is get your tumor tested," he implored. "Talk to your doctor to get your tumor tested in the most comprehensive way possible."

Suddenly, thanks to Deborah and Josh and their company, the medical profession woke up to the database approach to curing cancer. The National Cancer Database now contains more than thirty-four million records, representing more than 70 percent of all newly diagnosed cancer cases. The National Cancer Institute's Cancer Genome Project contains 2.5 petabytes of data from eleven thousand patients. So-called next generation sequencing makes mapping cancer genomics faster and more accurate. A company called QCI offers a database linking patient tests to their genetic alterations and all existing literature about known and emerging treatments for those alterations.

But to Deborah it remains personal.

When Dana performed the song "Now and Forever" in that performance two months before she died, she sang the lyrics:

> *Now and forever*
> *You are a part of me*
> *And the memory cuts like a knife.*

"If this type of genomic testing had been around," Deborah muses, sixteen years later, "Dana might have been saved."

KEY POINTS IN CHAPTER 16

- Matching is a kind of transitive property magic with data. If two databases share a few fields—like name and address—then data from one database can be "walked over" to another.

- This is one of the most important uses of data I see in my work. Because it means different data types can be blended, even if they are completely unrelated. Each new data type you add adds insight to the original database.

- The common fields that allow the matching, in the business, are called match keys, or linking variables.

THOUGHT STARTERS FOR YOU

- The concept of matching implies that you are starting with a preexisting database. So let's do the same here: What databases do you have now that are useful in your mission. A list of your organization's locations? Your customers? Your donors?

- What data can you match to that original database to make it more insightful? Are your locations in flood zones? Are your customers young or old, rich or poor? Repeat customers or flighty?

- What decisions can you make once you have added the new insights?

WHERE DO WE GO NEXT?

Once we've anchored our data to an identity and matched it to new and meaningful data sets, now we can really make it powerful. Two of the most potent ways of using data remain. The next, scoring, is maybe the most essential of all. You will notice echoes of multiple superpowers here: Crystallizing complex information as well as directing resources to where they are most needed and, indeed, to the hierarchy of reality-to-AI. Because "scoring" enables us to take a bewildering mass of undifferentiated options and ascribe meaning, value, and difference.

CHAPTER 17

Scoring

The Loneliness Score

A dam Greene knew what he had to do.

They sat on his business partner's 57th Street terrace, Adam and the three other founding partners of their investment firm. Manhattan splayed out below. The skyscrapers. The luxury apartments with the potted Japanese cedars. The plunging concrete canyons. The four of them, these business partners, had succeeded. They had launched one of the foremost green energy funds in the US. They had made money. Only . . .

Only when Adam's father had recently become ill, it had triggered something. Adam's father had been a fighter pilot, a salesman, a poker player, an *extrovert*, the kind of grandfather who showed up at his grandson's 6:00 a.m. hockey practice so perky, so *on*, that he'd crack up the other parents, still sipping their first coffees, with stories of the old days in Brooklyn.

But after Adam's parents had made the choice to move to New York City from their home of several decades, and then Adam's mother died, his father withdrew. Adam, a caring son, tried to help. He made introductions. He encouraged his father to rekindle old friendships. Maybe a program at the Jewish Community Center? Or the YMCA? But Adam was forced to watch, helplessly, as his father withdrew deeper into himself and eventually succumbed to dementia.

Loneliness.

Adam Greene believed he'd watched his father die of it. And now he couldn't stop trying to understand how, and why, loneliness had killed his father. Adam's head wasn't in the financial game anymore. Distressed assets? Merchant banking? Who cared, when loneliness—so corrosive that the United States Surgeon General published a report on it calling it an "epidemic"—was feasting on millions of people around him? Adam had been obsessing over articles and research about loneliness. One thing he had not been obsessing about? Their investment partnership.

So, that day on the terrace, Adam quit.

"They were my friends," he said of his three business partners. "We had worked together since the late 1990s."

But he had to do something.

"I really want to be figuring this out," he remembers thinking at the time, about the condition he felt had robbed him of his father. "Even though I don't know what this is."

INVISIBLE THINGS ARE scary. Film nerds know this. In the 1975 classic *Jaws*, the great white shark, for most of the movie, is just a fin or ominous music or bubbling water. It's not until minute eighty-one (out of a two-hour movie) that the shark breaks the surface, and everybody screams.

Loneliness has a *Jaws*-like quality.

First, it is deadly. Loneliness—defined as having few social connections or connections that are not supportive or inclusive—is more predictive of premature mortality than smoking fifteen cigarettes a day, drinking six drinks a day, being obese, being physically inactive, living with air pollution. It increases the risk of heart disease by 29 percent and the risk of stroke by 32 percent. Painfully, for Adam Greene and his family, it increases the risk of dementia in older adults by 50 percent. Why is this the case? Loneliness puts the body in a state of alert. "You have to deal with everything on your own" is the message the body receives. Cortisol, norepinephrine are stimulated. A kind of survival stress, in other words. It places wear and tear on the body.

But loneliness is also hard to detect.

How do some people travel on their own for months at a time, through strange lands, and still feel poised, centered, stimulated, and "Nonlonely" (to use an oddly appealing term of the psychology experts)?

While others like Mr. Greene Sr. can have a loving family, live in the middle of New York City—with millions of people and theaters and museums and restaurants and temples and parks—and feel utterly alone?

Adam Greene decided he was going to hunt the great white shark of loneliness. (I promise that's the last *Jaws* reference.) He raised seed money. A friend fed him a company name—they would call it Klaatch, after the coffee klatches they remembered their mothers and grand-mothers belonging to, where you'd drink coffee and gossip, connect. They partnered with a nonprofit called JASA, which runs affordable housing in New York City. They sent out flyers to the residents. They recruited seniors to join. Klaatch formed groups. Klaatch established a twelve-week program. Klaatch offered coach-led, peer-to-peer, one-hour sessions. Seniors, in small groups. Some groups fell a little flat—the personalities didn't click. But sometimes it went the other way. The group connected.

If you watch videos of seniors reflecting on the Klaatch program, you can see it. One of the interviewees was a silver-haired woman with a brainy air and the dark-framed glasses to go with it.

"I discovered other people like myself. Single women, who had lost their partners. We all got the *New York Times* every morning. We all watched Rachel Maddow. We meet on Sundays and have lunch. We're getting to the point we're planning on going across town, to go to the movies."

Listening to her, you can tell that going to the movies is a big deal.

There were multiple cases like this. Success stories. So the Klaatch team went to measure the impact they could see with their own eyes. Surely the seniors' level of loneliness had improved.

But . . . bupkes. Nothing.

No change in the loneliness scores.

"The scores didn't match what was visibly happening in the group," Adam remembers, with frustration. "How the hell am I going to measure whether our program works?"

WHY DO WE score things?

We know the term best from sports, where teams "keep score" of a game. When we keep score, we give that game a quantified, numerical label: Argentina 3, France 3. The word itself comes from Old Norse, *skur*, which is a little closer to *scar*, "to mark something." Back then they would create notches in a stone, for counting.

So we are taking a thing without much identity—a stone; a bunch of people kicking a ball around—and giving it a numerical label.

And why is that useful?

We are moving a thing from a state of ambiguity (where we know nothing) to a state of knowledge (where we know something).

You arrive at your friend's house in the middle of the game. Buncha people are already sitting on the sofas eating chips and chugging Corona Premier. What is the first thing you ask: What's the score? It's almost proverbial. Without the score, the game has no narrative. It's a scrimmage; it's a practice; it's a warm-up.

With the score, you have context. Who's dominating? Who's the underdog? Who's going to stage an upset?

• • •

MIKHAEL BORODIN USED to sit near my desk at our digital advertising start-up. Mikhael has a bearish quality. Maybe because he is Russian. Maybe because he used to wear those stiff, short-sleeved office
shirts, the kind that practically beg to have pens hooked over the breast
pocket, that seem so . . . Russian, or not American, anyway. And those
shirts revealed his burly arms. But Mikhael has a big, warm smile,
which you want when the guy you're dealing with has multiple degrees
in physics and he is your VP of data science.

Mikhael's job was to get people to click ads.

He used about a terabyte of data to do so.

But the way digital advertising works, each ad was a fresh start. A
blank slate. A web page—say CNN.com—would load on your computer, your browser. There was a little window in the page where the ad
went. The website of CNN.com would execute code on the page that
said, "Call the ad server, we need an ad here." And our company's ad
server would have the chance to serve an ad. The way the technology
worked, we didn't *have* to serve the ad. We could turn down certain
opportunities. We could, for instance, choose to serve an ad on the
dating site OKCupid instead.

It was Mikhael's job to make sure that people clicked on the ads we
served as frequently as possible. Because the advertisers *loooved* getting
those clicks.

But remember, each ad opportunity was a fresh start. Fresh, meaning the publisher wouldn't tell us, "Oh, this guy is an ad clicker." But
they would give us inputs. When the publisher asked us to serve an
ad, it would feed us certain information. What website is it? CNN
or OKCupid? What operating system is their computer running
on—Apple (iOS) or Microsoft (Windows)? What time of day is it?
What day of the week is it? What's the ad size—is it a big banner ad
or one of those slim little french fries at the bottom of the screen? Is

it being served on a laptop or a mobile phone? Had we already placed cookies on the browser, or were we seeing them for the first time?

(Mikhael's English was more or less perfect, but when he talked about "cookies," he pronounced it *cook-iss*. I loved that.)

This is the key to scoring: You need what the practitioners call training data.

You need to have lots of situations where you have information about what comes before, also known as predictive data: What website are you visiting? What operating system do you have? And then data about what happens afterward: Did you click? The more instances you have of both those things, the better you can predict what will happen next. It's not going to be perfect. But it's going to be "better than guessing," as David Miller, the data scientist I quoted in a previous chapter, used to say.

Mikhael wrote algorithms that decided whether the ad opportunity had a high probability of clicking or a low probability of clicking.

He *scored* each ad opportunity.

What we found was that despite having a whole terabyte of data, and a Russian physicist to write an algo, two things predicted a click. First, if the ad was served on a mobile device. Because people accidentally thumbed the ad instead of the button they wanted to push. Second, if it was served on dating or gaming sites. Because, presumably, there was a lot of swiping and poking going on that resulted in accidental clicks. (The advertisers didn't seem to care that most clicks were accidental. But that's another story.)

Predicting clicks on banner ads—perhaps not such a glamorous or miraculous example. At least, not in terms of serving humanity. But, on a data level, there *was* something of a minor miracle afoot. We served millions of ads a day. Tens of millions per month. And each time, Mikhael's algorithm would make a guess.

"OKCupid, on a mobile device? High probability of clicking!"

"CNN.com, on a desktop? Low probability of clicking!"

Millions of times a day, we were moving our clients from a state of zero knowledge to a state of knowledge. We were estimating. We didn't *know* who would click the ad. But we could make a good guess. An informed guess. And now the client knew something useful.

Thanks to Mikhael scoring all those cook-iss.

FOR ADAM GREENE, trying to score loneliness, there were more substantial challenges.

First, the psychology community had long since settled into a standard measure of loneliness. It was developed in 1978. Based on—as so many psychology innovations seem to be—testing done on undergraduates at the university where the psychology professors in question happened to teach. They worked up the loneliness test on 259 undergrads at UCLA. The test was twenty questions. It asked you some deep, intense stuff. Like if you felt "starved for company" or if "people are around me *but not with me*." (Emphasis mine.) This came to be known as the UCLA Loneliness Scale.

But this had challenges too. At twenty questions, and a four-point answer scale (often, sometimes, rarely, never), it's an elaborate test. It requires explanation. It's the kind of test you need to administer in the clinician's office—difficult to administer to lots and lots of people. A three-question version was developed. Better.

Still, for Adam, how would they administer a test like this to dozens of seniors? Are they going to wheel everybody down to the psychology lab? But what if the seniors had mobility aids—walkers and canes and oxygen tanks? So the Klaatch team started what they called "the friendly phone call." They would dial up the senior, at home, ask how it was going, administer the three-question test. Problem solved. The seniors liked the calls. Who doesn't like someone checking on them? Talking about themselves a little? The Klaatch team made the calls and administered the three-question UCLA test "pre and post," as we say in the research biz. Before and after. To measure change.

But the seniors' changes in social connectedness that Adam and his team observed were *still* not reflected in the scores.

This was due to another, even tougher, challenge. What the experts call *response bias*.

If someone asks you a question like "Are you starved for company?" chances are you will respond defensively. "Absolutely not. I'm fine. I'm not *starved*!" It's almost insulting. You will respond in a way that protects your ego. It takes an enlightened individual to answer personal questions without bias.

What that meant was, Adam's seniors were probably inflating their preprogram scores. In other words, when asked, before the program, whether they were lonely, they defensively said no, I'm not lonely. And this *raised their baseline*. This meant that even if Klaatch's one-hour, coach-led, peer-to-peer program made a bunch of New York seniors feel more connected to other people—and substantially improved their lives—the test would still look flat.

Adam did his homework and realized that he was not the only one facing this problem. A group of Finnish researchers had replicated these same results—these same problems with loneliness scores—in an academic study. The Finnish psychologists had pumped up more than a hundred Finnish seniors with art therapy and writing therapy and group therapy and had seen friendships born and connections made; and, when it came to measuring results, bupkes, zilch, or as they say in Finland, *ei mikaan*. No change in the loneliness scores.

Adam needed a way to score loneliness *passively*.

And that was when he thought about the phone calls.

Remember that friendly phone call? The one they placed to the seniors in the comfort of their own home? Where they asked the three-question UCLA loneliness test, but also got the senior chatting?

What if they carefully transcribed the words, the actual language, the senior was using and scored the transcript based on how the types of answers reflected the seniors' loneliness? Klaatch had hundreds of interviews recorded already. They could use textual analysis to find indicators of loneliness *without directly asking about it.*

That would be passive. The senior picking up the phone wouldn't know which vocabulary would correspond to what loneliness score. They would just be talking. There would be no way to game the test. No response bias.

Adam would still have the seniors' actual answers to the actual three-question UCLA loneliness test. So he wouldn't be losing that data. And he could add another ingredient. Something straightforward, like how much that senior had joined in the Klaatch programs. Attendance! That's a metric that goes back to kindergarten. Simple.

This is exactly what Adam did. He combined a textual analysis of the phone calls, the answers to the classic three-question UCLA test, and attendance. And he created his own loneliness score.

"Lo and behold, what we were finding was an exact match between the qualitative and the quantitative," Adam said. In other words, the new scores accurately reflected the improvement—or lack thereof—the Klaatch team could see for themselves.

Klaatch now possessed data about the thing they were trying to predict: Loneliness. They could see, right before their eyes, the seniors' new connections. Their mood. Their engagement. All the ways they acted, or didn't act, like Adam's father in the years before he died.

This score had made the invisible visible.

WHEN YOU TALK to Adam Greene, he bursts with energy. He is middle aged, in good shape, with gray hair, entering that time of life where many men focus on their golf game and waiting for the first grandkid. Instead, Adam is running an early-stage start-up. He is hustling. When he speaks about his loneliness score, and solving the problems of scaling it—Can they reach more and bigger senior residences? Can they use AI to score more seniors?—his eyes get a glow I've seen in the eyes of many entrepreneurs.

Is it the satisfaction of helping to heal the disease that afflicted his father? Maybe. What I see is that *game-on* flicker of an athlete taking the field. A lust to make a difference. "All the lonely people," as the Beatles sang. All that invisibility. All the blankness, the defiant problem that stretches from the Bronx to Finland. Solving that, with something as simple as a score, fills Adam Greene with passion and purpose. "It's the most rewarding thing I've ever done," he says.

For the older woman in the Klaatch program, that score was measuring real change.

"My husband passed away two years ago. Within a year, I lost many of my closest friends. I have withdrawn from a lot of stuff. To find this kind of a group," she says, referring to the senior programs administered by Klaatch, "was a miracle."

A few minutes later, she adds a comment, with only-in-New-York timing.

"My knees still ache," she says.

KEY POINTS IN CHAPTER 17

- Scoring is the essence of data. We look at many objects or phenomena that confuse us. And we create a methodology to have those blank objects tell us a story.

- Klaatch offers programs to make seniors more connected. But to determine if their programs worked, they needed to score people for loneliness. They created a methodology to do this using diverse inputs like interview transcripts and program attendance.

- Scoring is also predictive. A good example of this is digital advertising, where companies want to predict which users will click on an ad. They take inputs like content types, device type, and operating system and score a user for high or low likelihood for clicking.

- In both examples, data inputs and scoring conjured some invisible, hard-to-pin-down, and important attribute—lonely, clicker.

THOUGHT STARTERS FOR YOU

- In your world, how can you score things to make a valuable prediction? Does this slide show leukemia? Is this script in my giant submission pile a hit? Which sex worker websites are run by human traffickers? (Yep, I went back there.)

- This is absolutely the domain where AI helps apply these judgments at massive scale.

- The data you possess informs your ability to make these judgments. What data do you have that can act as a "truth set" to train your model or your score? Do you have a thousand slides that were leukemia and a thousand that weren't? Great, now you can score a million assays and automate your scoring.

WHERE DO WE GO NEXT?

With two chapters left, we now make a slight pivot. "Certification" is not about something you do with data. Certification is a role data plays. Once you have identified a thing and scored it (for instance, as grade AAA), now what? What can you do with that score? What role can that score play in the economy, in society?

CHAPTER 18

Certification

The Pope of Meat Grading

He was only a fictional character. Yet he had a massive impact on the real world. He exposed a corrupt industry, and he forced the president of the United States to pass new laws.

His name was Jurgis. He was a Lithuanian immigrant, newly arrived in Chicago. He and his family found what they thought would be honest labor in the Chicago slaughterhouses. Instead, this is what they saw:

> There would be meat stored in great piles in rooms; and the water from leaky roofs would drip over it, and thousands of rats would race about on it. It was too dark in these storage places to see well; but a man could run his hands over these piles of meat and sweep off handfuls of the dried dung of rats.

Jurgis's family saw waste bins dumped into fresh meat and then "sent out to the public's breakfast." They witnessed putrefying beef dressed up for sale using tricks with borax, color, and brine. Rats in the sausage.

This is the world of *The Jungle*, written by the journalist, novel-ist, and socialist Upton Sinclair. I think many more people have read about this book than read it. And you kind of forget, despite its fame as a work of "muckraking"—a word you usually follow with the word *journalism*—that *The Jungle* is a novel. As a piece of fiction, its social impact can be rivaled only, maybe, by *Uncle Tom's Cabin*. Its publica-tion led to public outcry and a feisty correspondence between Sinclair and President Theodore Roosevelt. Roosevelt—no friend to social reform—sent inspectors to confirm Sinclair's accounts of the Chicago slaughterhouses. Roosevelt promised: "The specific evils you point out shall, if their existence be proved, and if I have power, be eradicated." In 1906, Roosevelt proved as good as his word. He signed the Meat Inspection Act and the Pure Food and Drug Act, which conjured into existence the United States Food and Drug Administration.

The whole process took less than a year and a half.

These events turned the meat production process on its head. Now, instead of the dark storage rooms Sinclair describes, there is a new kind of expert. One who not only looks *at* the beef being prepared for "the public's breakfast" but *inside* it, with a kind of elaborate craftsmanship we might associate with winemaking or bending maple wood to make violins.

These, of course, are the meat graders.

IN TEXAS, ON US Route 83, you can keep your accelerator stamped down for miles. You might roar past the Cowboy Creek exit, which is the turn for Briscoe.

In America, there may be no more distant place from Chicago's frigid winds and ill-lit warehouses than Briscoe, Texas. In Briscoe, there's nothing but sun. The temperature hits ninety degrees in May. The tree cover isn't. It's grass—green in spring, other times brown—stretching out to a horizon so wide you feel like you've stepped into a geometry problem. There's a windowless country store with a couple abandoned gas pumps; a school; and that's it.

But nearby is the combination farm and ranch that Larry Meadows grew up on. He helped his mother gather eggs to sell and dipped hundreds per day into a vinegar solution to sterilize them. He helped his father raise cattle and hogs to "slaughter size" and truck them to Oklahoma City for sale. This is the kind of background, in other words, you'd expect from the man who later became, basically, the pope of US meat grading, running the national program for twenty years.

Larry explains the high end and the low end of beef grades to me. Now retired, he is as affable as they come—sheen-bald, wire-rim glasses, lots of grandaddy pride. And an accent so Texas that when he speaks, my East Coast–biased interview transcription program keeps adding extra syllables.

"Wagyu beef has so much fat you can barely see the red," he says, explaining the high end of the meat grades to me. "When you eat it, it's like eating butter. If you eat it real hot, it's delicious. As it gets colder, it gets a little too buttery for me." He explains that the cows used for Wagyu beef are a specific breed. You couldn't get just any cow to that level.

And then there's the other end of the spectrum. "As a cow gets really, really old, when she's like fifteen years old and she's really thin?" Larry tells me. "She may be a canner."

He is referring to the specific meat grading range that spans prime (steak house steak, the kind so furry with fat they hang it in the window to get you drooling), then choice, select, standard, commercial, utility, cutter, and at last, canner. There's nothing wrong with canner, mind you. Unlike the world of *The Jungle*, this isn't a safety inspection. That function is fulfilled by the USDA Inspection Services. This—what Larry does—is a quality score. Larry describes with some pride the meat that's used in the national school lunch program. It uses canner-grade beef: "It's beef that's cut in three-quarter-inch cubes. It's put in a can with a half a percent salt tablet and cooked in its natural juice. The meat gets really soft, and you get those natural flavors."

What determines the grade of beef, according to the USDA, is several very specific factors, each with what you might call a vectoring system, a "high to low" score.

The principle metric for a meat grade is how much marbling there is on the beef—that is, the amount of fat within the muscle. USDA marbling scores range from slight to small; then modest; moderate; slightly abundant; and finally, moderately abundant. (There's no "buttery" level.)

Then there's color. Larry rattles off the shades for me: "Grayish pink and light grayish pink and moderately grayish pink and then light cherry red, red, moderately red, dark red—we got a ton of different levels of colors."

Then there's texture, which ranges from fine (that's what you want, when the fat is little flecks inside the meat), to medium, to coarse (where the fat is in big, hard globs).

Then there's the age of the animal. This seems like it would be the most obvious, so obvious that you wonder why it's part of the score. I mean, presumably the farmer who raised the cow would know how old it is, right? So where's the mystery? But remember, this is happening at industrial scale. The cows are now carcasses, stripped of hide and head and hoof, and hanging in colossal warehouse-sized meat lockers at thirty-four degrees Fahrenheit on a mechanized chain, six thousand hanging there at a time. The meat graders that Larry used to supervise, with their white smocks and blue hard hats and boots—they're not going to call the rancher and ask the cow's birthday—they need an objective way of assessing the age of the animal. Even if it's not as accurate as, say, knowing that Bessie came mooing into the world on April 1, 2024, it's a process that's applied to all carcasses, so it's consistent. (Larry claims that he can tell "within a month or two" the precise age of an animal.) And how they do it is someone takes an air pressure power saw and splits each carcass down the spinal groove. And then someone else "ribs" each carcass—that is, makes a cut—between the lumbar vertebrae and the thoracic vertebrae, exposing the cut bone. And then someone else—the meat grader—looks for the level of ossification—the degree to which a sprightly young cow's cartilage has turned to bone. The more ossification, the older the animal.

Then Larry, and the teams he used to lead, would stamp the meat with its grade—stamp it right there on the carcass—with the grade of the meat: Prime, choice, canner. And that grade determines the price. The price is published every week in a report from the USDA. Yesterday's pricing sheet from Des Moines, Iowa—labeled the USDA BEEF CARCASS PRICE EQUIVALENT INDEX VALUE—told me that a four-hundred-pound carcass labeled prime should fetch $277.24, and the same size in select costs $231.06.

And in case, all this time, you have been wondering why I am writing in such depth about meat, I'm about to tell you.

Or Larry is:

"I've always believed, coming from a farm background, I wanted to do the best job possible for that farmer. Because that farmer spent two years raising the animal to get it to slaughter."

By that point, the farmer has a lot at stake. But market dynamics can be distorted when the seller, or the buyer, has too much power. Or when there is no objective means of assessing the value of a commodity. But in Larry's view, the USDA fixed that.

"We created trust in the system. That rancher felt good about us establishing the price—because he was paid fairly. We were a third party coming in there between two, really, conflicting parties—the buyers and sellers. And we would say, 'This is what it is, and this is the price.' You're treated fairly [as a seller]. You're treated fairly [as a buyer]. Because we were independent. I mean," Larry says, "it's all about pride."

In other words, Larry steps back and sees something here that would have made Jurgis Rudkus happy:

Fairness.

. . .

THE DATA HERE—the score that Larry and his meat graders provided—is secondary to the *role* that Larry played. The role of certifier.

When a third party plays a neutral role, creates a score, then makes that score public, it's a powerful position for data.

When S&P or Moody's gives a company a bond rating—now that they are, presumably, honest brokers again—they make a market for that company to borrow money. The company couldn't represent themselves as effectively. ("Here are our rosy financials!") Everyone would assume they were biased. This was what Henry Varnum Poor accomplished. He knew the railroads would fudge their numbers. So he gathered the numbers himself and checked them himself. He was *such* a railroad nerd that when he published metrics in his *Manual*, everybody figured the numbers were accurate—or as accurate as they could possibly be.

That was the role Susan Whiting and Nielsen played in TV ratings—an impartial party between buyer and seller to declare how large a TV audience was so the network could sell advertising based on the size of its audience.

Organizations like the Better Business Bureau play this role certifying businesses as honest brokers and grading (among other things) how they handle consumer complaints. Consumer Reports plays this role in declaring consumer products safe.

New York City places inspection grades in restaurant windows declaring a restaurant an A, B, or C grade for passing its health inspection.

It's not all just practical matters, either—counting TV audiences or food violations. A nonprofit named JUST Capital was founded on the notion that "we have put so much emphasis on profits, it's like we've ripped the humanity out of our companies," according to its founder, the investor Paul Tudor Jones. So JUST Capital went about scoring the morality—the goodness, the justice—of all the companies in the top stock exchanges. They set about scoring companies from AbbVie to ZoomInfo on how well they treat their workers. Does the company pay a living wage? Support workforce retention? Provide benefits and work-life balance? Protect worker health and safety? They pore through company filings to understand whether they have performed a pay-gap analysis based on gender or race. Whether they publish their minimum hourly wage. Whether they adhere to an international standard of occupational health and safety. They consult third-party data firms to understand whether each company pays a living wage and, if so, whether it is above or below the median of their industry.

And that's just the worker's scores. They also evaluate the company's impact on the environment, customers, communities. Then JUST Capital publishes its findings every quarter. It publishes an index for investors who want to invest in the companies who are the most "just."

Can a company declare, themselves, that they are just? They would all like to. But we wouldn't believe them.

THE TRICKY PART about playing the role of the certifier is that the folks you are certifying might not like the grades you give them. We saw that in the chapter about counting, when the Nielsen Ratings faced criticism for getting TV ratings wrong.

The obligation for the certifier, then, is to do two things.

First, to sweat the details. If a normal data person is already a burrower—someone who gets into the details of things and roots out the truth—then a certifier must be just a little bit more passionate, more obsessed.

Second, as much as possible, the certifier must be transparent about how they arrived at their conclusions. JUST Capital, for instance, publishes a detailed methodology, showing factor by factor how they arrive at their scores for "renewable energy percentage" or "paid parental leave policy."

For Larry Meadows, his source of expertise was a conclave the USDA would arrange twice a year. And the way Larry describes it, there is something Vatican-like about it. The three national supervisors, who oversaw all the meat grading in the United States—millions of cows and steers evaluated—would come together in Omaha, Nebraska. They would travel on Monday. Stay in Omaha for the week and evaluate carcasses. Three master craftspeople, alone with their tools: Hard hat, white smock, boots, clipboard, and a camera—and, of course, beef carcasses hanging from hooks. And the national supervisors would take careful notes. If select has three degrees of marbling, and you can score each degree on a 100-point scale, well, what *was* small, modest, or moderate, really? And then the three national supervisors would get together and compare their notes. There would be differences. One supervisor would think that carcass number seventeen was a select / small / 90 and the other supervisor would think carcass number seventeen was a select / small / 60. And they would revisit the carcass and reconcile these differences to agree on a standard. Then the twenty-five supervisors below them, who had also all flown in on the Monday, came into the plant with blue hard hats and smocks and boots. And they would all be shown the new, true metrics. The updated, right way to look at meat. The new standard for the whole country for the next six months. And they would duly photograph all the carcasses and laminate all those photographs or, nowadays, pipe them into a mobile device, so that all the graders could carry around the pictures and know what a select / small / 60 looked like. And on Friday, everybody would fly home. They called it the National Correlation.

Yes, of course, there are now more cost-efficient ways to accomplish this. This year, the USDA launched a "remote beef grading" program where you can take an apparatus attached to an iPhone and message in your beef pictures to a remote beef grading expert and get meat grades without everybody traveling to your plant. Which, indeed, seems efficient. But, as in all technological advances, you do feel something gets lost. Larry started his career when Texas Tech asked him to judge their yearly contest for raising cattle. And then there was the decades-long career as a supervisor and leader so committed he was simply known as "Chief." And then there's the moment I imagine, of Larry at the National Correlation, in a hard hat and his wire-rim glasses, in a smock that normally is meant to keep your clothes clean of blood but suddenly in this context feels like the smock of a scientist, leaning into the meat, squinting, probably, bringing a lifetime of expertise to that single judgment.

Exactly who you want as a certifier.

KEY POINTS IN CHAPTER 18

- Certification is a role data plays between parties with conflicting interests.

- The data is gathered by a party with no interest in the advantage of one party vs. another.

- Larry Meadows, while admitting that generally he wants to get the farmers a fair deal, and while having a farming background, has no bias I know of for any carcass or cattle rancher. (This is where S&P failed during the 2008 financial crisis. They were being paid by one side of the transaction and let it sway their certifications.)

- Then the scores created by the certifier are published. And this often sets a value, or is an important input to set a value, on a thing both sides care about.

- Culturally, this tends to create obsessive people who care about the minutiae—in a good way—in their area of expertise.

- The certifier also has pressure to remain fair in their judgment, because their role is an ongoing and public one. They must maintain neutrality between multiple parties or face criticism of unfairness from the aggrieved side. In the chapter on counting, we saw how Nielsen was under pressure for bias from TV ad sellers and was forced to make public adjustments.

THOUGHT STARTERS FOR YOU

- The role of a certifier is a very specific and powerful position in a marketplace. It can be played by government or commercial entities. But it's not a casual undertaking.

- It's also an obvious area to look for bias, as consumers and citizens. Just how are my credit scores generated, anyway? Or my university's rankings established? From what data? Who supplies it? Who checks it? What power of redress do I have if it's wrong?

- More about this in the conclusion of the book.

WHERE DO WE GO NEXT?

In our last chapter, we look at another critical way we use data: To measure performance. How do we know if something works? How do we use data to know whether we got the answer right?

CHAPTER 19

Performance

King Ben

F or a hot second, it felt like a second chance.

It was summertime in Connecticut. Not quite the New England weekend superwealth paradise of Martha's Vineyard. But a halfway-there version—a hundred miles short and still on the mainland—a quirky community where there's a bandshell with a Jimmy Buffett cover band on a Friday night, and there's a pizzeria at the corner of the tiny town intersection and a couple of swanky shops for the weekenders to buy Brie sandwiches and beeswax candles.

In June, the lawn around the gazebo in the postage stamp public park pops with green. And the whole place vibes on *water*. The town overlooks the Long Island Sound, a great scoop of salt water that ends in the Vineyard before opening to the big Atlantic. A dozy river rolls into the sound, where folks bring long-necked nets and tie raw chicken legs with string to go crabbing. There are more marinas than parking lots, and everybody has a boat, and on a fine day, folks will grab a cooler and folding chairs and hop on the whaler and go putt-putting around on the water. That June, Sue Stein was just getting back together with her husband, Tom. Sue and Tom had three boys together, ages five to twelve. Tom had just moved back in after a two-year separation. Summer had begun in earnest. Maybe this was going to be a season of second chances, even redemption.

That Saturday, Sue took their oldest son to his piano lesson. Tom said he would watch the other boys—Jimmy, their middle son, and Ben, their youngest, who was five.

When Sue returned from the piano lesson, the house was empty.

"Where is everybody?" Sue remembers thinking. "There was no message."

Finally, she heard from Tom.

The first thing he said when Sue picked up the phone was:

"Ben's really hurt."

It turned out Tom had taken their boat out. He had taken Jimmy, five-year-old Ben, two other friends of Tom's, and those friends' kids. Later, Sue learned that Tom and his pals had been drinking. Beer cans all over. Tom wasn't the greatest with a boat to begin with. Not because he was incompetent. Because he was arrogant. "The other guy will move," Tom would say. And that's just what had happened. They had been passing under a bridge, where the wide water narrowed to a couple of lanes under the archways, and where you had to be careful with the timing of boats coming the other way. And maybe Tom wasn't paying attention. Or maybe Tom was buzzed. Or maybe Tom was thinking, *The other guy will move*. But the other guy didn't. The other guy's boat struck Tom and Sue's boat in what was effectively a head-on collision.

Sue remembers the conversation with icy precision.

"How hurt?" Sue asked her husband. "What happened?"

Tom told her: "It was an accident."

"Well, is Ben going to be okay?"

Tom said, "We don't know."

Struggling to control her rising fear, Sue persisted: "Is Ben going to *die?*"

Tom repeated: "They don't know."

"And my stomach hurts," Sue told me later. "Have you ever heard the term *turning to stone*? Like getting that cold feeling of nothingness. And in that moment, I thought—well, I blamed Tom. I thought, *I hate you*."

When the boats collided, their son Ben had been standing in a doorway. The force of impact had rammed Ben's head against the bow-side doorframe. Hard impact. Ben had bounced to the other side of the small doorframe and struck his head again on the stern side. Another impact. Then the momentum from *that* blow bounced him back *again* to the bow side. Three impacts.

Ben had been medevacked to the nearby hospital. He was in a coma. Sue arrived and resumed her interrogations, this time, of the doctors.

"They told me, 'We can keep him alive.'

"And I said, 'What does that mean?'

"And they said, 'We'll know more every couple of hours.'

"And I said, 'Well, is he going to be a vegetable?'

"And they said, 'We don't know.'"

THE BRAIN IS the most complex organ in the body. It contains eighty-six billion neurons. Between these, there are an estimated one trillion neural connections. When someone gets a head injury like Ben's, the real damage is not from injury to the skull but from injury to the brain. The head rapidly accelerates and decelerates. The soft brain tissue strikes the hard bony structure of the skull. The complicated wiring of the brain is damaged. A vast array of complex problems follows, from memory loss to blurred vision, double vision, memory problems, concentration problems, dizziness, nausea, light sensitivity, sleep disturbances, depression, and PTSD.

And in those first moments of treatment—which usually happen in a busy emergency room—the diagnostic tool that the treating doctors have is called the Glasgow Coma Scale, or GCS. Because it is named after something, and it's an acronym, and it is the classic metric for traumatic brain injury, it sounds authoritative, which it is, and cutting edge, which it absolutely is not.

"We're still using diagnostic tools that were developed forty years ago," says Geoffrey Manley, a top neurosurgeon in traumatic brain injury.

What the Glasgow Coma Scale does is measure whether you are totally unconscious or alert enough to cry in pain. It buckets people with traumatic brain injury, or TBI, into three descriptions: Mild, moderate, or severe.

You rattle and smash the trillion connections between eighty-six billion neurons, and the only diagnosis available is *mild, moderate, or severe*?

This explains why Sue Stein kept hearing the words *we don't know*. Sue was experiencing, firsthand, this horrible mismatch between the trillion-connection complexity of traumatic brain injury and the tools with which doctors must use to assess TBI.

You can argue that this problem is harder than most emergency medical challenges because of the complexity of the brain. How can you predict an outcome when there are a trillion inputs?

But it is far from the only problem.

Another is that the medical establishment had, sort of naturally and understandably, sifted itself into separate and noncooperating groups. Doctors and clinics tended to cluster around their patient *types*. Some specialists treated military injuries—soldiers from Iraq injured by improvised explosive devices sent home with PTSD. Then, there were the sports people. Football linemen crunching skulls; or lacrosse, where high school girls use three-foot slingshots to whip around a ball of hard rubber with a concrete core, and nobody wears a helmet. Then, at last, civilian. Skateboarders and scooter crashers. Active grandpa taking a header on the tennis court.

Finally, there was the challenge of time scale. With heart disease (for instance), if your patient comes in with a heart attack, you know your outcome—live or die—within an hour or two. The causes might have involved a lifetime of smoking and steaks. But you capture that easily with an interview of the patient or family or looking at a blood test. In TBI, the equation is turned upside down. The *injury* happens fast and is easily described. The *outcome* stretches out for, potentially, decades, playing out, hidden, in the folds of the brain.

Between the neurological complexity, the divisions in the medical establishment, and the time scale of the outcome, we can sympathize with the ER doctor—especially when faced with a terrified and furious mother like Sue Stein—and their stammering answer, "We don't know," or, "mild, moderate, severe."

As Manley puts it, rather gently: "Are there better tools we can be using in this space?"

GEOFFREY MANLEY IS a busy man. He is not just a neurosurgeon. He's the head of neurosurgery at San Francisco General Hospital. He's the codirector of their Brain and Spinal Injury Center. He's a prolific researcher. He's one of those public spokespeople for a problem who might, in some other universe, be dull and cautious; but Manley is the opposite—unaffected and natural, so passionate about treatments and patient care, so overcaffeinated and battery surcharged, that terms and acronyms and metrics and cases come pouring out of him without punctuation.

He is also, believe it or not, a former garage mechanic. Manley had dropped out of high school to help support his family by working in a local auto shop when, one day, the Toyota he was fixing turned out to belong to a microbiologist at the University of Kentucky, who was impressed, befriended young Geoffrey, and convinced him that even though no one else in the Manley family had ever been to college, Geoffrey could make a go of it.

In the garage, Manley would have been familiar with automotive diagnostic tools. The car comes in. You know something is wrong, but you don't know what. The car is vastly complex with multiple systems at work, all hidden under the hard shell of the auto body. You plug the vehicle into the tool. Then the diagnostic machine monitors the car's systems and spits out a list of problems. A diagnosis.

Why wasn't there something similar for traumatic brain injury?

Why wasn't there a system that could give Sue Stein the answer to her question? Which was, simply, "What's going to happen to my son?"

DIGITAL ADVERTISING SEEMS trivial compared to these important medical questions. Yet there is a principle in digital advertising that illustrates what Manley and others are trying to achieve.

And that is the idea of *performance*.

Digital advertising beats medical questions if not in seriousness then in the abundance of data. Digital advertising is swimming in data. On any given day, a digital publisher might be running a hundred ad campaigns, and each of those hundred ad campaigns might be running millions of ad impressions. Each of those ad campaigns becomes, in effect, an experiment.

Maybe the advertiser wants the people seeing the ad campaign to "visit my website for a free trial!"

The advertiser spent a whole bunch of money on the ad campaign. They paid a creative team to come up with the ad. And maybe it was a TV or video ad, so there was a shoot with sets and actors, which are expensive; and they had to license music, which is expensive; and they had to pay a postproduction team to edit the ad, and then they had to pay the media company to run the ad. They're out a lot of cash. So the one thing they always want to know is:

Did it work?

Was it worth it for me to spend millions of dollars to try and get people to my website for a free trial? So, back in my Samsung team, Nelson and Freddie again, and their crew of fine analysts, would dive into the data. And they set it up like a scientific experiment.

We know this group of people, Group A, were exposed to the million-dollar ad campaign.

And they know this group, Group B, didn't see the ad.

Nelson and Freddie know this because the digital systems—we call them ad servers—know where they delivered the ads and where they didn't.

Then, if the advertiser tells us who visited their website, we can see whether Group A, the group who saw the ad, visited the website more than Group B. And if they did—well, the ad worked. The advertiser is happy.

This is, simply, the scientific method. Setting up tests and using controls to discover cause and effect. Yet this advertising example tells us something important. It tells us that you don't need lab coats and research grants to learn something useful about cause and effect. *Performance* is one of the most powerful ways of thinking about data. It's another example of data giving us the tools to ask questions that otherwise seem impossible to answer.

A nonprofit I volunteer for creates garden spaces in cities. They asked me to help them think about what the climate impact is of installing a garden in a bleak urban hellscape. It seems impossible to answer—until you find a metric that tells you what the impact on local temperatures is of turning a hectare of paved space into a hectare of green space. Suddenly, you know.

A foundation measures the cause and effect of carbon in the oceans.

A start-up measures the impact of road repair on transportation.

An AI tool tells a golfer how changes in her golf swing will affect her power and distance.

How could we know the cause and effect in these invisible phenomena?

It starts with finding all the data you can about this subject, which, at first glance—a golf swing? city potholes? gardens?—seems ridiculous and impossible to measure.

GEOFFREY MANLEY AND a group of specialists got tired of living in a world where they didn't know answers to even the basic questions for their TBI patients—"What's going to happen to my son?" So, at last, the military and sports and civilian people pooled their resources and created a database of traumatic brain injuries. "Most of us used to compete against each other for a very small pool of grant money," Manley says. "What we found is that, working together, we're getting further than working independently." They found a home at the UC San Francisco Brain and Spinal Injury Center. They named themselves TRACK-TBI, standing for Transforming Research and Clinical Knowledge in TBI. The group secured funding.

But what they mainly secured was data. They enrolled eighteen Level I brain trauma centers across the country, from Seattle to Miami, to contribute data about symptoms, CT imaging, clinical information, blood specimens, genomic data, even socioeconomic data, for about three thousand TBI patients. They even persuaded the families of deceased brain-injured patients to donate actual physical brains so they could do high-resolution MRIs.

The genomics, the socioeconomic data, the symptoms at the time of injury was intake data—the long list of items that might be a cause in the cause-and-effect dynamic. But they also gathered *outcomes* data. Data about what happened months, even years later.

At last, they were able to link cause and effect. At last, the team was able to make a linkage between that fraught and attenuated span between the moment the patient entered the ER and what their life would be like later. To figure it out, the research team, in effect, jammed the data into a supercomputer. They used machine learning to sort out the causes and effects. They found that features that were observable in the ER, like degree of consciousness, severity of intracranial injury, preexisting mental health conditions, preexisting medical conditions, and socioeconomic factors could in fact predict the patient outcome. And the algorithm found *nineteen* variations of the possible outcomes. Not three. Not just mild, moderate, or severe—but specific predictions of sleep problems at six months out. Vision problems at three months out. Disabilities. They could answer the question—or at least answer it better—"What is going to happen to my son?"

If the TRACK-TBI approach, and all its innovation around detecting causes and predicting effects, had been available years before, it all might have helped Sue Stein.

But it wasn't.

BEN CAME OUT of his coma. Sue and Tom, not surprisingly, did not last as a couple. Ben made it back to school. He grew into a man. He's now thirty-three. He cannot read. But he can drive, and he has a job in Ken's Krew, an organization that helps disabled people find work in Home Depot. He competes fiercely in the Special Olympics. He is opinionated, fastidious, judgmental, driven. Along the way, Ben had this teacher who really got him. In the classroom, the teacher would say, "In your kingdom, Ben, you can do what you want—but this is not your kingdom." The family loved that because Ben's stubbornness was notorious at home. The name stuck. *King Ben*. Now, every Halloween, to celebrate the affectionate poke, Ben dresses as a king. He sits in the yard on a lawn chair like a throne wearing a costume crown, ermine, and red cloak, his rich brown beard seeming like part of the costume. He beams, handing out candy to the trick-or-treaters.

As I listen to Sue tell me what she went through on that horrible June day—and all the battles she fought with surgeries and shunts to drain brain fluid and medications and schools and programs and lack of programs—as I hear her fret about Ben's future ("Here I am—I'm sixty-eight; I gotta figure this out for him"), I wonder how much the supercomputer's model would change if one of the inputs, one of the intake data points, could be: *The patient has one tough mother, who loves him.*

KEY POINTS IN CHAPTER 19

- A scientific experiment—a test group and a control group—can measure performance with data.

- This requires an abundance of experimental data, as exists in digital advertising.

- In medicine, however, the availability of data can be a challenge. In the world of traumatic brain injury, specialists needed to pool resources and gather special funding to have plentiful "experiments"—in this case, actual patient data.

- Once gathered, however, the data can help make linkages between cause and effect: Inputs and outcomes.

- We can apply this approach to numerous areas of human endeavor. What is the impact of an urban garden? Of adding CO_2 to the oceans? Of moving your hips in a golf swing?

THOUGHT STARTERS FOR YOU

- Ask the question "What is the impact of . . .?" and you know you are in the domain of performance.

- You realize the power of this question when you then ask yourself, *What is the impact of knowing the impact?*

- Can I sell to more clients if I can tell them the impact of my services? Can I tell families what's going to happen to their injured family members in the ER? Can I tell my government what's going to happen to the ocean if we keep our current practices?

- Begin asking those two impact questions about your domain. Start framing ways to answer "What is the impact of . . . ?" by designing experiments or gathering data about results. And think about the impact of impact, for you.

PART FIVE

Conclusion

There's no earthly way of knowing
Which direction they are going!
There's no knowing where they're rowing,
Or which way the river's flowing!
Not a speck of light is showing,
So the danger must be growing,
For the rowers keep on rowing,
And they're certainly not showing
Any signs that they are slowing . . .

—ROALD DAHL,
Charlie and the Chocolate Factory

When I was ten, at Virginia summer camp, I was a fat kid who could barely swim. Naturally, they held our swimming instruction in a murky lake teeming (I was certain) with venomous cottonmouths, with a rope marker for turnarounds a remote mile away, and a merciless instructor. After an hour of laps my heart would slam so hard I thought I was going to die right there on the dock, and I developed a hatred and suspicion of the element of water. I was like, *First* Jaws *and now this?* Only years later—after many, less traumatic experiences in shallow, clear pools—did I reconcile myself to swimming and decide it was not some kind of trick for killing children.

My wish for you is that you have familiarized yourself with the element of data and that, in reading this book, your journey to comfort and confidence has been faster than mine with water.

It is good timing for you to gain that confidence. Data is at the heart of everything related to artificial intelligence, which is on the front page of the business press every day. And, as I hope you now believe, data is indeed like an element, one that is all around us and invisible, ours to harness if we choose.

It is also a field evolving at a furious pace. Steadily accelerating from the time of John Graunt (1650s) to the time of John Tukey (1950s) to what is now a dizzying time with unimaginable achievements of data and AI being announced every fifty days—or even fifty hours. I believe, therefore, it is worth looking forward. Not because I believe I can predict the future—predictions are like popcorn: Irresistible, irresponsible, and never filling—but because I am detecting some of the themes in data that will shape our world.

Reality to Data

Yes, we have together explored many stories demonstrating how omnipresent data is in the twenty-first century. Yet think of how much human experience data does not capture. How much territory Alan Turing's poor old robot must still cover to understand sex, sport, and the rest of human experience.

Yes, Geoffrey Manley is helping build a symptoms database for traumatic brain injury. But what about Waldenstrom's, a rare blood cancer? Or Aarskog syndrome? Or Zellweger spectrum disorder?

Yes, Christy Lewis is building a database of polluters. But what about a database of corrupt insurance practices? Or toxic bosses?

It's important to keep in context how we build databases.

Databases are built by people or machines doing something boring: Labeling data.

Think about all those Nielsen Families in chapter 12. They're sitting down every day and filling out an exam booklet about their TV viewing. They're labeling data. They're taking their own TV viewing—something that happens organically and without thinking or observation—and they are intentionally observing it and turning it into data. Or Adam Greene's loneliness scores: Built on phone calls, each one recorded, and then scored by a person or a machine. In both cases, the labeling must occur thousands of times for it to be meaningful as a database.

I call this general area "reality to data." Because if we want our analytics and AI to be smarter, and tell us more things about reality, well, our tools need something to work with. So there will be pressure on start-ups and technologies that accelerate the speed with which we convert "reality to data."

A Dutch company called Send AI has built tools that take piles of messy documents and, in effect, reads them and adds them to a database. A start-up called Nanonets does the same thing with invoices. It sounds like some horrible summer job you would get in the '80s:

"Take this massive pile of invoices and type them into forms." It used to be called "data entry." Now it's called "annotation," which sounds so scholarly—but isn't. For some, data labeling jobs are horrible and exploitative: There are now "call center–like offices" placed all over the globe, *New York* magazine reported, with workers making "$1.20 an hour."

Yet to have an impact on wider ranges of human experience, one way or another—through AI or sheer, boring labor—we must convert new spans of reality to data. For a leader, this may mean focusing on converting *your* reality to data. Delving into *your* specialized knowledge and experience—the reality that lies around you every day as you go about your business or leading your mission-driven organization—and converting that into a source of power.

Data Is Scarce

Many large language models are now competing for attention and for share of the rapidly evolving market for AI: GPT, Grok, Palm, Llama, Gemini, Mixtral, to name a few. With all these models gobbling all the available data, could we run *out* of data?

A team of researchers dug into it. They refer to the open internet as a "stock" of data. At first, and for many years, they point out, the stock doubled every year, until it started slowing down in the 2010s. Now, they say, the entire publicly available internet contains about thirty-three billion terabytes of data. And they project that the average large language model will consume about that amount within a few years—sometime between 2028 and 2032. So GPT, Grok, Palm, and Llama will eat until they are full, or barely full, and by 2032 there will be nothing more for them to consume. We will have run out. The silos and warehouses will be empty.

There are aspects of this that I find silly. Data is not like food, where if you run out you starve. Data makes a model smarter and more accurate—the difference between a model hallucinating, or being "off," versus accurately anticipating what you want from it. The burden is on the model to get smarter with the superabundant data it already uses. In other words, "running out of data" is a matter of math people running out of imagination. Thirty-three billion terabytes should be plenty to train any model.

Yet the argument does force us to think about our "data stock" in stark terms. While data seems as abundant as air, in fact, data is subject to the forces of supply and demand, like any commodity. We might not have access to data that would solve an important problem! Or such data might exist, but it might be tucked away in the possession of people who might not wish to part with it. Or this data might exist, but someone might have developed it at great expense, so that person wouldn't want it scraped for free off the internet.

Data Tracking Data

A few days before the new year in 2024, the *New York Times* filed a complaint against OpenAI, claiming that OpenAI's models were "built by copying *millions* of *The Times*'s copyrighted news articles, in-depth investigations, opinion pieces, reviews, and how-to guides." (Emphasis theirs.)

Suddenly, with large language models, journalists and other content creators face the same problem that regular consumers of Facebook did in the Cambridge Analytica scandal. Namely, they face the reality that technology companies can scoop up the data we create and use it, and make a profit on that use, seemingly without permission and without disclosure.

But the large language model version of this problem makes it all much clearer. Because you know who owns the data.

In the past, it was fuzzy. When I search for a product, or look up a store in a mapping app, is the record of that action my intellectual property or the app's? I mean, I was using someone else's product when doing so—somebody's search bar or mapping app. So, even though the data says something about me, is that my data or the search company's data?

But if I write an article, and the *New York Times* publishes that article—well, there is an established legal idea about intellectual property. The article is the shared copyright of me and the *Times*. OpenAI cannot use it without permission. Or, at least, they can't do so without me complaining and publicly calling them a thief.

One major challenge here is the power disparity between a Facebook, or an OpenAI, and the rest of us. These are multibillion-dollar companies who can mop the floor, legally, with pip-squeaks like us. When you see the *New York Times* take them on and it still doesn't quite seem like a fair fight, it drives this home.

Second, there is the challenge of secrecy. It takes a lot of sophistication and effort to track down these companies' efforts. The *New York Times*—with over a thousand reporters, many of them world-class investigators, not to mention their legal team—was able to track down the use of its articles only indirectly, by tracing the handful of sources OpenAI disclosed it was using to train GPT-3.

What about the rest of us? How can we track down which data of ours Big Tech is using?

Here is a conceptual solution.

There is this pompous word in the art world called *provenance*—which I have heard people pronounce with a frenchified emphasis on the last syllable, which really makes it pompous—which means "custodial history." It's the record of who owned a work of art, ideally from its creation to the present moment.

Back in the analog era when you received a confidential report, or a Hollywood screenplay only a limited number of people were allowed to read, the pages would have a stamp on them in the background: CONFIDENTIAL, COPY 11. That way, if the report of the script leaked, everybody would know you, shameful number eleven, were the leaker.

We can combine these two concepts to initiate a data provenance system. Our data—for instance this book or an article written by a *Times* journalist or, if we wanted to go that far, even our searches and our location pings on a mapping app—can be stamped with a watermark, an invisible unique ID, akin to CONFIDENTIAL, COPY II. The watermark is unerasable. We will always know when we are being mimicked or copied or reproduced as a robot version of ourselves. We will audit the giant companies and understand to what extent they have bred our intellectual DNA into their robot flesh farms.

The *Times*'s great journalism—even when flattened to tokens, to digitized, numerical versions of itself—is great, and valuable, data. And the opportunities to use and make money from great data are innumerable.

Data Is Abundant, or the 8 Percent

If the *New York Times* believes its data (unwillingly) helped OpenAI build a multibillion-dollar business, then what might its data have achieved on its own? Or maybe it's better to ask, what if every organization in the United States—and the world—started thinking of their data as an untapped asset, what kind of value could they create for themselves? (Not for the bad actor taking it from them.)

I will answer this question from a domain I know well, which is digital advertising.

Years ago, call it 2012, I started hearing about Amazon hiring friends of mine to build an advertising business. Nowadays—with Amazon airing *Thursday Night Football* and running ads on its Freevee TV services—this might be unsurprising. Yet they so carefully wove their advertising into the user experience on their app and website that you might have missed it in the early days.

For advertisers working with Amazon, the attraction was never *just* the crunching, grunting glory of professional football. Or even being able to reach customers right there while they were shopping.

It was the data.

Amazon knew I had just bought Lavilin 72h deodorant or a forty-inch Honeywell room fan (white) or a pair of black ASICS Gel Nimbus 25 running shoes.

And maybe now, using that data, Nike could try and sell me running shorts, or Black & Decker could try and sell me a freestanding air conditioner, or Old Spice could try and sell me cologne. So those brands might run an ad campaign with Amazon.

And when Amazon had finished running the ad campaign for those brands, they could tell Old Spice how much cologne they had *sold* as a result of running the ad campaign. Because Amazon runs the ad system. And they have everyone's shopping data right there. So they know when you saw the ad and when you bought something. And advertisers love this. Think about how much better that is than running an ad on TV and the newspaper and then waiting with bated breath to see if people walk into your store. Maybe, doing it the old-fashioned way, you would know an ad worked—if enough people walk in the storefront waving your newspaper ad. Then, yes, you'd know there was a connection. But Amazon could count all the times an ad viewer bought an item, every time. They would be able to say, "Your ad campaign cost you $1,000 and you sold 416 items," and it would be an incredibly powerful way to sell advertising.

So Amazon did that. So successfully, in fact, that the business grew to nearly *$47 billion.*

This was 8 percent of the company's revenue. If we assume that the revenue translates directly to the market capitalization, or stock price, of Amazon—which I think is a safe assumption—then *that one use of data* translates into about $150 billion in value.

That's a significant boost, even for a company of Amazon's size.

I believe that many, many companies possess data they can use this way. No one, of course, will quite have the depth and scale of Amazon's data, or that of any of the Big Tech firms (Google, Meta, Netflix, OpenAI, and so on).

But relative to their organization's size? Absolutely. And the relevance—again, proportionate to that organization's mission—should be just as potent. An organization exists because it serves a certain set of customers, or "stakeholders" (to use the tedious economics-sounding term), well enough to make a profit or to fund itself in other ways. They're doing something right. And whatever it is doing well, creates data.

Travel companies know how people spend money on trips. Banks know how people spend money on everything. Transportation organizations know where people go and when and what times of day. Real estate companies know the volume and price of home sales, by property type, by ZIP code, by square footage. And then all this data can be supplemented: There is free satellite data from the government. Organizations can ask users to register products or sign up for promotions or take surveys and volunteer information about themselves. Usually, they will do this to know and communicate with their customer better: To focus on their core business. But what if they treated that data as an asset? What could the 8 percent solution be for that company? An additional, but potentially still core, way to use their data?

Amazon, arguably, is only helping its vendors by offering advertising: "Advertise on Amazon.com, sell more product; you, the seller of the product, make more money, Amazon makes more money, and more customers get connected to products they want." So, even though their advertising business seems like a sideshow, it supports the main business. (Which is no doubt why it has worked so well.)

For other organizations taking the 8 percent approach, some starter questions are:

- What do I know about my stakeholders? What domains—in physical or professional terms—do I have expertise in?

- If I took that knowledge as a starting point, how can I extend or expand my mission?

- Who else cares about those same issues, activities, or stakeholders? How can I help those other parties learn more, while staying true to the mission and the spirit of my stakeholder relationships and the obligations I have to my domain of expertise?

- How can I collect data about my expertise and make it simple enough for others to use responsibly?

- How can I make revenue, gain funding, or accelerate the traction of my organization by taking any of these steps?

If we translate the 8 percent factor to the US economy, then there is a latent $2.2 trillion in growth hiding in plain sight ($2.2 trillion is an 8 percent increase in US gross domestic product). A vast lift to everyone's fortunes.

All we require is for organizations to pay attention to their data.

The Data Advocate

I'm all for organizations making money and fulfilling their mission with data. Yet I believe data has an equally untapped role in our society—namely as a monitor of corporations and governments on behalf of the consumer and the citizen.

Let's start with the problem.

Most of our interactions with corporations and governments are hidden. Vague. Messy. Big, unanswered questions loom over these relationships. With the government: You're taking a whacking huge slice of my paycheck every week. Are you spending it responsibly? With corporations: Are they treating me fairly?

As an example: How do I interact with my health insurance company? My experience is: Someone in my family has an appointment with a doctor. Somehow notes on the diagnosis and treatment reach my insurance company, with a price attached. The insurance company decides what they will pay the provider. They pay it, and I pay the rest.

That's the consumer experience.

And we will stick with that perspective. Because what is important here is the point of view of the nonexpert.

From the consumer perspective, the opportunities for the insurance company to exploit the situation are abundant: Mainly in their ability to not pay and to force me to pay.

How do I, the consumer, know that my denied claim was justified in its denial?

How do I know the amount the insurer offered to pay is a fair amount?

Further, how do I know how well my insurance company treats all its other customers? For instance, if I have a bad experience and the insurance company refuses my claim, and I fight it, and I find they made a mistake—was that a one-off error? Or is it something systematic—that is, the insurance company just denies claims in great swathes, letting the most pissed or most poor or most particular customers catch them out—but doesn't worry about the lazy and passive customers who they treated equally unfairly.

The journalism organization ProPublica has reported on this phenomenon. So we know, in this case, that this is happening. But so what? You read an article about insurers denying claims, you recognize you were likely a victim of it this week and last week and the week before—what are you going to do about it? And how could data help?

Let's perform a thought experiment to determine how we might address this problem.

The first thing that needs to happen is to turn all that reality into data. What's the reality we're concerned about? How many claims that deserved payment were denied. How many claims that deserved a fair payment were paid out too low. What is a fair payment—for where I live and the cost of living there. How many times does no payment, or underpayment, happen for a particular insurance company.

How might we approach this as a data problem?

We would need, what we call in the business, a "truth set": A set of data where we know the answer is right, so to speak, and where the answer is wrong. In this case, it would mean: A database matched between diagnosis and payment, where we *know* what is correct for the insurance company to pay, and a set where we *know* it is wrong for the insurance company *not* to pay.

We would then need a truth set for payment amounts: How much is correct for an insurance company to pay, given an area's cost of living.

Then we would need a large database of claims—which ones were rejected, which ones were paid, and at what price. We might gather this through surveys, which would be difficult. But maybe with AI tools we could recruit a panel of insurance customers who would use their smartphone to take pictures of their insurance statements and send them to us. Then the AI could parse the images and turn them into formatted data for analysis.

This would be our sample. It would need to be large enough that we had a sufficient sample, on a sufficiently wide enough variety of claims, for all the main insurance companies.

But if we had that, we would be able to score each insurance company's performance as a payer. How many claims were they paying fairly versus denying unfairly? How often were they paying a fair price? We could publish these metrics, this report card. The bad actor companies would be shamed. The good actor companies could brag. All the companies would grumble that with all this transparency they have to stop profitable practices and take a hit to their margin. Then all the companies would be clever—because they were forced to—and think of new ways to make profits, hopefully in ways that do not harm the customer. The beauty of capitalism.

The point is that we could use data in this fashion—and in a thousand similar examples—to make the world a better place.

There are, naturally, challenges to doing this.

First, people have limited attention. So if some little organization dumps out an Insurance Fair Payment Score into the world, who is going to pay attention? It takes money and resources and effort to make people care—marketing and PR.

Second, it's tricky to make a business model work, and a data business is no exception. This is why, in the chapter about crystallizing complex information (chapter 11), we see how S&P got into trouble making money from selling bond scores. The people who benefited from getting a bond rated were *the people issuing the bonds*. It created a conflict of interest, with massive and tragic consequences.

But who else is going to pay? In our thought experiment, who is going to pay? The insurance company? Why would they pay to have themselves monitored?

Would the consumer pay? Almost certainly not: Health insurance is already expensive as hell. Maybe employers, as they evaluate insurers for a big multiyear deal? Also probably not; their interest is to get the lowest price, not scold their bidders.

The one area where it feels like this model almost broke free was in ESG investing. ESG, which stands for environmental, social, and governance, is an approach to investing that focuses on the social good of the companies people invested in. Setting aside all the debates on the issue—who among us will define *good*? And is this even the right role for an investor?—the *data* aspect was promising. A cottage industry for data sprang up, focused on scoring companies for doing the right thing. Bingo!

Only . . . who paid?

Who paid was a bunch of Wall Street analysts.

Did they have an interest in publishing and promoting that information? Of shaming and rewarding companies for doing the wrong or right thing?

You already know the answer. Wall Street banks and investment funds are in the business of having a secret formula for how they invest so that they can buy securities cheap and sell them expensive. If everyone knows the information—well, from an investing perspective, it's now useless. Everybody knows. The knowledge is priced into the stock. Boring. So where ESG ended up is a massive amount of powerful information about the good and bad behavior of companies, paid for, and locked up, by people who wish to keep the information secret.

This leaves us with a slim lane of nonprofit and B Corporation operating models where data advocacy can exist. There must be many examples I don't know about (and would love to hear about). But here are a few wonderful examples:

- Tree Equity Score. An organization that scores how well cities provide tree cover—essential to moderating local climates as temperatures rise—to underrepresented groups. Newark, New Jersey, gets a 73; not great. Leafy Charlottesville, Virginia, gets a 100. They overlay the data on maps in reassuring green or scary orange.

- Ad Fontes Media. A B Corp that uses panels of readers across the political spectrum to score news organizations based on their political bias and how reliably those news organizations represent facts. The *Wall Street Journal* podcast, *WSJ: The Journal,* represents the peak of integrity. *The Jimmy Dore Show* is the low point of unreliable and left biased, and Alex Jones represents the low point on the right. All displayed in an interactive grid.

- CharityWatch.org monitors six hundred charities that take more than $1 million in public funding and pores over their financial statements to evaluate how much each charity spends on overhead versus programs and how much they spend to raise $100 (presumably to detect when they're just throwing parties to raise pennies). Each organization gets a tidy scorecard with an overall grade and two pie charts.

I should note that all three organizations get top marks for tracking and crystallizing—distilling complicated information to one number, or a few—and deserve bonus points for clear visualization and open access.

I'd like to see a thousand more organizations like these. As data becomes cheaper to acquire, store, and process, more clever people who understand data and wish to do good will embrace data advocacy and use the power of omniscience to help shed light on the vague and messy interactions we have with powerful, well-funded, well-hidden people and organizations.

In Closing

Fear is limiting. Fluency is power. Over the course of this book I hope you have absorbed enough stories about data to feel more fluent, and feel more power. At a minimum, I hope you feel empowered to ask questions about where data comes from and how it is used. And simply to feel in your bones that you can understand data—and that no person, or no usage of data, is so clever that it cannot be explained in plain English. Perhaps you even feel a level of mastery. That spending time with all these data experts—from John Graunt and Henry Varnum Poor to Sharon Greene to Deborah Morosini—has rubbed off on you. And that now you have a tweaky little voice in your ear that thinks in terms of data superpowers and data uses that can guide you to realize more potential for you, your organization, and even our world at large.

If any of this now applies to you, congratulations. You are a data person.

INDEX

AbbVie, 232
abstraction. *see* stacking
Ad Fontes Media, 263
advertising
   Amazon, 257–58
   digital, 219, 242
   television, 126–27
AGI (Artificial General Intelligence), 54
AI (artificial intelligence), 41–54, 251, 253
Akerlof, George, 128–30
Albertsons, 194
Aldi, 194
Alphanumeric Television Interface Controller (ANTIC), 44–45
Alum Rock earthquake, 185
Amazon, 160, 203, 256–57
American Economic Review, 128
American Railroad Journal, 141, 144
Analytical Pyramid, 48–49, 54
annotation, 253
anomalies, 179–87
ANTIC (Alphanumeric Television Interface Controller), 44–45
Antigone (Sophocles), 16
AOL, 105
Apple TV, 125
Artificial General Intelligence (AGI), 54
artificial intelligence (AI), 41–54, 251, 253
Asteroids (video game), 44–45
asymmetry, information, 128
Atari, 44–45
Autonomous Underwater Vehicle (AUV), 133
Avangrid, 131

Balderrama, Carlene, 137–38, 147
Balderrama, John, 138
Battle of Thermopylae, 114–15
BCD (Bureau of Communicable Diseases), 110–13, 116–19
B2C (business to consume) magazines, 141
Bedrock, 131
Berners-Lee, Tim, 20–21
Better Business Bureau, 232
biases, 156, 173
Bilenker, Josh, 207–8, 209–12
Bleier, Tom, 180–82, 184–85
Boeing, 191
bond ratings, 232
Borodin, Mikhael, 219–21
Boston University, 201
brain, 239–41, 244–45
$BRCA_1$ gene, 208
Bureau of Communicable Diseases (BCD), 110–13, 116–19
Bureau of Labor Statistics, 166, 173–74
business to consumer (B2C) magazines, 141

Caesar, Julius, 15
calculations, in AI, 45–46
Calhoun, David, 191–92
Cambridge Analytica, 79, 254
Campbell's Soup, 194
cancer, 208
Cancer Genome Project, 212
CARFAX, 129
central processing unit (CPU), 45
CERN, 20

certifications, 227–36
CharityWatch.org, 263
Chiau, Charles, 131–33
Chomsky, Noam, 161
climate change, 168, 176
Climate TRACE, 94–95
Clinton, Bill, vii
clustering, 51–52
CNN, 219
Coca-Cola, 61
Colossus computer, 38
Columbus, Christopher, 103
Comcast, vii, 72–73
commodities, 165–66
Conference of Parties (COP), 170
consistency scores, 184
Consumer Electronics Show, 183
Consumer Price Index (CPI), 166, 168,
    172–74
Consumer Reports, 232
COP₂₁, 170
COP (Conference of Parties), 170
Corbet, Kathleen, 138, 147
Cornell University, 100
cortisol, 217
COVID-19 pandemic, 109–11, 116–19
CPI (Consumer Price Index), 166, 168,
    172–74
CPU (central processing unit), 45
cuneiform writing, 158–59

Dahl, Roald, 57, 249
dark room problem, 125–31
data, 99–107
    abundance of, 256–59
    advocating for, 259–64
    anomalies in, 179–86
    and artificial intelligence, 41–54
    and certification, 227–35
    complex information in, 137–47
    counting in, 153–63
    data people and, 71–81
    and data science, 27–39
    defining identity in, 189–99
    in everyday life, 3–12
    influence and importance of, 251
    introduction and influence of, 6–7

matching with, 201–12
in omniscience, 87–95
performance and, 237–45
and privacy, 59–68
problems solved with, 123–33
raster, 102–3
resources directed from, 109–20
scarcity of, 253–54
for scoring, 215–24
throughout history, 15–24
tracking data with, 254–56
tracking with, 165–77
vector, 103–4
databases, 252
data entry, 253
data person
    bad, 77
    defining, 72–74
data science, 34
data storage, 16–17, 44
decidability, problem of, 37
dementia, 217
Department of Health and Mental
    Hygiene, 111
Dia Beacon, 189
Dickinson, Carol, 179, 181
Dickinson, Scotty, 179, 181
digital advertising, 219, 242
DiMare, Anthony, 131–33
direct mail marketing, 203
Discovery+, 125
Disney+, 125, 126
DNA, 208
Don't Count Us Out coalition, 156, 162

earthquakes, 179–80, 179–82, 184–85, 185
eBay, 184
ECLS (Electronic Clinical Laboratory
    System), 111
Eddy, Walden, 145
electricity, 5–6
electromagnetic energy, 182
Electronic Clinical Laboratory System
    (ECLS), 111
enumerators, 18, 21–22, 28, 49–50
ESG investing, 262
ETV6 gene, 210

Eurgertes, Ptolemy, 23–24
Everett, Caleb, 158, 160

Facebook, vii, 79–80, 160, 255
Facebook Beacon, 79–80
fairness, 230–31
farms, wind, 125
fault lines, 182
fear, 264
fiduciary, 80–81
FoDA (The Future of Data Analysis), 33
Food Lion, 194
FourSquare, 9
FOX, 156, 159, 162
Fred Hutch, 209
The Future of Data Analysis (FoDA), 33

GCS (Glasglow Coma Scale), 239–40
GE (General Electric), 191–92
Gemini, 253
General Electric (GE), 191–92
General Mills, 194
genes, 207–8
geophones, 185
Glasglow Coma Scale (GCS), 239–40
Glick, Barry, 100–104
Goldman Sachs, 166
Gomez, Aidan, 42–44, 45
Goode, Brendan, 183–84
Google, vii, 45–46, 104–5, 160, 203
Google Maps, 11
Gotham Center, 110
GPS, 8
GPT, 253
GPT 3.5, 46
grading, remote beef, 234
graphics processing units (GPUs), 45
Graunt, John, 28–30, 251, 264
Green, Roger Lancelyn, 85
Greene, Adam, 215–18, 221–24, 252, 264
Greene, Sharon, 109–11, 113, 116, 119
Grok, 253

HBO MAX, 125
head injuries, 239–41
Hewlett, Freddy, 73
Hilbert, David, 37

Hoffman, Rhona, 189–91
Hollerith, Herman, 17–19, 49–50
Hospitality Design, 141
hot spots, 116
HTML (hypertext markup language), 21
HTTP (hypertext transfer protocol), 21
Hudson, Henry, 103
Hulu, 125
human trafficking, 71–72, 75–76
Hutchison, Allie, 186
hypertext markup language (HTML), 21
hypertext transfer protocol (HTTP), 21
Hy-Vee, 194

Iberdrola, 131
IBM (International Business Machines),
    19
ICD (International Statistical
    Classification of Diseases and Related
    Health Problems), 197
"idea of three," 158
Iger, Bob, 192
inflation, 166–68, 172–75
Inflation Reduction Act, 168
information asymmetry, 128
injuries, head, 239–41
intelligence, machine, 43
International Business Machines (IBM),
    19
International Statistical Classification
    of Diseases and Related Health
    Problems (ICD), 197
Introduction to Mathematical Philosophy,
    158
Ishango Bone, 157

JASA, 217
Jaws, 216
Johns Hopkins University, 207
Jones, Paul Tudor, 232–33
Journal of Political Economy, 128
The Jungle, 228
JUST Capital, 232–33

Ken's Krew, 245
Klaatch, 217, 221–22
Kodak, 181

Kohlberg Kravis Roberts (KKR), 64
Kraft, 61
Kroger, 194

Landsat 8, 89–90
Large Hadron Collider, 20
large language models (LLMs), 42, 160
larotrectinib, 207–8
learning, machine, 51
Leonidas, 114–16
Lewis, C. S., 1, 91–93
Lewis, Christy, 87–88, 252
LeWitt, Sol, 189–91, 198
Library of Alexandria, 16, 23–24
light detection and ranging (LIDAR), 51
linear television, 126
linguistics, 161
LinkedIn, 203
lists
    compilers of, 204
    subscriber, 193
Llama, 253
LLMs (large language models), 42, 160
LMNA gene, 210
Local People Meter, 155–56
location data, 7
Loma Prieta earthquake, 179–80, 185
loneliness, 216–18
Lovelace, Ada, 38
Ludt, Steve, 44
lung cancer, 202–3
Lyman, Bill, 77–78

machine intelligence, 43
machine learning, 51
magnetometers, 185
Manley, Geoffrey, 240–42, 244, 252
MapQuest, 102, 105
marketing, direct mail, 203
matching, 201–12
match key, 206
McCormick, Gavin, 88, 94
Meadows, Larry, 228–31
meat grading, 228–30
Meat Inspection Act, 228
medical conditions, 10
medications, 207–8

metadata, 16
Miller, Dave, 31–32
Miller, David, 220
MIT Technology Review, 186
Mixtral, 253
Moffitt Cancer Center, 209
monopiles, 132
Morgan Stanley, 166, 172–73
Morosini, Deborah, 201–3, 208–12, 264
Morosini, Helen, 202, 208
mortgage crisis, 138
Murdoch, Lachlan, 162
The Myths of the Norsemen, 93

Nabisco, 194–95
nacelles, 132
Nanonets, 252–53
National Cancer Database, 212
National Cancer Institute, 203, 208, 211
National Comprehensive Cancer Center,
    209
National Correlation, 234–35
*Natural and Political Observations Made
    Upon the Bills of Mortality* (Graunt),
    29
NBC, 156
Netflix, 125
neurons, 239
new movers, 204–5
New Yorker, 161
New York magazine, 253
New York State Department of
    Agriculture and Markets, 112
New York Times, 141, 254, 255–56
Nielsen Company, 30–31, 60–62, 79–80,
    162, 191, 232
Nielsen Families, 156, 252
Nielsen Media Research, 154
Nike, 257
norepinephrine, 217
NTRK fusions, 210–12
NTRK gene, 207–8

Ohion State Department of Agriculture
    Commodities Report, 165
oil deposits, 124
OKCupid, 219

INDEX

O'Keeffe, Georgia, 198
OpenAI, 254–55
Orsted, 131
Orwell, George, 198

Palm, 253
Paramount+, 125
Paris Climate Accords, 170
particle colliders, 19–21
Pennsylvania Railroad Company, 142
Pepys, Samuel, 29
performance, 242–45
Piggly Wiggly, 194
Piraha, 160–61
plagues, 27
Planet, 90–93
Pollock, Melissa, 173, 175
Pollock, Missy, 165–66
Polo, Marco, 103
Poor, Henry Varnum, 139–47, 192, 232, 264
Poor's Manual of Railroads, 145–46
Powell, John Wesley, 89
Price, Vernon D., 145
Princeton University, 36
privacy, 79–80
problem of decidability, 37
Procter & Gamble, 61, 194
Progressive Grocer, 141, 193–94, 196
Project Atlas, 59–62
ProPublica, 260
provenance, 255
Publix, 194
punch cards, 18–19
Pure Food and Drug Administration, 228

QCI, 212

RADAR, 51
Railroad Gazette, 141
Railroad Record, 141
railroads, 140–47
Railway Times, 141
raster data, 102–3
ratings, bond, 232
"reality to data," 252–53
rectifiers, 233

remote beef grading, 234
response bias, 222
Review of Economic Studies, 128
Roosevelt, Theodore, 228
RR Donnelley Corporation (RRD), 102–3
Russell, Bertrand, 158, 161

Safeway, 194
salmonella outbreak, 112–13
Samsung, 125–31, 127, 183, 242
San Andreas fault, 181
San Francisco General Hospital, 241
San Francisco Giants, 179
SatScan, 112, 118
scientific method, 243
scoring, 215–24
seismic surveys, 124
SendAI, 252
Shakespeare, William, 151
Sinclair, Upton, 228
Smith, Kurtwood, 144
Smith, Winston, 198
S&P. *see* Standard and Poor's
Spartans, 114–15
Spatial Data Systems, 103–4
Speedeon, 205–6
stacking, 52
Standard and Poor's (S&P), 138–39, 146–47, 232, 262
Stein, Ben, 238–39, 245
Stein, Sue, 237–39, 245
Stein, Tom, 238, 245
Steinkamp, Roderic, 191, 198
Stellar Solutions, 185
Stewart, Jimmy, 180
Stew Leonard's, 194
stock prices, 166
Stone, Nelson, 125–26
storage, data, 16–17, 44
storage capacity, 44
streaming television, 126
subscriber lists, 193
substitution bias, 173
surveys, seismic, 124

Tabulating Machine Company, 19

Taylor, Scott, 192–98
TBI (traumatic brain injury), 240–41, 244–45
TDLinx, 192–93, 196
television, 126
television ads, 126–27
That Seventies Show, 144
"The Market for 'Lemons'" (Akerlof), 128
Time magazine, 138, 193
Topaz Systems, Inc., 9
TPM$_3$, 210
tracking, 168–72
    climate change, 168, 176
    defined, 168
    inflation, 166–68, 172–75
TRACK-TBI, 244
trade magazines, 141
training data, 220
traumatic brain injury (TBI), 240–41, 244–45
Tree Equity Score, 263
triangulation, 8
Trump, Donald, 116
trust, 80–81, 231
truth sets, 260–61
Tukey, John, 33–37, 251
turbines, wind, 132
Turing, Alan, 34–37, 41–43, 252

Uber, 7–9, 203
UC Berkeley, 182
UCLA, 221
UCLA Loneliness Scale, 221
UC San Francisco, 244
Uncle Tom's Cabin (Sinclair), 228
UN Framework Convention on Climate Change (UNFCCC), 171–72
Unilever, 61
United Nations, 170–72
United States Geological Survey (USGS), 89–90, 181
universal record locator (URL), 21
University of Miami, 158, 160
URL (universal record locator), 21
USDA Inspection Services, 229–30, 231, 234

USGS (United States Geological Survey), 89–90, 181
US Postal Service, 205

Variety, 162
Vattenfall, 131
vector data, 103–4

Wall Drawing 118, 190
Wall Drawing 448, 190–91, 198
Wall Street Journal podcast, 263
Walmart, 194
watermark, 256
WattTime, 88
Waze, 105
Welch, Jack, 191
Whiting, Susan, 153–54, 156, 162–63, 232
WHO (World Health Organization), 10–11
Whole Foods, 194
Wilbur, Elisha P., 145
wind farms, 125
wind turbines, 132
World Health Organization (WHO), 10–11
writing, cuneiform, 158–59

Xerxes, 114–15

ZoomInfo, 233
Zuckerberg, Mark, 80

JUSTIN EVANS is a twenty-year veteran of the data and technology industry, whose innovations have generated hundreds of millions in revenue for Fortune 500 companies such as Samsung, Comcast, and the Nielsen Company, as well as venture-backed startups. In addition to his business work, his mission as a writer and communicator is to demystify data and AI, and to empower any leader to use their "data superpowers." He is a frequent conference speaker, the author of The DataStory substack, as well as *The Little Book of Data* (HarperCollins Leadership) and two novels, one of which, *A Good and Happy Child*, was named a Top 100 Book of the Year by the *Washington Post* and optioned by Paramount Pictures. Justin is a Phi Beta Kappa graduate of Columbia University and was a Dean's Scholar at NYU Stern, where he received an MBA. He lives in New York City.